Greenhill Books

BATTLE
OF THE
BULGE

ALTERNATE HISTORY
FROM GREENHILL BOOKS

DISASTER AT D-DAY
The Germans Defeat the Allies, June 1944
Peter G. Tsouras

FOR WANT OF A NAIL
If Burgoyne had Won at Saratoga
Robert Sobel

GETTYSBURG
An Alternate History
Peter G. Tsouras

THE HITLER OPTIONS
Alternate Decisions of World War II
Edited by Kenneth Macksey

INVASION
The Alternate History of
the German Invasion of England, July 1940
Kenneth Macksey

THE MOSCOW OPTION
An Alternative Second World War
David Downing

THE NAPOLEON OPTIONS
Alternate Decisions of the Napoleonic Wars
Edited by Jonathan North

RISING SUN VICTORIOUS
The Alternate History of
how the Japanese Won the Pacific War
Edited by Peter G. Tsouras

THIRD REICH VICTORIOUS
The Alternate History of
how the Germans Won the War
Edited by Peter G. Tsouras

COLD WAR HOT
Alternate Decisions of the Cold War
Edited by Peter G. Tsouras

DIXIE VICTORIOUS
An Alternate History of the Civil War
Edited by Peter G. Tsouras

BATTLE
OF THE
BULGE
Hitler's Alternate Scenarios

Edited by Peter G. Tsouras

Greenhill Books, London
Stackpole Books, Pennsylvania

Battle of the Bulge:
Hitler's Alternate Scenarios
first published 2004 by Greenhill Books,
Lionel Leventhal Limited, Park House,
1 Russell Gardens, London NW11 9NN
www.greenhillbooks.com
and
Stackpole Books, 5067 Ritter Road,
Mechanicsburg, PA 17055, USA

Text and Maps © Lionel Leventhal Limited, 2004

British Library Cataloguing in Publication Data
Battle of the Bulge : Hitler's alternate scenarios
1. Ardennes, Battle of the, 1944-1945 2. Imaginary histories
I. Tsouras Peter
940.5'4219348

ISBN 1-85367-607-1

Library of Congress Cataloging-in-Publication Data
A catalog entry is available from the library.

Typeset and edited by Donald Sommerville.
Maps drawn by John Richards.

Printed and bound in Great Britain by
MPG Books Ltd, Bodmin, Cornwall.

CONTENTS

ILLUSTRATIONS

MAPS

Key to Military Symbols Used in Maps

⊠	infantry unit	X X X X X	army group or front
⊠	mountain infantry unit	X X X X	army
		X X X	corps
⊠	airborne infantry unit	X X	division
⊠	motorized infantry unit	X	brigade
		I I I	regiment
⊘	tank unit	I I	battalion

THE CONTRIBUTORS

CHRISTOPHER J. ANDERSON is a lifelong student of World War II, editor of *World War II Magazine* and consulting editor of *MHQ: The Quarterly Journal of Military History*. He is the author of several volumes in Greenhill Books' series, *GI: A Photographic History of the American Soldier*.

JAMES R. ARNOLD has written more than 25 military history books on topics ranging from the Napoleonic Wars to Vietnam. He has contributed chapters to the Greenhill alternate histories *Rising Sun Victorious* and *Dixie Victorious*. His most recent book is *Marengo and Hohenlinden: Napoleon's Rise to Power*. He is currently finishing a Civil War era novel, *The Cost of Freedom*.

KIM H. CAMPBELL was a regular officer in the United States Army serving 13 years in combat arms and intelligence. For the last 13 years he has been a senior intelligence analyst with the Air Force Intelligence Analysis Agency. He holds a master's degree in strategic intelligence and a BA in European history. He has written numerous articles on military operations for official United States Army and Air Force publications. He has been a student of military history for nearly 40 years.

DAVID ISBY has written and edited over 20 books, including (by Greenhill), *G.I. Victory* (with the late Jeff Ethell), *Fighting The Bombers*; *The Luftwaffe Fighter Force: The View From the Cockpit*; *Fighting the Invasion, Fighting in Normandy*; and *Fighting the Breakout*. He has contributed to several previous volumes of alternative history published by Greenhill including *Cold War Hot*; *Rising Sun Victorious*; and *Third Reich Victorious*. He has designed 19 conflict simulations and holds two Charles Roberts awards for excellence in the field. A Washington-based national security consultant and attorney, he holds a BA in history from Columbia University and a JD from New York University. He was awarded the title "bourgeois falsifier of history" by the Soviet government (pre-glasnost).

DR SEAN M. MALONEY teaches Contemporary Warfare in the War Studies Programme at the Royal Military College of Canada and is currently the Strategic Studies Advisor to the Canadian Defence Academy in Kingston, Ontario. He served as the historian to the Canadian Army's NATO forces at the end of the Cold War and is the author of several books, including *War Without Battles: Canada's NATO Brigade in Germany 1951–1993*, the controversial *Canada and UN Peacekeeping: Cold War by Other Means 1945–1970*, and the forthcoming *Operation KINETIC: The Canadians in Kosovo 1999–2000*. A habitual traveller, Dr Maloney has conducted extensive field work on Canadian operations in the Balkans, Middle East, and Southwest Asia. He is currently completing a book on Operation Enduring Freedom in Afghanistan.

JOHN PRADOS is an analyst of national security based in Washington, DC. Prados holds a PhD from Columbia University and focuses on presidential power, international relations, intelligence and military affairs. He is author of a dozen books, including titles on World War II, the Vietnam War, intelligence matters, and military affairs, including *Combined Fleet Decoded: The Secret History of U.S. Intelligence and the Japanese Navy in World War II*; *Hoodwinked*; *Lost Crusader: The Secret Wars of CIA Director William Colby*; *White House Tapes: Eavesdropping on the President*; *The Hidden History of the Vietnam War*; *Operation Vulture*; *The Blood Road: The Ho Chi Minh Trail and the Vietnam War*; *Presidents' Secret Wars: CIA and Pentagon Covert Operations from World War II Through the Persian Gulf*, among others. He has contributed chapters to 14 other books, and entries in four reference works. Prados is a contributing editor to *MHQ: The Quarterly Journal of Military History*, and a contributing writer to *The VVA Veteran*.

LIEUTENANT COLONEL PETER G. TSOURAS, USAR (ret) is a senior analyst with the Defense Intelligence Agency in Washington. Formerly he was a senior analyst at the U.S. Army National Ground Intelligence Center and the Battelle Memorial Institute. He served in the Army as an armor officer in the 1st Battalion, 64th Armor Regiment, in Germany and subsequently in intelligence and Adjutant Generals Corps assignments. He retired from the Army Reserve in 1994 after serving in Civil Affairs. His assignments have taken him to Somalia, Russia, Ukraine, and Japan. He is the author or editor of many books on international military themes, military history, and alternate history, including numerous features in History Book Club and The Military Book Club. His books include *The United States Army: A Dictionary*; *Operation Just Cause*; *Military Lessons of the Gulf War* (all with the late Bruce W. Watson); *Changing Orders, The Evolution of the World's Armies 1945 to Present*; *Warriors' Words: A Quotation Book*; *The Great Patriotic War*; *Disaster at D-Day: The Germans Defeat the Allies*, *Gettysburg: An Alternate History*; *The Anvil of War*; *Fighting in Hell*; *Military Quotations of the Civil War*; *The Greenhill Dictionary of Military Quotations*; *Panzers on the Eastern Front: General Erhard Raus and His Panzer Divisions in Russia*; *Rising Sun Victorious: The Alternate History of How the Japanese Won the Pacific War*; *Third Reich Victorious: How the Germans Won the War*; *Dixie Victorious: The Alternate History of the Civil War*; *Alexander the Great: Invincible King of Macedonia*; and

Montezuma II and the Fall of the Aztec Empire. He has written numerous book chapters as well as articles which have appeared in the U.S. Naval Institute *Proceedings*, U.S. Army Command and General Staff College *Military Review*, *Military History Quarterly*, and *Military History Magazine*.

ANDREW UFFINDELL is a British military historian. His publications include *The Eagle's Last Triumph: Napoleon's Victory at Ligny, June 1815;* and two books written with Michael Corum, *On the Fields of Glory: The Battlefields of the 1815 Campaign* and the *Waterloo* guidebook in the Battleground Europe series. He has contributed chapters to two books of alternative history: *The Napoleon Options*, edited by Jonathan North, and Peter Tsouras' *Dixie Victorious*. In addition, he has written a chapter for *Napoleon: the Final Verdict* and edited a volume of essays by the late Jac Weller, *On Wellington*. His most recent publications are: *Great Generals of the Napoleonic Wars and their Battles, 1805–1815* and *The National Army Museum Book of Wellington's Armies*. Among his published articles have been an analysis of friendly fire at Waterloo and studies of the Franco-Austrian War of 1859. He has also served as editor of the *Newsletter of the Society of Friends of the National Army Museum*.

CHARLES VASEY LLB FCA FTII is an itinerant finance director and game designer/publisher based in London. After reading law at London he qualified with Binder Hamlyn and worked with KPMG in both taxation and corporate finance before starting his own business. A man of frighteningly few achievements he has written for *Military Modelling*, *Strategy & Tactics*, and publishes intermittently his own magazine *Perfidious Albion*. He has published a number of boardgames on such disparate topics as Mars-la-Tour 1870, Biblical warfare, Tsushima, and the English Civil War.

INTRODUCTION

All wars generate their fair share of controversies over the roads not taken, the failure of vision, and the opportunities missed – and often missed by an eyelash. The great wars, because they involve such great stakes and affect so many lives, are especially rich in such controversy. Those issues do not merely echo through history – they resound like trumpets and drums, muted perhaps by time, but still clear and intense if you listen closely. For those with that special keen ear, there is much to learn in how the balance of history clangs one way or another by the weight of an eyelash on the scales.

This year's sixtieth anniversary of the Battle of the Bulge, also called the Ardennes Offensive,[1] presents the timely opportunity to examine not only the great German gamble of December 1944 but the preceding operations that led to that point beginning with the landing on D-Day in June. The colorful guise of alternate history is the medium through which the workings of history are illustrated.

The historian Geoffrey Parker notes, "'Counterfactual' calculations have, of course been scorned by many historians – especially by those who believe that major events must stem from major causes. Two centuries ago, however, Samuel Johnson eloquently demolished these doubts:

> "It seems to be almost the universal error of historians to suppose it politically, as it is physically true, that every effort has a proportionate cause. In the inanimate action of matter upon matter, the motion produced can be but equal to the force of the moving power; but the operations of life, whether private or publick, admit no such laws. The caprices of voluntary agents laugh at calculation. It is not always that there is a strong reason for a great event. Obstinacy and flexibility, malignity and kindness, give place alternately to each other, and the reason of these vicissitudes, however important may be the consequences, often escapes the mind in which the changes are made."[2]

There has been no greater stage for the demonstrations of Dr Johnson's statement than the Northwest Europe Campaign of 1944–45. Like pearls strung on a thread, the controversies of this campaign follow it from beginning to end. These are not merely the arguments of old soldiers reliving the time when their lives burned with an intensity they would never again achieve and academic historians who never feel any passion at all as they disturb the dust of their books. These controversies had price tags measured in human lives in the hundreds of thousands to the millions. They each represent a road not taken, a road that would have likely led to an earlier end of the war from the early fall of 1944 to the early days of 1945. The consequences of those roads not taken were enormous, not only in their butcher's bills but in the entire political and military nature of the postwar world. If the war had ended in September or January, how many lives would have been saved? How many fewer would have died in the last frantic slaughters in the Holocaust? Surely, the quarter million casualties on both sides suffered in the Ardennes would have been avoided.

This book explores such episodes in this mighty campaign, the critical decision nodes that were influenced by the proverbial eyelash.

This team of British, Canadian, and American military historians, explores the alternatives to the major decisions of the Northwest Europe Campaign of 1944–45. We have written on the premise that history, as Dr. Johnson, explained, does not run along a well-worn groove. It is a continuously shifting synthesis of chance, design, character, accident, and luck both good and bad. History is a constantly shifting array of decision nodes – the ultimate game of choice and chance based on strategy and guessing in the dark.

Clarifications

The ten chapters in this book do not form a continuous thread or single plot line. Rather they are the stories woven by ten authors each charged with examining a different episode in the Northwest Europe Campaign of 1944–45 in the light of the very real potential for different outcomes. Each is self-contained within its own alternate reality.

Our accounts of this alternate reality naturally need their own explanatory references, which appear in the endnotes that follow each chapter. The use of these "alternate reality" endnotes, of course, poses a risk to the unwary reader who may make strenuous efforts to acquire a new and fascinating source. To avoid an epidemic of frustrating and futile searches, the "alternate notes" are indicated by an asterisk (*) before the number of the endnote within the notes themselves. All works appearing in the bibliographies included separately in each chapter are, however, "real".

Also, to assist the reader, the names of military units of the Western Allies are given in Roman type and the German units in *italics*.

The Chapters

The chapters are presented in chronological order. Thus David Isby begins the book with his chapter, "Monty's D-Day: Caen and Beyond." The failure to take Caen on D-Day, as was planned, was a crucial failure that allowed the Germans to contain the Allied beachhead for almost two months. Isby takes an institutional approach as he examines the training, leadership, and experience of the British and Canadian Armies and compares them to the Germans, to see where the eyelash might have fallen on the scales of this battle.

Chapter Two, "By the Throat: Decision at Falaise" centers on the battle of the Falaise Pocket in which the German *Fifth Panzer* and *Seventh Armies* were almost bagged in their entirety. Those many thousands who escaped the trap were the cadres that rebuilt the *German Army* in the West and thus enabled Hitler to keep the war going until the spring of the next year. Yet the Allies came so achingly close to snapping the jaws of the encirclement shut on these men. The Allies stumbled, and the Germans escaped to fight again. The laurels of victory were dangling before Bradley, Montgomery, and Eisenhower. Had any of them reached out a finger's length more... ?

After Falaise the Allies found themselves on the horns of a dilemma. Both Patton and Montgomery vigorously presented plans in which their armies would be given logistic priority to make a single, killing thrust into Germany. History offers few more splendid opportunities, for the *German Army* that struck so hard three months later in the Ardennes did not exist. It had to be rebuilt from the survivors who escaped the Falaise Pocket. But Eisenhower pleased neither Patton nor Montgomery when he decided to proceed slowly on a broad front.

"Patton and the Narrow Thrust" by James Arnold picks up the challenge to show what might well had happened had Eisenhower allowed the marriage of the splendid opportunity with the perfect man.

Montgomery was as surely disappointed as Patton with Eisenhower's decision. He, however, as an army group commander had much more freedom of action and fashioned a consolation prize in Operation Market-Garden to seize the Rhine bridges and drive into Germany. Sometimes, such an exercise in alternate history demonstrates exactly the opposite of the accepted "what ifs" as Andrew Uffindell writes in "A Backdoor into Germany: Monty Bounces the Rhine."

These first four chapters address the opportunities that presented themselves to the Allies prior to Hitler's desperate gamble in the Ardennes. These chapters all concerned opportunities fumbled by the Allies. Hitler's gamble, however, was the great attempt to reverse the course of the war in the West in a single decisive blow. Now it was the Germans who raced for the golden prize. As the Allies at first reeled from the blow, then stood fast, and finally counterattacked, the prize remained in play. Christopher Anderson keys on the bone in the German throat as their Panzers drove for the bridges over the Meuse in his "The Race to Bastogne: Nuts!" In reality, the arrival of the 101st Airborne Division to Bastogne was in the nick of time but the division's journey was fraught with delays and misunderstandings, any one of which would have detained it until too late.

Sean Maloney in his "Blunting the Bulge: From the Maas to the Meuse with the First Canadian Army" provides a Canadian option to the Battle of the Bulge that was well within the realm of the possible. It was one that would have made the Allied effort almost entirely a North American one.

Montgomery enters the fray again and plays a plausibly better hand in Charles Vasey's "Go Home. This is our Goddam Show!" while staying in character enough still gratuitiously to insult the Americans whom he had helped.

John Prados in "Operation Herbstnebel: Smoke Over the Ardennes" shows the limitations of the German plan even if more of the breaks fell their way. He writes, "The German offensive at the Battle of the Bulge is very interesting from the standpoint of casting an alternate reality. First of all, not very much needs to change for the outcome to be different. The German preparations, while not flawless, were close to optimum for generating a surprise." He throws into the mix a greater degree of surprise, well within the possibilities.

Kim Campbell's "Holding Patton: Seventh Panzer Army and the Battle of Luxembourg:" takes on a subsidiary operation, that of the German Seventh Army on the southern flank of the offensive and plays out its potential to spoil Patton's famous relief of Bastogne.

The last chapter assumes as its starting off point a German victory in the Ardennes, the capture of Antwerp and the trapping of a million Allied soldiers in a small pocket in Holland. "Ardennes Disaster: The Iron Curtain Falls on the White House" paints the political convulsions that would have rippled from the Ardennes through London and Washington and even Moscow to then wash back on the fighting forces now stretched desperately thin across the front. Early January 1945 finds Churchill driven from office and Franklin Roosevelt dead of a stroke. Charles De Gaulle remains the only Western national leader with clear strategic and political vision. Then, things start to go really bad.

Peter G. Tsouras
Alexandria, Virginia
2004

Notes

1. In American usage it is known as the Battle of the Bulge; British, Canadian, and German histories refer to the Ardennes Offensive.
2. Geoffrey Parker, *The Grand Strategy of Philip II* (Yale University Press, New Haven, 1998) p. 293. Samuel Johnson's quotation is cited as "Thoughts on the late transactions respecting Falkland islands" (1771) in Samuel Johnson, *Political Writings*, X 365–6.

1
MONTY'S D-DAY
Caen and Beyond

David C. Isby

It was the combination of the man and the moment. General Bernard Law Montgomery, brought back from command of the victorious Eighth Army in North Africa and Sicily, was now the Allied Ground Forces Commander, directly under General Dwight Eisenhower, the Supreme Allied Commander in Europe. Montgomery was "doubled hatted," also commanding 21st Army Group which included the British and Canadian Armies that were being committed to Operation Overlord, the D-Day invasions that would commence the liberation of the continent.

Montgomery had direct access to Winston Churchill, Britain's wartime prime minister, and as a senior general who had delivered victory where his predecessors had been defeated, his views carried a great deal of weight with the Allied and British political and military leadership. Britain's continued status as a world power, both in its dealings with its wartime U.S. and Soviet allies and in the postwar world, would depend on it being able to continue to demonstrate that its military capabilities were key to both wartime victory and postwar stability.

A great deal was at stake on D-Day, not all of it apparent on the battlefield. The goals were much broader than those shown by the phase lines on the planning maps: the creation of a viable beachhead that would include the liberation of the ancient Norman cities of Bayeux and Caen on D-Day and would set in motion events that would lead to the defeat of the German armies in France and the Allied breakout from Normandy. Montgomery was uniquely positioned to make it happen.

Resources

To make the liberation of Bayeux and Caen on D-Day more than a mirage would require more than winning that day's battle on the beaches and moving inland. It would require having the invading forces capable of taking the objective. D-Day was not a wargame to be won by the better commander, it was to be the culmination of years of making decisions and of preparing forces for battle. The results of 6 June were determined by decisions made long before that both empowered and limited commanders and planners alike.

Churchill came to the support of Overlord reluctantly. He believed that Britain's resource shortages mandated a minimum-risk strategy on the battlefield. The Anzio invasion in Italy had demonstrated the risks inherent in an amphibious operation. It had been carried out on a basis of risk-minimization in execution, but in eschewing the risks inherent in a rapid advance on Rome, it accepted those associated with a longer battle of attrition. Churchill carried away from Anzio a reluctance to invade northern Europe. Another lesson was that concentrating on getting ashore was not enough and that forces had to push inland quickly. The need to prevent politically unacceptable defeats in the course of even a victorious campaign in order to maintain Britain's status as a great power and to stave off war-weariness in a country stretched thin by years of rationing, shortages and bad news was seen by Churchill as more important than the absolute cost of the victory in the west.

The politics that limited Montgomery on D-Day were not all of Churchill's or even Britain's making. The British and Canadian forces lacked many of the hard-earned advantages that allowed their predecessors in 1918 to defeat the German Army in the last hundred days of that war. For one thing, there was no ANZAC Corps available to Montgomery. One way to have been more assured of a successful landing and move inland would have been substituting for the two British lead divisions, the 50th and 3d Infantry Divisions, the 2d New Zealand Division (with its organic armored brigade) and the 9th Australian Division. Given time to train together and plan, reinforced with British corps-level assets, that would have been a corps to rock the German defenses. But it was not to be. The 2d New Zealand Division remained in Italy, 9th Australian Division in New Guinea. Their absence weakened British landpower for the invasion.

Compounding the pressure on Montgomery to use his forces effectively was the lack of confidence in the U.S. Army that permeated the British political and military leadership. Based in part on U.S. setbacks in the opening stages of the Tunisia campaign and compounded by what the British saw as a critical lack of combat experience on the part of U.S. senior commanders, it was thought that Montgomery's armies represented the best chance of being able to engage the Germans at anything like parity. The British had noted with concern the deficiencies of U.S. divisions training in Britain, but the rapid learning curve and success of those in combat in Sicily and Italy, being further away, had received less attention.

Some of the decisions that constrained Montgomery on D-Day were those of resource allocation, such as how many landing craft, especially the all-important tank landing ships (LSTs) would be built in the U.S. and Britain. The shortage of LSTs and other key amphibious warfare resources was to limit the force that could be put ashore on D-Day and in the critical weeks of the build-up that followed. There was nothing Montgomery, or any other general, could do in 1944 to create more landing craft even though this was the resource that most directly determined battlefield success.

Britain had put a preponderance of its resources into its part in the combined bomber offensive against Germany. This was seen, in the years before D-Day, as the main British strategic front against Germany and held open the prospects of victory without having to repeat the costly battles of attrition on the Western Front in the First World War that were needed to defeat the German Army. Repeating such costly victories would have been seen as unacceptable, both in Britain and in the eyes of those it needed to convince of its continued viability. R.A.F. Bomber Command absorbed quality personnel and resources that could otherwise have improved the ground forces. Again, there was nothing any general could do in the months before D-Day to change this situation.

Yet Montgomery was able to do a great deal to redress the impact of these long-standing resource allocation decisions. Churchill's (and Montgomery's) successful actions to get U.S. agreement to postpone Operation Anvil, the invasion of southern France, mitigated the landing craft shortage. Originally scheduled to be simultaneous with Overlord and so directly in competition for landing craft and other assets, Anvil was now postponed for some two months.

Montgomery was also able to help push the decisions re-allocating the direction of the bomber offensive. Over the objections of their commanders, the bombers would be used against transport targets in France and occupied Europe in the months preceding D-Day and, after the invasion, would be available for attacks on targets near the front lines. This was reflected in the decision on 25 March 1944 to redirect the bombers onto the transport network in France.

These two examples of many showed that, even while Montgomery could not undo long-standing resource allocation decisions, he had considerable weight in deciding how these resources should be used in assuring the success of Overlord.

Men And Units

Montgomery could change only a few things for D-Day.[1] He could insist on more combined arms training. He could insist that key tactical maneuvers on D-Day, including the liberation of Bayeux and Caen, be rehearsed time and time again in comparable countryside in England. He could insist that effective tactics for the *bocage* country of Normandy be worked out and rehearsed in parts of England where there were similar hedgerows, transforming farm fields into miniature fortresses. He could sack commanding officers who proved "sticky"—in the euphemistic idiom of 1944—in offensive tactics.[2] Yet the British did not have large numbers of suitable candidates for battlefield command, the Canadians even fewer.

Montgomery could match "horses for courses." Even if he could not have 9th Australian Division in the first wave to move inland, he could choose which troops went ashore and when, to ensure that there would be effective combined-arms mechanized forces moving inland. Again, he could go to Churchill and push for more resources: to deploy more ships offshore for long-range naval gunfire support; to concentrate troop carrier and transport aircraft from the Mediterranean and U.S. training bases to increase the number of airborne forces in the initial invasion; to get the U.S.A.A.F. and R.A.F. bombers to handle some of the resupply mission for the airborne forces.

Montgomery would have to change the way he personally did business and not insist on the rigid top-down control that had allowed him to turn the situation around in North Africa and put his stamp on the Eighth Army. Montgomery's self-confidence was perhaps the one inexhaustible resource available to the British Army on D-Day. But it needed to be big enough to admit of inputs from other sources than the man himself, from the lessons of the Eastern Front, from the recovered lessons of 1918, and ways to maximize them, as Field Marshal William Slim later explained:

> "Commanders at all levels had to act more on their own; they were given greater latitude to work out their own plans to achieve what they knew was the Army Commander's intention. In time they developed to a marked degree a flexibility of mind and a firmness of decision that enabled them to act swiftly to take advantage of sudden information or changing circumstances without reference to their superiors."

Thus, faster decision making in response to the faster tempo of war required decentralized control.[3]

While more resources could be made available for Montgomery's actions on D-Day, what could not be changed were the British and Canadian ground forces with which he would have to fight. Both political considerations and the purely military decisions on operations, tactics, training and doctrine limited the effectiveness of these forces. In 1944, the British and Canadian Armies were still paying for 1919–39 and their countries' failures to come to grips with the evolving realities of modern war in those years. The increased tide of materiel and the victories in North Africa, Sicily and Italy had not addressed the root causes of repeated British military failures in the opening years of the conflict.

While the British and Canadian divisions waiting for D-Day in England may have had months or years of pre-combat training more than the German divisions they would have to defeat, they were putting in place flawed solutions. The important thing in determining the outcome in Normandy was training. The commanders could not ask any unit to carry out on D-Day actions they had not performed many times before. This included the invasion, the exit from the beaches, and the marrying up of individual units into combined arms task-organized forces.

British and Canadian training had concentrated on the difficult and highly specialized requirements of the amphibious assault itself. The Canadian 9th Infantry Brigade went so far as to announce that it intended to confine its

training to the invasion and not having to fight the remainder of the war.[4]
Despite the importance of combined arms tactics demonstrated in North
Africa, British and Canadian battalions and, with few exceptions, brigades
were single-arm and tended to train that way. Despite many lessons from
North Africa recognizing the importance of having tactical commanders able
to take charge and fight combined arms battles, in the garrison conditions of
wartime England, rigid top-down control by higher level commanders—
desperate to keep their jobs—was the rule.

The Germans, despite their crippling shortage of material and human
resources, could build on pre-war investment and doctrine improved in
combat in the *Blitzkrieg* years and on the Eastern Front. The German
commanders the British and Canadian forces would be opposing on D-Day
and in the subsequent weeks had all been trained against them in North
Africa, or in the fighting on the Eastern Front. The Germans had one
advantage that no other major combatant in the European theater possessed:
the ability to train commanders against forces other than Germans. The
tactical and equipment inadequacies of their pre-1942 opponents allowed the
Germans to build tactical and operational skills and confidence in their
leaders, even as the strategic disaster that awaited Germany loomed closer.

The British and Canadian Armies were trying to solve an operational
problem—beating the Germans in Normandy and liberating France—by
treating it as a tactical problem. Yet, tactically, the British and Canadian
Armies did not have the solution to dealing with an intact German defense.
This provided a great incentive to gain objectives in Normandy before the
German defense was able to solidify, or to take measures, whether through air
bombardment or bold and decisive ground maneuver, to prevent the defense
from solidifying.

German defensive tactics were good. They had been markedly superior to
those of their opponents since at least as far back as 1916 (and were to remain
good to the end of the Cold War). Even when carried out by a greatly
outnumbered force—including the remnants of units hit by massive artillery
or air concentrations—the Germans could slow advancing Allied forces long
enough for reserves to be brought up. The lessons of Tunisia, Sicily and Italy
had demonstrated that attacking Allied infantry, even when they had the
weight of numbers and were supported by excellent and plentiful artillery,
could be held to slow rates of advance and heavy casualties by the combination
of skillfully positioned and camouflaged general purpose machine-guns with
interlocking fields of fire, snipers, and minefields. These were backed up by
equally skillfully used AFVs and anti-tank guns that could limit the ability of
Allied armor to clear away these defenses. Mortars provided the German
defense with a responsive indirect fire capability. The Germans also
demonstrated that, even when Allied infantry were able to prevail against
these economy-of-force defenses, they were often deprived of their gains by a
counterattack before they could consolidate and reorganize. German tactics
had been evolving. While the British and Canadian forces in England had

been training to defeat a defense based around towed anti-tank guns as their primary tank-killing weapon—as the 88mm gun was in North Africa—the Germans defense was strengthened by an increased reliance on self-propelled anti-tank guns, while their infantry had more hand-held anti-tank weapons such as the *Panzerschreck* rocket launcher.

German armies were only defeated by pulling them apart. In the longer term, the ability to conduct their effective defensive tactics would have to be defeated by attrition but there would not be time for attrition on D-Day. The ability of Allied firepower superiority to unravel the German defensive tactics was limited. The combat units were not heavily armed enough and had to rely on "outside" firepower from higher levels, which mandated top-down planning to make sure the firepower was delivered in an accurate and timely manner and avoided fratricide. This required that advancing troops keep to a precise schedule, even if this meant forgoing opportunities to advance when offered by enemy battlefield weakness. The British and Canadians had made advances in battlefield command and control, but they had not solved the problems of integration and coordination. The British and Canadian Armies in England had not been the beneficiaries of the same sort of technological advances and rapid tactical innovation that had marked those countries' air forces and navies in the preceding years. In part, this reflected resource allocation decisions that often put the armies in third place. It also reflected the ambiguous high-level political support for the mission—decisive battle in Northwest Europe—that these armies would be committed to.[5]

The leading cause of problems is solutions to other problems; the problems with the British and Canadian Armies that inhibited their ability to carry out high-tempo combined-arms mechanized operations were solutions to the problem of how to avoid the (politically unacceptable) losses of 1916 on the Somme and 1941–42 in the desert. The British and Canadian doctrine of "metal before muscle," intended to minimize casualties in the short term, played to their strength (flexible and powerful artillery) rather than weakness (shortage of infantry replacements). It also incorporated lessons from Alamein, Tunisia and Italy, where effective artillery and air support, more than bold and decisive maneuver, had made advances possible. The British had solved the problem of uncoordinated weak combined arms mechanized "Jock columns" "swanning off into the blue" in North Africa and being defeated in detail by Rommel by insisting on detailed pre-planning. While this made possible the strong top-down control Montgomery used successfully at Alamein, it also prevented rapid maneuver or infiltration. It provided minimal scope for initiative, even though the tactical commanders who remained were more experienced than those who had often been defeated by the *Afrika Korps*. Pre-planned timed air and artillery strikes prevented a repetition of experiences in North Africa where the artillery had been forced to withhold fire when British and German armor had been intermixed. Yet this in practice prevented tactical—let alone operational—exploitation or even seizing opportunities.

Raising the tempo on D-Day would have required highly developed tactical skills and experience that were too often lacking in the British and Canadian forces training in England, or even in those divisions that had returned from the Eighth Army for the invasion. Systematic application of lessons learned was attempted—many British and Canadian units in England received training from veterans of North Africa—but too often fell short. "Without the correction of fundamental doctrinal flaws, other areas of innovation—organizational and training reforms or better weaponry—can only marginally improve an army's combat capabilities."[6]

Too often lessons learned in other combat zones were not allowed to contradict received wisdom providing by the army training establishments. What the British and Canadians did not manage was to set up a "feedback loop" that would lead to doing things better. Most important was that this was applied at the operational level as well as at the soldier and tactical level. What they lacked was assurance that the Germans could be beaten in a mechanized battle and a viable model of how to do so. This had not been provided by El Alamein or Tunisia. There was no equivalent of the 1943–44 campaigns in Burma, which showed that the Japanese were not invincible in the jungle. The model remained Alamein, avoiding weakness in mobile warfare through methodical advance and weight of materiel.

It was unlikely that the deficiencies in British and Canadian tactical training and doctrine could be remedied in time for D-Day. But there were ways around this. The Soviets had demonstrated this since Stalingrad when they cut off and captured large German formations. The Germans' tactical superiority there did not give them victory. The most potentially significant solution Montgomery could have helped bring about to improve his armies was to define an effective operational doctrine which, previously, had been basically unknown outside the German and Russian forces. Even had Montgomery been willing, the lack of a sound doctrinal foundation to build on precluded his putting in place an operational-level solution to his force's tactical limitations.

Some things could be changed. The need for improved staff work—especially intelligence—to make sure that Allied material superiority was not wasted was one way the British and Canadian Armies could be made more effective. This was a key combat lesson in North Africa, when poor staff work contributed to many of the British tactical defeats. It was also an area where the British and Canadian forces had too often failed to come up to the level of professionalism they had achieved in 1918.[7]

The willingness to maximize the potential impact of air power on the battlefield was another area where North African experience offered the potential for improved near-term effectiveness, without the large-scale changes that Montgomery lacked time to implement.

It had taken until 1942 for the British to get back to where they were in 1918 in terms of air-ground cooperation.[8] The British had developed tactics for effective air-ground coordination and direction of close air support by the time of Alamein. In Tunisia, the use of air-direction "tentacle" links and "cab-ranks" of fighter bombers in holding patterns over friendly territory until a target was located had been successfully demonstrated. However, despite this capability, training forward air controllers to operate with forward deployed forces had lagged in the United Kingdom. It proved to be difficult to assure reliable air–ground communications. But this was an area where combat lessons could be identified and investments in training and resources could provide results that would yield increased combat effectiveness, even when large-scale re-equipping or re-training was not feasible.

Bomber Command itself was no longer the blunt instrument that its own leaders claimed it to be. In the transport campaign before D-Day, when collateral damage concerns placed a premium on accuracy, the use of skilled crews from the Pathfinder Force and navigational aids had allowed the R.A.F.'s heavy bombers to strike targets at night with a circular error probable (the distance around the aim point where half the projectiles impact) of under 300 yards. If matched with good intelligence—it was easier precisely to locate targets such as marshaling yards rather than troops in assembly areas—the R.A.F. heavy bomber force was capable of more than carpet-bombing.[9]

Yet the bombers' potential impact on the results of D-Day would require not only integrating them with the ground forces' scheme of maneuver, but doing so while the R.A.F. leadership was opposed to such support, which was considered a diversion from the strategic bombing campaign. The pre-bombing transport campaign met with resistance for the same reasons. Yet, while the bombers would be required to continue their interdiction attacks, the initial stages of the invasion allowed bombers to hit enemy concentration areas in ways that neither the close air support mission or later stages of the campaign would make likely.

Turning Intentions into Battlefield Reality

Montgomery stressed the importance of highly aggressive mobile execution of the plan on D-Day, to act with forces well trained in offensive tactics. He made inputs throughout the planning process, dating from when he first saw a draft of the plan at Marrakech in 1943.[10] Montgomery may have had a reputation from his methodical operations in North Africa and Sicily. Yet at his 7 April briefing at St Paul's School, London, he emphasized the importance not only of methodically using Allied numerical and material superiority to defeat the German defenders but also of using bold and decisive maneuver. Montgomery stressed it was important to threaten breakouts both from the U.S. and British ends of the beachhead.[11]

Similarly, Montgomery sent a message to his subordinate army commanders, Lieutenant General Omar Bradley (commanding the First U.S. Army) and Lieutenant-General Miles Dempsey, (commanding Second [British] Army) on 14 April:

"Having seized the initiative by our initial landing, we must insure that we keep it. The best way to interfere with enemy concentrations and countermeasures will be to push forward fairly powerful armoured force thrusts on the afternoon of D-Day… The whole effect of such aggressive tactics would be to retain the initiative ourselves and to cause alarm in the minds of the enemy… Armoured units… must be concentrated quickly… Speed and boldness are then required and the armoured thrusts must force their way inland… I am prepared to accept almost any risk to carry out these tactics."[12]

Montgomery had impressed on his army commanders the need to link up the beachheads as quickly as possible, but that they must retain the initiative, recognizing that while the Allied forces would be vulnerable to counterattack while they "get the whole organization sorted out and working smoothly; while this was happening there was a danger of the enemy catching us off-balance."[13] Montgomery said of the invading forces at a 15 May briefing that they must be:

"…sent into this party 'seeing red.' Nothing must stop them… We must blast our way ashore and get a good lodgment before the enemy can bring up sufficient reserves to turn us out. Armoured columns must penetrate deep inland and quickly on D-Day… We must gain space rapidly and peg out claims well inland."[14]

This stated the commander's intention in no uncertain terms. Without the ability to execute the commander's intention, it was no more than rhetoric, a broad yet empty goal. Preventing them from executing the commander's intention were both external constraints and the nature of the British and Canadian Armies themselves. The sheer importance of the decisions made about executing the invasion itself and getting the Allied forces ashore tended to obscure others about how those forces would fight to achieve their objectives once they were ashore. The results of D-Day depended heavily on decisions made long before H-Hour or when the first live rounds were chambered.

The Bomber Attacks 5–6 June.
On the night of 5–6 June, the R.A.F. Bomber Command pre-invasion attacks, originally intended to be aimed primarily at the coastal batteries and the beach defenses, were instead re-targeted at German reserve units in their assembly areas, especially those of the 21st Panzer Division. The location of these positions had been determined in the preceding weeks by making a priority of the fusion of air reconnaissance, reports from the French resistance, and wireless signal intercepts.[15] The accuracy possible at short ranges using navigational beacons transmitting from the UK or close to the coast using the bombers' own equipment (the coastline was visible on the bombers' H2S radars) meant that the bombers could threaten battalion-size assembly areas

as well as large conurbations. Unlike the beach defenses, these were not near the coast, putting a premium on the Pathfinders of 8 Group of R.A.F. Bomber Command. The strikes ensured that the hours of darkness would not be used for preparing a rapid reaction move or launching a counterattack against the Allied paratroopers, but recovering from the results of bombardment.

Punishing strikes were inflicted on several of *21st Panzer Division*'s battalions. But several other attacks missed their targets altogether. They either had too large a target location error to inflict any damage on the target unit or the Pathfinders had been unable to mark the location of the target. This change of the Bomber Command D-Day mission represented an awareness that the real threat to the British accomplishing their D-Day aims was not the beach defenses, which could be countered by more effective use of naval guns, but mobile forces able to counterattack and defeat British spearheads advancing inland or to penetrate to the beachheads.

The hours preceding D-Day would be one of the last times when targeting German reserve units rather than static defenses would be possible, as they would likely move before they would be targeted. However, even though the losses were not as large as had been hoped, the German reserve units were disorganized by the effects of the bombardment and were less able to intervene when the orders came.

The Airborne Invasion

Operation Hillman, the British airborne invasion on D-Day, was intended to anchor the potentially vulnerable left flank. It including the seizure, by glider-delivered troops, of what became known as Pegasus and Horsa bridges. The airborne troops were given an additional mission, however: seizing key objectives in and around Caen, an element revived from earlier planning for the Normandy invasion.[16]

Because the lightly-equipped 6th Airborne Division was thinly stretched in its existing mission, this meant that forces had to be added to the air invasion. This, in turn, meant that more aircraft had to be provided but this was possible. A U.S.A.A.F. troop carrier wing was pulled out of the Mediterranean (along with the British 1st Airborne Division it was to drop). Other transport aircraft were combed out of home-based American units. While these did not have crews trained to drop paratroops, they could be used for resupply. R.A.F. and U.S.A.A.F. bombers could also be pressed into service to drop supply and weapons canisters.

Because of the importance of the airborne drops to the British plan, there had been a high-level assessment of their strengths and limitations ordered directly from Montgomery. This had led to the decision to equip the airborne troops with large amounts of U.S. equipment stripped from divisions waiting in England for the later stages of the build-up. The British airborne soldiers had little time to train on U.S. bazookas and tactical radios, but it was better than going into battle with their own inadequate kit. Tactics were also modified to the extent possible at the last minute, with special reference to airfield seizure. The German tactics of 1940–41 were reviewed, with reference to the drops in the Netherlands and Crete. Additional glider pilots were trained in diving, tactical approaches to small landing zones.

The elements of the British 1st Airborne Division that were sent into the Caen sector followed the model of the 6th Airborne Division on the flank, modified to take the stronger expected resistance into account. The last-minute requirements for tactical adaptation were better received by the combat veterans of the 1st than the 6th, who had years of exercising in England to prepare them for their mission.[17] The drops were timed to follow closely the bomber strikes on flak concentrations and the German reserve unit positions.

The airborne drops were marked with confusion. Despite the extensive use of R.A.F. Bomber Command pathfinders with the troop carriers, many of the paratroopers were scattered. The multiple R.A.F. bomber attacks also compounded the situation. The central assault was on Carpiquet airfield, built on a plateau southwest of Caen that overlooked the Orne valley. Following a high-altitude bomber attack on the airfield, a battalion-sized parachute drop seized the airfield, landing while the outnumbered garrison—*Luftwaffe* flak troops, a *Waffen-SS* flak platoon and howitzer battery—were emerging from their slit trenches.[18] The paratroopers removed obstacles on the main runway for a glider-borne force, already in the air. If this force had not seen the marker flares showing that the runway was clear, it would have had to divert. The flares were set out at the last minute and the gliders arrived, bringing in a force from the divisional reconnaissance squadron with heavily armed gun jeeps.[19] These were to dash to take the Orne River crossings in Caen itself and hold them until the other 1st Airborne Division units could form up and reinforce them. At the other drop zones near Caen, casualties were heavy. But the *coups de main* to seize the Orne River bridges near Caen, succeeded, as did the smaller force from 6th Airborne at Pegasus Bridge.

D-Day: Invasion

On the three British and Canadian beaches—Sword, Gold and Juno—the landings ranged from the near-unopposed in places to the heaviest fighting of the day outside of Omaha Beach. Here was an area where the extensive investment in, and training for, beach landings, especially capability provided by the specialized AFVs of the 79th Armoured Division, paid off.[20] Once ashore, the challenge was to build on this dear-bought success.

One of the improvements to the invasion plan had been an increased number of warships for the shore bombardment mission and incorporation in the tactics for cooperation with the ships of the lessons learned from Sicily, Salerno, Anzio, and especially the U.S. experiences in the Pacific. The reinforced bombardment ships were as concentrated offshore as they were to be off Iwo Jima in 1945. Each division had a battleship (or cruiser substitute) inshore for close support. Each assault battalion had "its" destroyer supporting it, which the battalion had rehearsed and trained alongside. More ships pulled in for shore bombardment duties; assault battalions had better reinforced naval gunfire teams to direct the fire of "their" destroyers against German strongpoints.

But even where improved fire direction tactics and training knocked out strongpoints that could have otherwise delayed the invasion, there was little that could be done about the congestion at the beach exits and the delays of moving inland. While many of the assaulting infantry battalions were able to infiltrate around continued German resistance or blocked beach exits and advance to their assembly areas inland, there was no way this could be done with the vehicles landing on the beach. There, the delays in getting moving proved to be a critical factor, even with improved coordination between beachmaster parties and the specialized tanks to create routes off the beach.

The congestion on the beach was critical because, by noon, the second echelon of the invasion was coming ashore. This represented one of the most important divergences from the original plan, for instead of bringing ashore the third brigades and divisional assets of the three assault divisions, on each of the three British and Canadian beaches an armored brigade group was to be landed. Montgomery had decided to violate divisional integrity in his two British and one Canadian assault divisions. Rather than expecting the British 50th and 3d Infantry Divisions to push inland and take Bayeux and Caen respectively on D-Day, they would push forward to open beach area exits for these brigades to make a passage of the lines and continue the advance. The Canadian 3d Infantry Division would continue to push towards Caen, providing flank protection.

These stripped down brigade-sized combined arms mechanized forces were to expand the invasion inland and link up with 1st Airborne in the Caen sector. Each consisted of a regiment (battalion-equivalent) of Sherman tanks, a motorized infantry battalion, a regiment (battalion) of self-propelled howitzers, and a force of specialized tanks, flails for minefields and fascine-carriers to fill in anti-tank ditches.[21] The "cost" for putting these forces ashore was to delay a brigade of each of the assault divisions and many of the divisional assets, especially artillery and anti-aircraft units, until the next day.

To violate divisional integrity and ask the armored brigades to make a passage of the lines with the assault infantry divisions soon after they had moved off the beach and would doubtlessly be hotly engaged was something that seemed to turn against Montgomery's earlier successful generalship (though it owed a great deal to a time-compressed version of the tactics that proved successful during the break-in at Alamein). Yet Montgomery realized that if he was going to turn his commander's intention into more than rhetoric, his infantry divisions, wedded to battle drill and methodical advance (in the absence of 9th Australian or a comparable formation) and whose combined-arms training emphasized the use of Churchill tanks of the army tank brigades as part of these tactics, would not be able to push on to the objective. Even if ordered to make a rapid advance, they were too vulnerable to even small forces that would, with snipers, machine guns and mines, slow

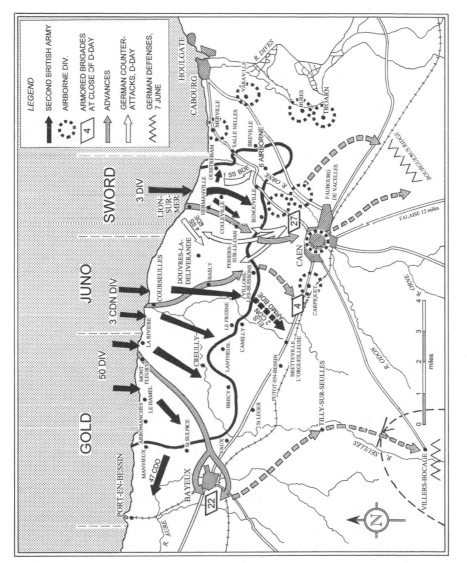

From the Beaches to Caen: 6–7 June 1944

their advance until German mechanized reserves could stop them and then deliver a counterattack. Montgomery realized that he could not ask infantry, even when given wheels and tank support, to do the job of a combined arms mechanized force.

The three (understrength) armored brigades that constituted the second echelon—22d Armoured Brigade from 7th Armoured Division on Gold Beach, 27th Armoured Brigade on Sword, 4th Armoured Brigade on Juno Beach—all had specific objectives for D-Day. All had been originally intended to come ashore late on D-Day or on D+1; the new plan just accelerated their landing, moving around LSTs rather than requiring additional ones. The 22d Armoured Brigade was to advance and seize Bayeux, opening the road to link-up with the Americans. Once reinforced with the rest of the 7th Armoured Division on D+1, it was to continue to drive deep into the German defenses, protecting the flank of Caen from the west and preventing the German defense from solidifying. It would be followed by an infantry division when landed. The 27th and 4th Armoured Brigades were to advance to link-up with 1st Airborne Division in its positions around Caen before it could be defeated by German counterattacks.

These brigades had practised the difficult passage of lines—moving through the attacking infantry—in repeated command post exercises with the assault division staffs. They had also rehearsed it in field training exercises, using parts of Sussex where the hills and hedgerow-lined roads were like those running towards Caen. Fratricide was a special concern, addressed by large formation recognition markings on jettisonable panels.

In many ways, the plan was for the application of a 1918 lesson on firepower and coordination, rather than looking to the speed and shock of the advance to prevent the Germans from reacting to block the drive inland. As in 1918, pre-planning and mission-specific training made coordination possible. Because German defenses were in depth, it was necessary to apply firepower throughout the depths of the defense near-simultaneously. Heavy guns did this in 1918. The alternative was to use the available firepower to crack the initial defenses then wait and consolidate—which the aggressive German defense was unlikely to permit to pass without a counterthrust—then crack the second line. Swift exploitation of the results of firepower was found to be vital.[22]

The 6 June 1944 application of firepower through the depths of the defense was marked by the re-appearance, during the afternoon of D-Day, of Bomber Command. Its second mission was to follow the pre-invasion strike that had hit the assembly areas of German units away from the beachhead. But, as it would be for the remainder of the campaign, the target location error was now greater and fratricide concerns would limit the ability of these bombers to be decisive. Locations where German reserves and artillery threatening the 1st Airborne paratroops at the airfield and the Orne bridgehead near Caen were likely to be positioned were selected as targets in the absence of timely reconnaissance. Because the paratroopers were holding relatively confined positions and were able to set up marker beacons for the bombers, the attacks were able to disrupt German counterattacks against them without fratricide.

Now, the challenge would be to use Allied firepower superiority to limit the counterattack capability of German reserves, especially those of the *21st Panzer Division* and reserve infantry units that might have left their assembly areas. While the ability to knock out large numbers of tanks with heavy bombers was as limited in daylight as it was in darkness, the objective was to hit areas where German forces could be expected to engage the advancing armored brigades, either with anti-tank fire or counterattacks with combined arms forces.

During the afternoon of D-Day the pre-planned strikes by heavy and medium bombers were intended to create destructive and demoralizing effects. For areas close to the battle, they needed to be coordinated with ground units, with offset distances to reduce the chance of fratricide. For the bombing of German reserve units, where the goal was to delay and disrupt commitment, this meant accepting lesser effects.

Well-trained and coordinated tactical airpower was required to engage relocatable targets (such as mobile *Kampfgruppen*) and those German forces within the stand-off distance imposed on the bombers. Tactical airpower, along with artillery (both long-range and self-propelled) would provide the firepower through the depths of the German defenses. The three armored brigades would provide the movement.

Close air support was instrumental in the deep advances made on D-Day. The advance of the 22d Armoured Brigade on Bayeux was delayed by congestion at the beach exits but it was successful. There was hard fighting when German reserves from *352d Infantry Division*, brought forward to reinforce the troops from the static divisions, were encountered in hasty defensive positions. A combined arms attack with close air support and direct support from the self-propelled howitzers was sufficient to bull through, though strongpoints remained to engage follow-on forces.

The two brigades advancing on Caen and the link-up with 1st Airborne were critical to Montgomery's D-Day goals. It was a maneuver they had exercised many times before, across comparable pieces of hedgerow-divided English countryside. The desert veterans of the 4th Armoured Brigade, advancing down the Basly road, met relatively light resistance. After a fire fight near Les Buissons, defeating forces from a static division and a counterattack from *21st Panzer Division*, they were able to use reconnaissance reports over the air control "tentacle" to infiltrate towards the paratroopers in Caen.

The 27th Armoured Brigade, advancing along the road from Lion-sur-Mer towards Caen, was engaged with German forces around the high ground east of Epron when the major German counterattack of D-Day was launched by elements of the *21st Panzer Division* from its open flank, supported by head-on attacks by elements of *12th SS Panzer* not "pinned" by the fighting around Caen.[23]

The main German thrust was launched towards the beaches, the decisive sector, hoping to overrun the landing areas and link up with isolated coastal strongpoints still holding out. Only a secondary thrust, advancing blind in the absence of effective German reconnaissance, consisting of one *Kampfgruppe* of the *21st Panzer Division* tried to flank the 27th Armoured Brigade. Again, the tentacle provided warning of the German counterattack. Close air support was called in against the attacking Germans. The survivors found themselves engaged by tanks in hull-down firing positions, the anti-tank guns of the motor battalion, and the protective fires of the self-propelled artillery. The German counterattacks failed.[24]

At the critical moment, the late-day reinforcing airdrop brought in additional forces that seemed, to the Germans, to be in a position to cut them off. Several of the 1st Airborne drop and landing zones were too close to the enemy to be used, forcing the use of alternatives in the 6th Airborne Division sector. But it was enough that the British forces held on. The link-up at the Orne River bridgehead in Caen and Carpiquet airfield to the southwest was finally carried out after dark.

The British achievement of their D-Day objectives, however, had its overall impact limited by the results on the other beaches. The U.S. advance inland from Omaha Beach had been slowed for a number of reasons, including the unexpected German resistance and lack of specialized AFVs. This left the British flank nearly open. It had the potential to limit Montgomery's ability to exploit the success gained on D-Day.[25]

However, Montgomery decided to use his forces—feeding them into the attack as they came ashore—to continue the advance while relying on follow-on forces arriving to backstop the German counterattacks. He would rely on Ultra intercepts of German orders for a counterattack, using Allied intelligence advantages to accept a degree of risk in order to turn his pre-invasion intentions into post-invasion reality.[26]

The successful advance on D-Day meant that there was more area for the build-up but also more front for the British and Canadians to cover. The situation in Normandy resembled that of the classic meeting engagement. Both sides could gain an advantage by getting forces into battle earlier. It says much for the effectiveness of the Allied air interdiction campaign and the effects of the strategic air offensive on the German petrochemical industry that the Allies were able to maintain their advantage even though they had to bring their forces cross-channel.

The Germans were used to defending a long front through quick-reacting maneuver, with only a screen of static defenses to delay an attacker. They had been refining how to do this since 1916. But this was not something the linear-minded British and Canadian Armies were comfortable with doing and they remembered all too well the defeats Rommel dealt out to poorly trained commanders and units which had tried to emulate the brilliant advances of the original 7th Armoured Division of 1940 (which carried out magnificent offensive actions in the opening North African campaign of 1940–41) without first having its training and skilled personnel. While the advances on D-Day were assured by objective and mission-specific training, well-planned use of airpower, and fine fighting by the troops on the ground, especially the 1st Airborne Division's paratroopers, continuing to use superior intelligence to gain battlefield advantage would be more problematic. If the divisional and brigade commanders had all been combat veterans with their confidence sharpened by repeated exercises,[27] or if they all had access to the intelligence that went to the top levels of command, it might have worked better, but Montgomery, on 7 June much more than on 6 June, had to play the hand he had been dealt.

D+1 and Beyond

On 7 June, resupplied by airdrops in the morning, the 4th and 27th Armoured Brigades advanced from Caen to Bourguébus Ridge, southeast of the city, with its commanding fields of fire to the north and offering the position for the jumping off of an advance to the south, to Falaise and beyond, to Argentan. As ordered, they were to carry on the bold and decisive maneuver of D-Day, only this time there was no ability to coordinate through detailed advance staff work.

The Germans had only small forces on Bourguébus ridge, mainly the survivors of the previous day's fighting further north reinforced by a scratch collection of reserve units pushed forward. But this time there was no higher headquarters to coordinate the two attacking brigades, limited fire support because of the lack of pre-planned airpower and a shortage of direct support artillery ammunition. The British tried to "bounce" Bourguébus Ridge. In what amounted to two non-supporting attacks; each was stopped in detail. One was broken up by German forces still holding on to the Faubourg de Vacelles, across the Orne from the British positions in Caen. Because of fears of a counterattack against the positions around Caen, neither attack was pressed home. Instead both brigades withdrew into defensive positions.[28]

During the day, the advanced units of the British 3d Infantry and the Canadian 3d Infantry Divisions were able to advance to relieve the paratroopers, but neither side had a solid or cohesive front line. Allied intelligence superiority—Ultra decrypts and air reconnaissance—gave them a better idea than the Germans had of where the enemy's gaps might be found by quick-moving armored spearheads. In effect, Allied intelligence superiority provided a technological solution where the Germans were forced to put in place an operational solution to holding too long a front with scant forces.

The 22d Armoured Brigade did better on 7 June. With limited resupply, it was able to move off from Bayeux, where it was relieved by troops of the British 50th Infantry Division during the day. Moving south, it encountered German resistance around Tilly-sur-Seulles. Without artillery or air support, it was able to infiltrate around to Villers-Bocage, but there had to hold on, awaiting reinforcements and resupply and guarding the western flank of Caen. Here, the forces that had come ashore early on D-Day were reinforced with the remainder of the brigade, a further two armored regiments. Other elements of the 7th Armoured Division, now ashore, were following its route. Long columns of vehicles with Desert Rat insignia filled the few routes cleared of obstacles. On several occasions, they were forced to turn front to flank to engage German counterattacks. More Allied forces were coming ashore, as were supplies to restart the advance and headquarters to coordinate the forces.

On the other side, while every unit that arrived in Normandy was immediately being pushed into the front line, the German commanders immediately set about planning a counterattack. The British positions around Caen and their tank strength ashore required the commitment of the bulk of German armor to that sector, rather than against the U.S. advance towards the base of the Cotentin Peninsula. The immediate German goal was to penetrate between Caen and Bayeux towards the strongpoints bypassed on D-Day.

The British were able to seize the initiative. 7th Armoured Division was to move to Villers-Bocage, defeating any threat to the Caen area from the west, and then advance into the developing "Caumont Gap," several dozen square miles of terrain where there were minimal German forces holding the ground.[29] If the British and Canadian Armies were going to fight the way Montgomery wanted them to, the priority would be exploiting the Caumont Gap, not defending the hard-won gains along the Orne. The forces in and around Caen had to dig in and hold on against increasing pressure from *12th SS Panzer Division* and other German reserves. But the pressure on Caen was not to be relieved by committing forces into that battle, but by increasing pressure on the Germans elsewhere.

The first step in this was the Desert Rats' advance. This came to a halt with a counterattack by a numerically smaller German force against the spearhead 22d Armoured Brigade that had advanced as far as Villers-Bocage and was starting to head southwest for the Caumont Gap. As they had done so many times on the Eastern Front against Soviet tank penetrations with their flanks unsecured, the Germans were able to inflict heavy losses.[30] The British to the north—the rest of the 7th Armoured Division spread out in road columns stretching back towards Bayeux and the beaches—were unable to bring their superior numbers to bear against the Germans. Movement cross country ran into minefields at roadblocks and concealed anti-tank guns that were soon reinforced by German armor.[31]

Over the next few days, however, instead of withdrawing, the remainder of 7th Armoured Division tried to maneuver around the defeat. The result was a defeat reminiscent of the worst days in the desert in 1942. Another German counterattack, thrusting north of Villers-Bocage. cut off the spearhead. The Germans did not have enough mobile reserves available to complete the rout, but most of the Desert Rats' tanks that had not been lost in action had to be abandoned as their crews retired behind a rearguard position held by the division's lorried infantry brigade. Close air support inflicted substantial losses on the Germans, but with most of the British artillery still out of range of the advancing division, there was not enough firepower to defeat them. The attempt to make a broad and sweeping advance had ended up in defeat in detail. However, it did draw German reserves away from the Caen fighting, where the British positions were being solidified. However, the British were still looking up at defenses solidifying in front of them on the high ground south of the Orne valley.

The Results

The Germans—in the best traditions of their Eastern Front victories of 1943—moved immediately to launch an operational counterattack. In the days after 7th Armoured Division was in its losing battle or trying to move around the German threat to Caen from the west, they did not commit the forces arriving at the front to this battle, but concentrated them for a counterattack. Rather than pursue the Desert Rats towards Bayeux (and hit the anti-tank guns and supporting tanks of the 50th Infantry Division) other German forces struck north towards the road linking Caen with the beachheads, hoping to cut it or at least drive a wedge between the two potential points for a British advance.[32]

It was now the British turn to react. Alerted by Ultra to the planning for the counterattack, many of 21st Army Group's anti-tank units, now ashore, were brought forward into hasty defensive positions. Increased naval shore bombardment, accepting risks from German submarine and air threats, joined with tactical airpower to limit the German penetrations to insupportable advances by units that had infiltrated past British strongpoints towards the beaches.[33] The German chance to take advantage of the higher level of risks the British had been willing to take to achieve their D-Day advantage had passed. But the need to push the armored brigades forward into Caen to defend the paratroopers and the need for follow-on forces to fight their way forward prevented bolder British advances even if the troops had been trained for them and willing to carry out such actions. The ability of even small and disrupted German reserves to spoil the plans on which British coordination with air and artillery depended undercut the British chance to gain more than tactical advantage from their success on D-Day. The British chance for an operationally significant advance had passed as well.

Montgomery had tried to compensate for the limitations of his British and Canadian forces by planning, coordination, adding forces, and changing the focus of planning in training from the movement ashore to the movement to the first objectives. But no plan survives contact with the enemy, and the British and Canadian Armies, even with improved staff work, were unable quickly to come to grips with the opportunities that started to present themselves on 7 June. Examples were the failure to "bounce" Bourguébus ridge against a numerically weak German force and the punishment inflicted on the 7th Armoured Division when, trying to move with the high operational tempo Montgomery's intent demanded, it ended up being decimated by a smaller German force in a situation where neither Ultra, air reconnaissance, nor close air support could allow it to bring its superior numbers to bear.

The British success on D-Day led to higher casualties than might have been expected otherwise, especially among the paratroopers who to hold until relieved. Had they not been re-equipped at the last minute, even these skilled and determined soldiers might have been overrun. The seizure of the objectives on D-Day meant that there was a large beachhead for the build-up, removing some of the constraints that would otherwise have slowed the arrival of forces and supplies. But the most important advantages were that it prevented the cost, both in casualties and in morale, that a long battle of attrition in front of Caen would have entailed and, secondly, it showed that British and Canadian forces could find a solution to even the most clever and skillful German defense, given time, and that they could then exploit this with effective mobile combat.

The British success on D-Day made the U.S. fighting considerable easier. In the words of Omar Bradley:

> "Faced with the task of defending so tantalizing a route of advance to the Reich [Caen direct to Paris] the Germans could not be blamed for believing Monty might hope to force a breakthrough in the vicinity of Caen."[34]

Even after the First U.S. Army had taken St Lô, the Germans were not able to transfer armored reserves to meet the emerging threat in that sector.

The superior staff work and air-ground coordination that Montgomery was able to put in place before the invasion helped more than a commitment to effective mobile operations through improved coordination and planning in the battle of attrition that followed. This included several bloody repulses before much of the high ground outside of Caen, including Bourguébus ridge that stood near-empty on 7 June, was finally seized.

Much to the bitter disappointment of Montgomery, and Churchill who had backed him, there was no way around taking the German forces apart, unit by unit, a costly process. It was no consolation that even their German opponents did not have the tactics for combined arms offensives that could yield decisive breakthroughs against an enemy who was combat experienced and had armored and anti-tank reserves. The frustrations of the Germans at Kursk in 1943 were learned afresh by the British and Canadians in Normandy.

But that it was possible to do better was being demonstrated, even then, by the Soviet Army's destruction of Army Group Center and its offensive into Rumania. The most important result of taking Caen on D-Day was not the terrain gained and the hard fighting avoided. It was that the British and Canadian Armies were able to put in place a solution to the operational and tactical problem of how to prevail on the lethal battlefields of 1944–45 despite their own drawbacks and limitations. The British and Canadian forces, demonstrating the same sort of capability on a smaller scale and achieved through different reasons, were able to do their part when the U.S. breakout from Normandy, Operation Cobra, started on 15 July. In this battle the British and Canadians were able to breach the German lines and advance to beyond Falaise, closing the pocket on the German Army in Normandy and then keeping it closed.

The Reality

Wargamers often are guilty of trying to win games by using the tactics and thinking of a later era. Unless constrained by realistic limits on command capabilities and the imposition of the "fog of war" or restrained by what are known as "iron maiden" rules, they will gleefully have Frederick the Great's troops act like French revolutionaries or Stonewall Jackson's foot cavalry. Anyone postulating different potential outcomes needs to identify what can be changed and what cannot. Here, the British and Canadian Armies on D-Day are not shown acting like the German Panzer divisions at their most skillful. Nor were they going to fight the way 5th Guards Tank Army was doing at the same time on the Eastern Front. The historian also cannot criticize these forces for failing to metamorphose into their more effective late Cold War future selves, with reliable radios and more realistic training.

Rather, the success possible on D-Day is shown in some ways as embracing the lessons of previous combat. The changes postulated as making Caen on D-Day possible were all lessons that were inherent in the 1918 experience as well as in the lessons on combined arms operations and tactics that the German (and Soviet) armed forces had demonstrated throughout the Second World War. These were changes that could have been made even if the underlying failure to evolve in 1919–39 was not addressed.

The British experience of the earlier years of the conflict established foundations that improved operations and tactics could be built on. In 1940, the original British 7th Armored Division was probably better than any Panzer division, but it was the result of local adaptation by good, junior leaders. The British could not reproduce this hand-crafted success, still less were they able to define the ideas behind it and apply them to new war-raised mechanized formations, British and Canadian. In Normandy, from D-Day to the Falaise gap, they were trying to push through offensive operations with forces that were not prepared for them, lacked the replacements to sustain them and were fighting against unforgiving opponents.

The issue of Montgomery is critical to any consideration of British and Canadian performance in Normandy. He was identified with the forces under his command in a way that few commanders in later years would be. His two army-level commanders, Dempsey and Crerar, remain overshadowed by him. Indeed he clearly identified what the Allied plan needed before D-Day—yet he could have done more to bring it about.

It is apparent that Montgomery's ego remained a barrier to implementing many of these fixes. Yet there were broader deficiencies beyond Monty's combination of self-regard and admitted tactical skill. His army commanders, both meticulous planners rather than thrusting armored commanders, would not have been expected to provide this. It is hard to avoid concluding that the

German Panzer General Geyr von Schweppenburg's judgment on von Rundstedt "an infantryman of the last generation" applied also to Monty.[35]

An infantry commander of 1918 could have brought the British Army to Caen, even if it would then have been beyond its capability to use the advantages offered by Allied Ultra intelligence and superior mobility and German logistics weakness to exploit the Caumont Gap and defeat the German Panzer reserves in a series of mobile battles *en route* to Paris and the German frontier. That would have beyond the capability of any of the British or American ground forces in June 1944.

The Germans would have played it differently. As for the Soviets, they long taught the Normandy campaign after D-Day as a nadir of the operational art in their staff colleges. Their forces were used to wagering on big decisive advances. When they lost equally big they had to answer to Stalin, but there were, unlike for the Western Allies, no newspaper accounts to sting their political master nor voters to ask what was going on.

The important fact was not whether Caen was taken on D-Day. Such an advance would certainly have helped the situation on the ground and led to the breakout perhaps some weeks before it finally took place, but that depended on events remote from the British sector, such as the inflow rate over the beaches after the great storm and the results of the fighting on the Cotentin peninsula. But those were marginal advantages.

The improvement in the British and Canadian Armies postulated is not outside the capability of even a faltering British war economy and an army weakened by years of war and the loss of its best personnel and other claims on resources. Had the British and Canadian Armies in England in 1944 improved from their 1942 predecessors in the same way and degree as the British and Indian Armies committed to fight the Japanese did over the same time frame, it would have created formations that would have taken Caen on D-Day (and relieved Arnhem in Operation Market Garden).

What was most important is that had British and Canadian Armies been the kind of forces that were able to take Caen on D-Day, it would have meant that all of the Northwest Europe campaign would have gone better. The postulated armies that took Caen on D-Day would never have had the frustrations of Market Garden or the campaign for the Antwerp approaches that their real-world counterparts did. They would have been able to find ways to carry out their missions, given sufficient time for the in-depth staff work and coordination with airpower that would have meant that they would have fought with an effectiveness that matched their courage.

Bibliography

Bradley, Omar N., *A Soldier's Story*, Holt, New York, 1951.

Bradley, Omar N., & Blair, Clay, *A General's Life: An Autobiography*, Simon & Schuster, New York, 1951.

Cox, Sebastian, & Gray, Peter, *Air Power History, Turning Points from Kitty Hawk to Kosovo*, Frank Cass, London, 2002.

D'Este, Carlo, *Decision in Normandy*, Dutton, New York, 1983.

Ellis, L.F., *Victory In The West*, Volume I, *The Battle of Normandy*, HMSO, London, 1962.

French, David, *Raising Churchill's Army: The British Army and the War Against Germany 1919–45*, Oxford University Press, Oxford, 2001.

Hamilton, Nigel, *Monty: Master of the Battlefield*, McGraw Hill, New York, 1983.

Hart, Russell A., *Clash of Arms: How the Allies Won in Normandy*, Lynne Riemer, Boulder, CO, 2001.

Hart, Stephen Ashley, *Montgomery and "Colossal Cracks", The 21st Army Group in Northwest Europe 1944–45*, Praeger, Westport CT, 2000.

Isby, David C., ed. *Fighting in Normandy, The German Army From D-Day to Villers-Bocage*, Greenhill, London, 2001.

Jarmowycz, Roman Johann, *The Quest for Operational Maneuver in the Normandy Campaign*, Ph.D. Thesis, McGill University, 1997.

Montgomery of Alamein, Viscount, *Normandy to the Baltic*, Corgi, London, 1974.

Slim, William, *Defeat Into Victory*, Cassell, London, 1956.

Wilson, David Alan, *The Development of Tank-Infantry Co-Operation Doctrine in the Canadian Army for the Normandy Campaign in 1944*, M.A. Thesis, University of New Brunswick, 1994.

Wilson, John, "Too Many Died In Their First Battle," *British Army Review*, No. 131, Spring 2003, pp. 28–38.

Notes

1. In reality, he did not do the things listed in this paragraph.
2. As was done with a number of veteran divisions, including 7th Armoured and 51st Highland, after initial setbacks in Normandy.
3. Slim, *Defeat Into Victory*, p. 292
4. 9th Canadian Infantry Brigade War Diary entry of 15 September 1943 quoted in Wilson, *The Development of Tank-Infantry Co-Operation Doctrine in the Canadian Army for the Normandy Campaign in 1944*, p. 110
5. See generally: French, *Raising Churchill's Army*.
6. Russell A. Hart, *Clash of Arms*, p. 416
7. In reality, all the major British offensives after D-Day were undercut by flaws in staff work, especially intelligence and planning. Comparing the performance of 1944–45 British and especially Canadian corps staffs with their 1918 predecessors is often discouraging.
8. Brad Gladman, "The Development of Tactical Air Doctrine in North Africa," in Cox and Gray, *Air Power History*, pp. 188–206.
9. In reality, the army remained unaware of many of the RAF's capabilities and the RAF, especially Bomber Command, was anxious to get back to its "real war" and did not publicize this. Investment in the more flexible tactical air control procedures was also limited.
10. Hamilton, *Monty: Master of the Battlefield*. See parts five and six generally.
11. D'Este, *Decision in Normandy*. See chapters 6 and 12 generally.
12. D'Este pp. 80–1.
13. Montgomery of Alamein, *Normandy to the Baltic*, p. 50.
14. D'Este, p.86.
15. In reality, this was not done. D'Este, p. 124. No one knew or cared much where *21st Panzer* was stationed on D-Day.
16. D'Este, p. 35.

*17. Robert E. Urquhart, *Caen and Arnhem*, Royal Publishing, Los Angeles, 1995, p. 66.

18. Actual garrison strength from Jarmowycz, *The Quest for Operational Maneuver in the Normandy Campaign*, p. 67.

*19. John Allan Fairley, "Remember Caen and Arnhem, The Story of the 1st Airborne Reconnaissance Squadron," *Pegasus*, Aldershot, 1978, p. 44.

20. See generally Ellis, chapter IX.

21. These types of battlegroups were used on several occasions, such as by the Canadian 9th Infantry Brigade in D-Day and, following Normandy lessons, by the Guards Armoured Division in Operation Market-Garden.

22. Stephen Ashley Hart, *Montgomery and "Colossal Cracks"*, p. 11 and chapters 2–5 generally.

*23. David Iswitz, *"Panzer" Meyer, His Tactical Successes and Execution for War Crimes*, New York, 2002, Apologia Books, p. 333.

24. This is the counterattack that, in reality, hit the Staffordshire Yeomanry and the 2d Btn. King's Shropshire Light Infantry, both units in action for the first time. The repulse the Germans suffered is that described in Ellis, pp. 202–3.

25. Offered as reason in Hamilton, pp. 597–8, 623–6, 636–9, 648–9.

26. An example of when this was done by U.S. commanders is in Bradley & Blair, *A General's Life*, p. 259–60.

27. The common assumption of British high-level commanders pre D-Day, that their greater combat experience was critical in making their commands more effective than their U.S. counterparts, was not borne out by experience. Compare the real-world performance of Montgomery and his army, corps and division commanders in Normandy, to a man Great War combat veterans (with the exception of Major-General "Pip" Roberts of 11th Armoured Division), with that of Eisenhower, Bradley, and their U.S. counterparts, most of whom had not seen combat in the Great War.

28. In reality, there were many examples of scratch German forces defeating in detail poorly coordinated British and Canadian forces when artillery and air could not be effectively employed.

29. General der Panzertruppen Heinrich Freiherr von Lüttwitz, "The Gap at Caumont," in Isby, *Fighting in Normandy*, pp. 68–71

30. This is more costly than the historical Desert Rats' repulse at Villers-Bocage because it takes place two days earlier (with fewer British reserves) and because the Rats were trying hard to push into the trap. Ellis, p. 251.

*31. Michael Wittmann, *Last Hero In A Losing Battle: The Posthumous Autobiography of Michael Wittmann*, Gollancz, London, 1952, p. 242.

32. This is what General der Panzertruppen Leo Freiherr Geyr von Schweppenburg proposed on 9 June. Geyr von Schweppenburg, "Situation When Panzer Gruppe West Assumed Command," in Isby, *Fighting in Normandy*, pp. 90–2

33. This is a larger version of *21st Panzer*'s counterattack on 6 June.

34. Bradley, *A Soldier's Story*, p. 208

35. Geyr von Schweppenburg, "Panzer Tactics in Normandy," in Isby, *Fighting in Normandy*, p. 216

2
"BY THE THROAT"
Decision at Falaise

Peter G. Tsouras

Hitler's Headquarters, East Prussia, 20 July 1944

The wooden map storage hut[1] shuddered with the force of the explosion inside. Smoke and debris shot out its large windows. Inside was carnage, but a man stumbled out through the smoke, blackened, singed, and holding his arm. Hitler had survived the most serious attempt on his life.

The bomb itself had been confined to one small building in East Prussia, but its deadliest effect was to be on the quarter million German troops trying to keep the Allies from breaking out of the growing beachhead in Normandy.

> "Hitler's chronic mistrust and scorn for his generals now became manic. Throughout the Normandy campaign he had intervened in their decisions. Now he began to sweep aside the unanimous advice of men... unfailingly loyal to him in the past... and to direct the battle in a fashion that severed all contact with reason or reality."[2]

He retreated even more into the world were myth and will trumped mass and skill. Hitler's wounds were not even healed one week later when the Americans and Canadians would give him the supreme opportunity for such madness.

Down the chain of command many responded like automatons in carrying out his senseless orders. Others, like the commander of the *12th SS Panzer Division "Hitlerjugend"*, Kurt Meyer, were lost in that realm of madness as well. Meyer had not lost his warrior's wits, however. He had helped train the division's teenagers gathered from the *Hitlerjugend* (Hitler Youth) into living steel, echoing the Nazi motto to make men "as hard as Krupp Steel." He had grown from a Nazi street fighter in the early 1930s into one of the finest commanders of the war, becoming a legend on the Eastern Front in the *1st SS Panzer Division "Leibstandarte"* as "Panzermeyer." He had been selected to command the new *25th SS Panzergrenadier Regiment* of the *12th SS* as it trained. With his cadre from *Leibstandarte*, he hammered the cream of German youth into one of the most lethal fighting forces in the world. They had arrived in Normandy on the day after the invasion to snatch Caen from Montgomery's grasp and hold it for almost two months of a relentless bloodbath. Blood was the operative word. Meyer was lost in the Hitler world of blood, myth, and Aryan glory. He saw himself and his teenage warriors as the living embodiment of Siegfried and his heroes from the epic Neibelungelied. Like Siegfried, the *12th SS* was bathing in the torrent of the dragon's blood. The bloodbath of the dragon imparted invincibility. Like all myths, however, this one held its own doom, for as the red, hot blood flowed over naked Siegfried sheathing him in invisible armor, a leaf fell upon his back and shed the blood off a patch of skin.

Cobra, 25 July 1944

For almost two months the German *Fifth Panzer* and *Seventh Armies* had held the First U.S. and Second (British) Armies in a narrow beachhead after their spectacular landings on D-Day. The German soldier was at his finest in the desperate defensive fighting in the hedgerow country of inland Normandy. Repeated Allied lunges had been cushioned by the natural defensive nature of the Norman countryside stiffened by German valor and skill. The front appeared essentially static with heavy Allied losses for each yard gained. The British press had begun comparing the cost to the Somme, and Britain's manpower barrel had already been scraped clean.

American losses had been heavy, too, but the U.S. Army could afford it. Its new divisions were steadily stacking up behind the front. The First Army was preparing to split into two and give birth to the Third Army, to be commanded by the already legendary Lieutenant General George S. Patton.

British Empire reinforcements were also North American. Second Army had already given birth on 23 July to the Canadian First Army consisting of Canadian II and British I Corps and commanded by Lieutenant-General Henry Crerar. In addition to the British and Canadian units, the army included the Polish 1st Armored Division, and Belgian and Dutch units. With two new armies in the order of battle, army group headquarters were activated—the 21st Army Group for the British, commanded by General Montgomery, and U.S. 12th Army Group, commanded by Lieutenant General Omar Bradley. Montgomery was still in overall command of the Allied ground forces in the battle, but decision-making tended to be more and more collegial the more American divisions joined the fighting.

The plotters who failed to kill Hitler did not realize that the Allies had timed their major breakout from Normandy for the day after the Hitler was supposed to have died—21 July. But the weather delayed it four days provoking the comment from Bradley, "Dammit, I'm going to have to court-martial the chaplain if we have more weather like this."[3] The weather finally cleared on the 25th, and American storm broke.

Montgomery had planned all along to keep the attention of the Germans on his front centered on Caen. It was the closest point to the Seine and to Germany and good tank country. Almost all the German armor was massed there as well as the bulk of the German forces. Fifteen divisions faced the

British while only nine divisions faced the Americans. *Panzer Group West* (soon to be renamed *Fifth Panzer Army*) commanded by General Hans Eberbach, was concentrated against the British while most of *Seventh Army* under SS General Paul Hausser faced Bradley's Americans. Both armies fell under Field Marshal Günther von Kluge's *Army Group B*. Hausser's nine mostly infantry divisions had been bled dry in the fighting as the priority for heavy equipment went to those units fending off Montgomery's ponderous offensives. Bradley had worried that von Kluge's attention would drift over to the American build-up on the western end of the front. Montgomery, however, had done his work well. The German attention remained fixed on the British. The surprise would be total.

The surprise was also as crushing as it was complete. First fighter-bombers conducted pinpoint attacks on the German outposts followed by a massive pounding by 1,500 Flying Fortresses and Liberators over a front four miles wide. As the ground forces attacked, medium bombers hunted along the roads behind the front to paralyze the movement of reserves. The Germans had been stunned. General Fritz Bayerlein, commander of *Panzer Lehr Division*, wrote, "My front looked like a lunar landscape and at least 70 percent of my troops were out of action—dead, wounded, crazed or numbed."[4] Yet the remnants of the German front held on for two more days until men could do no more, and the front finally ruptured. Patton was now in control; the Third Army had sprung into life and was pouring through the gap in an endless stream of armored and soft-skinned vehicles.[5]

The broken German front snapped back east as the Third Army muscled it aside. Patton sent a corps west into Brittany and two more south and east to plunge into the depth of the German rear. Anyone reading a map would see that these spreading arrows were the making of a great encirclement. The deeper they went, the more constrained were the forces of *Army Group B* into a long sack with the British and Canadians to the north and the Americans to the south of it. The German generals at the front began looking over their shoulders to the narrow neck of the sack to the east—their escape route.

Hitler instead chose to see in all this a magnificent opportunity. The Americans were pouring through a relatively narrow gap between the German lines and the sea. Strike across the gap, and the Americans would be cut off. The American success would be turned on its head. The only problem was that Hitler was still thinking in terms of his early successes where the Germans had at least parity in forces and control of the air where they needed it. None of these applied now, but nonetheless his order went out on 2 August:

> "All available Panzer units, regardless of their present commitment, are to be taken from the other parts of the Normandy front, joined together under one specially qualified Panzer operations staff, and sent into a concentrated attack as soon as possible. The outcome of the whole campaign in France depends on the success of this attack."

Hitler concluded that the moment presented "a unique, never recurring opportunity for a complete reversal of the situation."[6] To support it he authorized the transfer of four divisions from the *Fifteenth Army* in northern France and Belgium now that the expected Allied invasion of the Pas de Calais region looked like it would never materialize. Two divisions went to Hausser and two to Eberbach. From *Army Group G* in the south of France came a Panzer corps for Hausser as well.

The long-suffering von Kluge was aghast at the order to transfer his Panzers for this operation. "Tanks are the backbone of our defense, where they are withdrawn, our front will give way... If, as I foresee, this plan does not succeed, catastrophe is inevitable." Hitler had already dismissed such remonstrations when he had sent his *OKW* (*Armed Forces High Command*) representative, General Warlimont, to von Kluge's headquarters with the instructions, "Tell Field Marshal von Kluge that he should keep his eyes riveted to the front and on the enemy without ever looking backward."[7] Known as "Clever Hans" (*Kluge Hans*, a play on his last name), the field marshal remained one of Hitler's favorite senior officers. "A non-smoker and a virtual teetotaller with a reputation for fearlessness, the brilliant field commander jokingly compared himself to Napoleon's Marshal Ney, 'the bravest of the brave'." He had visited Hitler on 1 July while recovering from an accident in Russia. At that very time the Wehrmacht's chief of staff, Field Marshal Wilhelm Keitel had phoned OB West (Supreme Commander West), Field Marshal Gerd von Rundstedt, to ask his recommendations regarding the serious situation on the Normandy front. Von Rundstedt had shouted over the phone, "Make peace, you fool!" Keitel had scurried to report this to Hitler, who immediately replaced von Rundstedt with the startled von Kluge.[8] Clever Hans would come to have cause to remember his predecessor's advice.

On the same day that Hitler gave his order, the Canadians had been hammering at the village of Tilly-la-Campagne south of Caen for the second day. Despite the most intensive bombardment and incessant ground attacks, the *Leibstandarte* clung stubbornly to the village. As one Canadian would write:

> "At 1800 hrs [6:00 p.m.] the Typhoons arrived and Tilly went up and then down in a mess of smoking rubble... Shortly afterwards our arty played terrifically heavy fire into the rubble and many air bursts were fired directly over Tilly as well. It is a seemingly impossible thing for anyone to live under such fire. Snipers continue to be very active and the seemingly impossible thing has happened because we are once again receiving MG fire from the slits at Tilly. The Hun is like a rat and comes up for more no matter how hard we pound him."[9]

The only thing that stood between a collapse of the front under relentless British and Canadian pounding was the hardbitten quality of units like *Leibstandarte*. That fact was only too well known to the tough, fighting commander of the *I SS Panzer Corps* and its two Panzer divisions—*Leibstandarte* and *Hitlerjugend*—Josef "Sepp" Dietrich. Dietrich had been an NCO in the First War, one of the few German tankers then, and then an old Nazi Party man and associate of Hitler from the early street fighting days. He was a notable fighting soldier but was out of his depth at senior command. He did, however, inspire great confidence in his SS men because of his pugnacious and down-to-earth character and his care of the troops. One observer had noted that he was no general but a realist. He had already come to the conclusion that Hitler's leadership was leading Germany to defeat. But even so, he was thunderstruck when told of Hitler's plan, which would leave him only three infantry divisions with which to fend off the new Canadian First Army.

> "I protested with von Kluge for over an hour about the impracticability of such an operation. I used every argument in the book. There was not sufficient petrol for such an attack; if three armored divisions were sent west it would be impossible to hold Falaise; it was impossible to concentrate so many tanks without inviting disaster from the air; there wasn't sufficient space to deploy so large an armored force; the Americans were far too strong in the south and such an attack was only wedging one's way tighter into the trap rather than safely getting out. To each of my arguments von Kluge had only one reply, 'It is Hitler's orders' and there was nothing more that could be done. I gave him what he wanted."[10]

Von Kluge worked miracles to concentrate his tanks for the attack. By night they slipped unnoticed away from 21st Army Group's front. First *Leibstandarte*'s battle groups departed like ghosts in the darkness, then *Hitlerjugend* followed on the night of 5 August as the newly arrived *89th Infantry Division* took their places. Panzermeyer had been afraid that his shrunken *Hitlerjugend* battle groups in corps reserve would have to stay in place when it was reported that a shortage of fuel had delayed the arrival of the *89th*. He had a few moments to contemplate the remnants of the division that had entered the battle in Normandy on 7 June. Then it was at its full establishment of 21,000 men and 220 tanks.[11] His boys had been magnificent—the pick of German youth—hardened like Krupp steel, fit and bronzed and utterly fanatical. For Meyer they were the perfect embodiment of the superiority of the German race. Now as his exhausted men waited in corps reserve, his two battle groups numbered barely 2,500 fighting men and 50 tanks. As usual he had prepared to place a number of liaison officers with the *89th* as it took over *Leibstandarte*'s front expecting that his division would remain in reserve. At the last minute, though, he received the word that the *89th* would arrive on time after all. The harried supply staffs had found enough fuel. Meyer recalled his liaison officers and set his division onto the road west to join the German Panzer concentration.

Operation Lüttich, 6–7 August 1944

Unbeknownst to each other in the first week of August, the staffs of the German *Seventh Army* and Canadian First Army were simultaneously working on plans for attacks that would overlap by only a few hours. Hitler had chosen Lüttich for the name of the operation to sever the American Third Army by driving to the sea at Avranches, the corner of the French coast where Normandy meets Brittany. Lüttich is the German name for the Belgian town usually known in English as Liège and was chosen to recall Ludendorff's speedy reduction of the Belgian forts there in August 1914. The Canadians chose Totalize as the code-name of their operation. Lüttich would begin in the late hours of 6 August and surge through the next morning. Totalize would begin late on 7 August and reach its crescendo the next day. Timing is everything, they say, and for the Allies the beauty of the unintentional timing was that the German Panzer forces would be committed and locked into action elsewhere when the Canadian hammer tripped.

The famed Ultra intercepts of German communications gave Bradley a heads up early on 6 August that a German attack was imminent. By correlating the German chatter regarding air attack operations in the vicinity of Mortain with the arrival of a Panzer division nearby, Bradley was able to send out a message late in the day that an attack was building. Unfortunately, it caught the U.S. 30th Infantry Division still short of the positions it was meant to occupy in the path of the German attack at Mortain. The Germans had paid enough homage to surprise to be rewarded that evening. They dispensed with the usual bombardment. They needed surprise and bad weather desperately. Once they were in the open, the Allied air forces would hunt them down. As it was, the five Panzer divisions participating in the attack had barely 200 tanks and assault guns.

The initial battle reports came in the early morning hours and were passed immediately to Hitler's *OKW* headquarters. Hitler habitually kept late hours and read them with trembling hands. His eyes gleamed as he turned to his staff, "I knew if von Kluge believed in this plan, it would succeed. We have destroyed one enemy division already."[12]

The *2d Panzer Division* had caught the 30th Infantry Division on the road on its approach march and as guides left behind from the 1st Infantry Division were showing the lead elements to their positions. The 30th was a good division, but did not stand a chance on the road as the Panzers ran over men and sprayed machine-gun fire into the ranks. The men fled into the dark countryside as the Panzers sped on. The 30th's broken and bloodied parts immediately began sorting themselves out to get back into the fight.

Moving up with *2d Panzer* was *Leibstandarte* and *Hitlerjugend*. The later was reinforced with the Tiger-equipped *Heavy Tank Battalion 101* and its famous tank-killer, Michael Wittmann. Leading *Leibstandarte*'s *1st SS Panzer Regiment* was the redoubtable Joachim Peiper. Only recently returned from hospital, he was his old bold self, a twin to Panzermeyer if ever there were one. As his attack moved forward at midnight, he watched an Allied night fighter come flaming down toward the head of his column as it moved through a defile. For a moment Peiper's heart was in his mouth as he realized that if it struck the lead tank, his regiment would be trapped in the defile behind it. At the last minute, the plane veered and crashed into the woods nearby to ignite a bonfire.

Morning brought thick fog which clung to the battlefield. It was in this soup that *Leibstandarte* and *Hitlerjugend* ran into Combat Command C (CCC) of the U.S. 3d Armored Division in a meeting engagement. For those who survived it, it would either be called the Fog Fight or *Der Nebelschlacht*. Tanks rammed each other and opened at point blank range. This gave the American Shermans with their low velocity 75mm guns parity for once with the more lethal long-barrelled German guns. At point blank range, the U.S. gun would cut right through a Panther's armor. Despite this, the experience of the SS was the trump. The hard school of Russia had prepared them for the grimmest fighting. Another trump was Michael Wittmann and his famed Tiger tank. Wittmann hunted like the beast his vehicle was named for, killing Sherman after Sherman until he nearly rivaled his score of British tanks in the slaughter earlier at Villers-Bocage. As the fog finally lifted at noon, the remnants of CCC pulled back. Now the two German units raced forward towards the sea only a few miles away.

Meyer's spirit soared as a young voice shouted over the radio, "Der See, der See!" (The sea, the sea!) The recon team had reached a vantage point where they could see the spires of Avranches, the glimmer of the bay beyond, and the roads jammed with American vehicles. Instantly the message flew to *OKW*. As Hitler basked in the adulation of his staff, swarms of Allied planes filled the air over the battlefield.

12th Army Group Headquarters, 7 August 1944

Bradley remained remarkably calm as the Germans cut their way towards Avranches that day. The events reaffirmed his belief that Ultra was not "the oracle of Delphi, but rather a marvellous source of intelligence to be evaluated and used tactically with utmost care."[13] The warning time had not been enough to organize a better response to the determined German drive. The situation was well in hand despite the German nearness to Avranches. Two U.S. corps had already wedged themselves between the Germans and the town. Patton's masterful nose for battle and the same sketchy Ultra warning had caused him to stop three of his divisions in the vicinity of St Hilaire just in case something might happen.[14] They made all the difference. The 30th Infantry Division had reformed around its regiments in the German rear and was making hell for the few follow-on German infantry units, and more importantly for the German supply columns.

Rather, Bradley was savoring the opportunity that had presented itself. He was in awe of this moment, though it did not stop him from working practically to take advantage of it. The next morning Bradley greeted the visiting Secretary of the Treasury, Henry Morgenthau, with the words, "This is an opportunity that comes to a commander not more than once in a century… We're about to destroy an entire hostile army."[15]

Bradley had already directed Patton to throw his XV Corps, commanded by Major-General Wade Hampton Haislip, north towards the vital road junction in the German rear at Argentan. Bradley told Patton, "We'll go as far as Argentan and hold there… We've got to be careful we don't run into Monty coming down from Falaise."[16]

Planning to Totalize, 29 July–6 August 1944

As Bradley spoke, Monty was indeed coming. His Canadian First Army was preparing to launch Operation Totalize to rupture the front and drive the 12 miles to Falaise, that other transport hub in the German rear, parallel to Argentan to the south. Bradley and Monty had quickly come to the conclusion that the already planned Totalize would fortuitously form the north pincer of a grand encirclement. Patton's XV Corps was already racing to be the southern pincer.

Major operations such as Totalize, however, cannot be ordered at the drop of a hat. Thanks to the foresight of the Canadian II Corps Commander, Lieutenant-General Guy Grenville Simonds, the Canadians would be ready at the right moment. Simonds' rise in the Canadian Army had been meteoric. The son of British Army officer, he had been born in Britain in 1903 but was raised in Canada after his father emigrated. He had made a name for himself for his knowledge not only of military theory but of the practical problems of modern war as well. This opinion was confirmed by his articles on mechanized warfare in the *Canadian Defence Quarterly*. He had been the youngest Canadian general officer when he took command of the 1st Infantry Division, and subsequently the 5th Armoured Division, in 1943 and had come out of the fighting in Sicily and Italy with a brilliant reputation. Promoted to command II Corps in early 1944 at the age of 40, he had led his corps in brutal fighting since D-Day and was spoiling to give the *coup de grâce* to an obviously overstretched enemy. Simonds was a man who could get things done in an original way.

On 29 July he had received instructions from General Crerar to plan major break-through operations on the axis Caen–Falaise. The next day Simonds told his divisional commanders that he foresaw that, if things continued to go well with the American breakout in Cobra, he would receive orders for a breakout attack through Falaise.

> "In this there would be 'no holding back whatever,' and no division would stop until every reserve had been exhausted. It would be necessary to accept casualties, but doing so would make it possible to finish the war quickly and thereby avoid the heavy losses to be expected from a struggle of attrition."[17]

Simonds recalled quite clearly Crerar's forceful guidance back on 14 May before the invasion that in such a "break-in" attack "a matter of highest importance is to get the infantry over and through the enemy's prearranged zones of defensive fire in the shortest possible time after the intention to attack is revealed."[18]

Later on 30 July Simonds presented Crerar with his initial requirements for the operation. He requested the strong reinforcement of his II Corps as well as "total" air support for two days. His corps already consisted of the Canadian 2d and 3d Infantry and 4th Armoured Divisions. Crerar readily augmented them with the British 51st Highland Division and 33d Armoured Brigade from British I Corps. He also added the Polish 1st Armoured Division newly arrived from England. Crerar arranged through Montgomery for the air support to be genuinely "total," siring the operation's code-name—Totalize.[19]

The following day he formally briefed Crerar, and on 2 August presented the written plan to his division commanders. The plan stated that the open ground to be covered was ideally suited to the defensive weapons of the enemy and that the persistent Canadian attacks to date had alerted the enemy to expect future ones.

> "In essence, the problem is how to get armor through the enemy gun screen to sufficient depth to disrupt the German anti-tank gun and mortar defence, in country highly-suited to the tactics of the latter combination. It can be done."

The plan keyed on the fact that the enemy defense would be "most handicapped in bad visibility—smoke, fog, or darkness, when the advantage of long range is minimized."[20]

The German defenses were in two parallel lines. The forward line ran May-sur-Orne—Tilly-la-Campagne—La Hogue. The second and less well-prepared line ran from Hautmesnil to St Sylvain. The critical terrain feature of the first line was map Point 122 on the Falaise road which bisected the Canadian direction of attack. A similar vital piece of terrain for the second line was also in the vicinity of Hautmesnil where the road passed over a knoll. It was clear from the nature of the terrain and the German defenses that two successive "break-in" efforts were necessary to rupture the front.

Simonds' plan stated that the key to the operation was to employ overwhelming air support to suppress the German defensive weapons while infiltrating ground forces through the defensive positions under conditions of poor visibility. Normally, formal assaults on both German lines would necessitate a pause between efforts that would dissipate momentum and speed. That could be avoided by infiltrating through the first German line and then have follow-on forces pulsed through the second line while other units were still clearing the first line.

Simonds proposed to implement the plan in three phases. In the first phase, the Canadian 2d Infantry Division and the British 51st Highland Division, supported by two armored brigades, would attack at night with no preliminary artillery support. The objective would be to cut through both German defensive lines to a depth of six miles. The attack would be preceded by a massive strike by heavy bombers. Only as the ground attack went in exactly one half hour later would it be supported by a "quick medium artillery barrage." The attacking infantry would go straight for the first objectives. Here Simonds introduced a vital innovation. The infantry would be mounted in improvised armored personnel carriers, converted Priest self-propelled guns. "The essentials are that the infantry shall be carried in bullet and splinter-proof vehicles to their actual objectives."[21]

The second phase would see the introduction of the fresh Canadian 4th Armoured and 3d Infantry Divisions to cut through the second German line to a depth of over 11 miles from the operation start line while supported by a massive heavy and medium bomber strike. Finally, in the third phase, the Canadian 4th Armoured and Polish 1st Armoured Divisions would shoot forward the final four miles to seize the high ground on either side of Falaise.

Late on 3 August Montgomery phoned Crerar to approve the plan and give him the target date of 8 August, which was subsequently moved up to the 7th as events further west at Mortain added to the increased urgency of the operation. The German front was creaking everywhere under pressure while Hitler persevered with Lüttich at the end of its long shriveling sack. The British Second Army was already attacking with some success with three corps on line to the west of Canadian First Army and was pivoting south and east. On 4 August Montgomery issued a directive to his two armies in which he stated that, "The general situation is very good" and that the German force was "in such a state that it could be made to disintegrate completely." Montgomery's appreciation of the situation had preceded Bradley's by three days before the German attack at Mortain. The Canadian objective was Falaise which would "cut off the enemy forces now facing Second Army and render their withdrawal eastwards difficult if not impossible."[22]

In what would become a famous statement, Montgomery said to the Canadian army commander,

"Do this, Crerar, and we will have Jerry by the throat."[23]

While the generals conferred, the workshops went into overdrive to convert the Priests by removing the guns and mantlets and welding armor plate over the openings. When the armor plate gave out, two plates of mild steel filled with sand were substituted. The Navy complained that Canadian soldiers were cutting plates out of stranded but reparable craft on the Normandy beaches. The 76 converted Priests were christened Kangaroos after the code-name of the conversion operation.

Perhaps an even more difficult task was the planning and coordination of the unprecedented night bomber supporting strike. Nothing like this had ever been done by night. However, Air Chief Marshal Sir Trafford Leigh-Mallory pushed things along and coordinated the meetings, the last one of which was held in England. Agreement seemed to have been reached when Crerar's representative and chief of staff, Brigadier Mann, was asked to present the plan the next day to Commander-in-Chief, Bomber Command—Air Chief Marshal Sir Arthur Harris.

It was late on 6 August, with barely a day before H-Hour, when the meeting opened. Harris stated simply that he would not approve the bombing because bomber pathfinding of the required precision "could not be done at night." Mann rose to the occasion and stated that since Harris would not support the already agreed upon plan, he would have to notify the First Army commander. He stated that he expected Harris would also personally notify the 21st Army Group commander—Montgomery. Harris replied that he had no intention of calling Montgomery. There was a long pause around the table as it become obvious that Mann had called Harris' bluff, a most noteworthy feat and one rarely accomplished. Discussions resumed and Harris' reservations were resolved to everyone's satisfaction.

As Totalize worked its way to its final stages, the German *89th Infantry Division* took over the front previously held by *I SS Panzer Corps' Leibstandarte* and *9th SS Panzer Divisions* sent off to take part in Lüttich. A Yugoslav deserter and a lost ambulance that drove through the lines tipped off the Canadians of the arrival of the new division. Simonds' intelligence staff believed that the SS units had merely moved into local reserve. Based on this information, Simonds revised his plan. Phase I would remain the same, but the two attacking divisions would press on to secure the second as well as the first German line. Canadian 4th Armoured and Polish 1st Armoured Divisions were ordered up to the corps start line and would pass through the lead troops to continue the attack in Phase II. The 3d Infantry Division would be committed from corps reserve at this point to secure the left flank of the armored divisions. British Second Army would already be giving a big assist with its ongoing attack by threatening the left flank of the Germans facing II Corps. Crerar's other corps, British I Corps, had been too weakened by units being detached to the Canadian corps to participate actively in the attack but would move forward to cover its neighbor's extending left flank.

Simonds had wanted a week to train his two front-line divisions on their Kangaroos. He got one day. The infantry of the 2d Infantry Division's 4th Brigade practiced from dawn to dusk mounting and dismounting from their strange new vehicles, though time was, of course, found for church parade. A brigade of Highlanders of the 51st were run through the ropes as well. Each division would have one mounted brigade and one foot infantry brigade.

The support services had been working without a break at the same time to distribute 205,000 rounds of artillery ammunition, 152,000 gallons of fuel, and 130,00 rations to the forward positions. They also delivered a further 1,067 tons of ammunition and 672 tons of fuel to be carried forward by the attacking forces.

Simonds was apprehensive about his follow-on armored divisions—they were both green. In the exploitation role, quick thinking based on sound experience would be vital. That was the rub. Experience weeded out the leaders who could meet this hard standard. How many opportunities would be lost while the Darwinian hand of combat winnowed out the failures? Could the cumulative effect of inexperience and poor leadership snatch victory itself away? For that reason, his address to his commanders on 5 August emphasized "the vital importance of keeping the initiative and maintaining the momentum of the attack." He hammered home the war winning opportunity that lay before them. As a final touch he called up the feats of their fathers as he noted that it was the eve of the anniversary of the battle of Amiens in 1918, "and I have no doubt that we shall make the 8th of August 1944 an even blacker day for the German armies than is recorded against the same date 26 years ago."[24]

Operation Totalize, 7–8 August 1944

Along the Canadian front the men could hear the throbbing vibration of a host of 1,020 heavy bombers—Halifaxes and Lancasters—as they converged over the German lines at H-Hour—2300. The ground transmitted the shock waves as they dropped 3,462 tons of bombs throughout the depth of the German positions. So much dust and smoke erupted from that hell that the follow-on bombers could not identify their targets and had to be called off. The R.A.F. and R.C.A.F. had lost only ten aircraft. At 2300 the ground attack divisions surged forward into the roiling darkness.

The cloak of night was thickened by a low ground-hugging mist, and the smoke of the bombing was added to inexplicably by German smoke rounds. Artificial moonlight, called "Monty Moonshine" was provided by searchlights shone at a low angle to help the attacking tanks which were also guided forward by radio beams, Bofors guns firing bursts of tracer along the axes of advance, and green marker shells fired onto the knoll at Point 122. Nevertheless, the attackers stepped off into chaos. The Germans in many places were shaking off the stunning air blow and coming out to fight.

The 4th Brigade plowed through the confusion with its tanks and Kangaroos, undeterred by failing to meet the letter of its movement plan from place to place. The battalions were supposed to pass west of Rocquancourt. Instead, the Royal Regiment of Canada drove east of it; the Royal Hamilton Light Infantry drove through it; and the Essex Scottish simply lost their way. Nevertheless, the brigade pressed on and ended up at its objectives all the same, testament to the power of determined forward movement.

The 6th Brigade went in on foot to dig the Germans out of the defenses the 4th Brigade had bypassed. In most cases, the Germans did not wish to cooperate. The luckiest battalion, the South Saskatchewan Regiment, had followed directly on the heels of the armored vehicles of 4th Brigade and walked right into Rocquancourt while the Germans still had their heads down. To the east, though, there was vicious fighting to take the neighboring villages. Les Fusiliers Mont-Royal could only finally subdue May-sur-Orne with flame-throwing Crocodile tanks. The Cameron Highlanders of Canada hammered their way into Fontenay-le-Marmion only to be surrounded by counterattacking German tanks bypassed by the initial advance. With their commander dead and the Germans full of fight, the situation was critical until Lieutenant R.R. Counsell, the carrier platoon leader, took his vehicles back to the battalion base. He loaded supplies and all the support personnel of the battalion and sped back with the reinforcements to keep the Germans at bay. They were finally relieved when the South Saskatchewans and a troop of the 1st (Canadian) Hussars cleared the Germans off the ridge north of the village with a large bag of prisoners.

The 51st Highland Division had a similar bag of luck and tough fighting. Their armored columns duly made their objectives, but the reduction of the bypassed German positions was a bloody affair. Tilly-la-Campagne proved almost as tough a nut as when the *Leibstandarte* defended it the month before. The 2d Battalion of the Seaforth Highlanders was repulsed in its first assault. It attacked again, this time reinforced with the regiment's 5th Battalion and a squadron of tanks. That was enough.

The armored columns had performed just as Simonds had expected and with relatively few casualties. In the 2d Infantry Division the three Kangaroo-mounted battalions of the 4th Brigade suffered only 7 dead and 56 wounded as opposed to the 68 dead and 95 wounded of the four foot-mobile battalions of the 6th Brigade.

Simonds had every reason to be pleased. Few plans had been executed with such success under such difficult conditions as the first two phases of Totalize. By the evening of 7 August, his two divisions had reached their objectives. Already the two armored divisions were moving up to the original jump-off positions of the two infantry divisions. If Simonds had been in the rear of the German *89th Infantry Division*, he would have been even more pleased. Crowds of demoralized German soldiers were drifting away from the fighting, something one German officer with four years of combat stated he had never seen before. The division's baptism of fire had evidently been too much. For all intents and purposes the *89th* had ceased to exist as a coordinated fighting formation.

As H-Hour (1315, 8 August) for Phase II approached, Simonds should have started to worry. His armored divisions were lagging in a growing traffic jam of thousands of vehicles. The artillery was also having a hard time moving forward to support the next phase. The *89th Infantry Division* may not have been responsive as a maneuver unit any longer, but surviving elements continued to fight, and sniping was a serious problem. The unit logs of the advancing divisions are full of exhortations to subordinate leaders that seemed to have had little effect in the confusion. The Canadians were also unaware that behind the breached German second line was another line coming into being manned by deadly troops of the Luftwaffe—General Pickert's *III Flak Corps*—fielding a lethal mix of dual-purpose 88mm anti-aircraft/anti-tank guns and 20mm anti-aircraft/anti-personnel guns. Simonds would have been even more concerned had he known that the *85th Infantry Division* was being directed to reinforce the *89th*. Its advance units were already reaching the forward area. Another flak battle group from *III Flak Corps* was also on its way from the Orne River nearby.

Nevertheless, the situation still seemed rich in opportunities. German resistance had crumbled, as far as could be determined. Best of all, there had been no appearance of elements of Dietrich's *I* SS *Panzer Corps*. The thunderbolt of Phase II was now about to be delivered by 687 American heavy bombers all across the front of the Canadian II Corps. The earth heaved as the streams of bombs hit a string of weakly held German positions. Unfortunately, gross errors led to the bombing of the Polish 1st Armoured and Canadian 3d Infantry Divisions. The Poles lost 315 killed and wounded and the Canadians over 100. The tactical headquarters of the Canadian division was also hit with great loss. Canadian military histories would make much of the contrast with the flawless bombing of the R.A.F. and R.C.A.F. on 7 August.

Despite the heavy losses, both armored divisions crossed the line of departure on time at 1355. They had barely advanced two miles when they ran into an anti-tank trap set by *III Flak Corps* that left the fields covered with pyres of burning Canadian tanks. Simonds ordered the divisions to continue their attacks that night, but nothing happened and instead the tanks harbored for the night to get some rest. Totalize seemed to have ground to a halt after such a promising start. The accumulation of friction, a tough enemy, and the inexperience of the troops had been too much for the green divisions. Simonds' temper almost got the better of him when he stopped to consider what the situation would have been like if the SS had entered the fight.

But there was still some steam left in Totalize. The commander of the 4th Armoured Brigade (4th Armoured Division) remained keen to fulfil Simond's timetable for Phase II and dispatched in the early morning a team of the 28th Armoured Regiment (The British Columbia Regiment) and the Algonquin Regiment to strike around the flank of the German positions in the villages of Bretteville-le-Rabet and Langannerie and drive to seize the high ground of Point 195 in their rear. From that position it would also dominate the highway to Falaise. The leading 28th was new to combat, the light in the early morning very poor, and the terrain not overabundant in easily identifiable landmarks. It almost immediately wandered off its course and began heading southeast instead of southwest. Bringing up the rear of the column was B Squadron. As the rest of the team headed off in the wrong direction, the squadron leader stopped to consult his map again. Clearly the column was going in the wrong direction. An exchange of signals halted the column and turned it around. B Squadron, now in the lead, headed southwest. By 0620 the team had secured Point 195.

The rest of the 4th Armoured Division attacked shortly thereafter and caught the Germans in a trap with the team on Point 195 firing into their rear. The German defense collapsed. Attempts to deploy *III Flak Corps* guns into Quesnay Woods on the other side of the Falaise Road from Point 195 failed as the gunfire from the 28th drove them off.

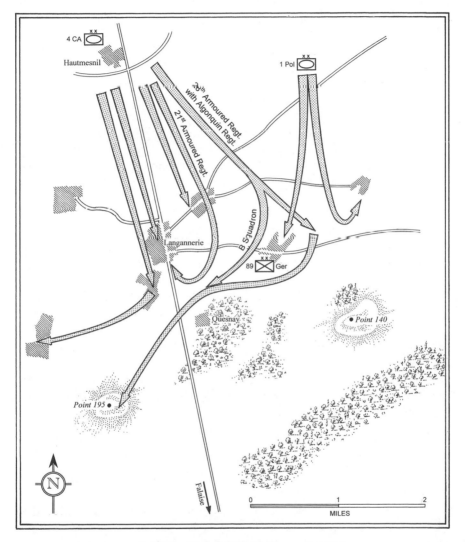

4 CA

Hautmesnil

1 Pol

29ᵗʰ Armoured Regt.
with Algonquin Regt.

21ˢᵗ Armoured Regt.

B Squadron

Langannerie

89   Ger

Quesnay

• Point 140

Point 195 •

Faîaise

N

0   1   2
MILES

Seizing Point 195: 9 August 1944

Now the two armored divisions raced forward to the Laizon River which angled towards the southwest. It was an obvious line of defense if the Germans could man it.

Sepp Dietrich knew a disaster when he saw it. The Canadian rupture of his *I Panzer Corps* front was now all too real. It was an SS Panzer corps in name only. His SS Panzer units had all been drawn off for that madman's gamble at Mortain. He was left with only the remnant of the *89th Infantry Division* and the *272d Infantry Division*, which had its hands full with holding the flank against the Canadian breakthrough. His only hope was the arriving *85th Infantry Division* and the battle group of *III Flak Corps* arriving from the Orne. He was desperately using the 88mm gun as a substitute for tanks but had to fight Pickert who seemed more interested in defending administrative areas in the rear. Dietrich feed the *85th*'s battalions into an improvised line one by one as they came up along the Laizon and begged Pickert to deploy his flak guns along that line as well. It was too late. The Poles bounced the river in the early afternoon, and the Canadians flowed down the highway parallel to the Laizon River towards Falaise.

Operation Lüttich Lingers, 8–11 August 1944

The gamble at Mortain still spun out its feeble life as the situation north of Falaise worsened. Hitler had been so aroused by the message from *Hitlerjugend*'s recon team that his gaze was fixed unalterably on success. He contemptuously ignored the increasingly frantic messages from von Kluge. The offensive had been stopped in its tracks, but the hapless troops wore a crown of thorns shoved down on them by relentless Allied air attacks. His request to move a Panzer group to deal with the Canadian drive was met only with suspicion of treachery. Von Kluge was so alarmed by the Canadian attack that he said to Hausser, "There is an enemy penetration at Caen such as there has never been before." Knowing that Lüttich was hopeless, he could not bring himself to cancel it outright, but he could put a brake on it.

> "I come to the following conclusion: We must make preparations tomorrow for the reorganization of the attack. There will be no continuation of the attack tomorrow, but we will prepare to attack the following day."[25]

Other senior officers begged Dietrich to approach Hitler to tell him that the situation was hopeless. Dietrich, "the realist" responded, "If I want to get shot, that's the way to do it."[26] The Panzers would not be moved back.

The Supreme Allied Commander, General Dwight D. Eisenhower, had arrived at Bradley's headquarters on 8 August and assured him that he could arrange an air resupply effort of 2,000 tons a day should the German attack actually cut off Patton's spearheads. Eisenhower would later write,

> "I was in his headquarters when he called Montgomery on the telephone to explain his plan, and although the latter expressed a degree of concern

about the Mortain position, he agreed that the prospective prize was great and left the entire responsibility in Bradley's hands."

Bradley's orders were to the point."The 12th Army Group will attack with least practicable delay, in the direction of Argentan to isolate and destroy the German forces on our front." The key role would obviously go to Patton whose XV Corps was striking towards the German supply base at Alençon beyond which he was to be prepared for further action against the enemy flank and rear in the direction of Argentan. Argentan was the key. The city was a vital communications center in the German rear. Significantly it was only 15 miles from Falaise. It was just north of Argentan that Montgomery had drawn the army group boundary .

Patton's XV Corps took Alençon on the night of 11–12 August and swept north 35 miles to take Argentan late in the following afternoon. Patton impishly asked Bradley, "Shall we continue and drive the British into the sea for another Dunkirk?"[27] Bradley's eyes must have rolled at another one of Patton's tactless but colorful comments. No, he responded. Stop at Argentan along the army group boundary. It would not be long before the Canadians closed the distance. They were banging on the gates of Falaise as XV Corps entered Argentan. Patton's diary entry for that day expressed his deep reservations.

"The corps could easily advance to Falaise and completely close the gap and thereby encircle two German armies, but we have been ordered to halt... I am sure that this halt is a great mistake, as I am certain that the British will not close on Falaise."[28]

The Battle for Falaise, 9–12 August 1944

Dietrich was in the thick of the fighting that threw the Poles back over the Laizon River on the night of 9 August. The *85th Infantry Division*'s battalions were well-led and aggressive, the result of months of hard training awaiting an invasion in the Pas de Calais. The 4th Canadian Armoured Division had also been stopped on the other side of the river where it crossed the highway to Falaise the next morning by *III Flak Corps*' guns less than four miles from the city.

Montgomery was animated by the success of Totalize to emphasize to Crerar that this was probably the critical moment of the war. After he took Falaise, he was to hold it with one infantry division and direct his armored divisions further southeast to Trun which would be the cork in the bottle holding the German armies. Simonds brought up his 3d Infantry Division out of corps reserve to take its place to the right of the 4th Armoured Division on the morning of 11 August. The 3d was a hard-bitten formation. It had landed on D-Day. The next day it had closed with the arriving *Hitlerjugend* in what would become one of the most vicious grudge fights in the war. Neither division took prisoners as they struck and stabbed at each other in the brutal fighting outside Caen. The 3d had had good teachers and was a formidable fighting force. Nevertheless, if asked, the division's unanimous opinion was that it would be better if it never ran across *Hitlerjugend* again.

Instead of *Hitlerjugend*, though, the *85th Infantry Division* was fully up in the line supported by dozens of *Luftwaffe* 88mm anti-tank guns. It had a strong position along a ridge that ran down the east side of the Laizon River. Simonds could see the roofs of Falaise in the near distance, and was determined not to be mocked by the prize any longer. This was no time to stint on the application of force. Again the ground vibrated to the engines of over a thousand heavy and medium bombers. The German line along the river was pounded in waves till it was smothered in a thick pall of smoke and dust. The Canadian artillery added to the pall with its own deluge of smoke shells.

Again the Canadians and Poles advanced just as the last bomb fell. The *85th* had been sorely wounded but was not dead. Flak nests brewed up a ring of Shermans around them. But the tide of Simonds' attack breached the river line quickly, rounding up 1,010 prisoners in the first hour alone.

The Canadians pushed south as the Germans slowly withdrew from one position to another, though the 4th Armoured Division's advance was slowed by the deadly anti-tank guns. The diarist of its 4th Armoured Brigade recorded, "It appeared that the enemy had once again established an anti-tank screen on the southern slopes of the high ground which the Armoured Brigade was unable to penetrate." They were barely a mile outside Falaise. To the west 3d Infantry Division was banging on the suburbs. But Dietrich was determined to hold on to the town as long as possible. Remnants of the *85th* and *III Flak* troops fought the Canadians house by house. Dietrich personally led the defense and poured every man—shoemakers, farriers, and clerks—into the fighting.

Night fell and was illuminated by the burning town, explosions, and flights of tracer rounds rising and falling over the inferno. Simonds had bigger fish to fry now that the 3d had locked Falaise in its death grip, moving his two armored divisions to link up with the Americans who, he had just been informed, were entering Alençon.

The fighting went on through the early morning as the 2d Infantry Division was committed to enveloping the town from the west. The last resistance, 60 Panzergrenadiers and a particularly resolute group of SS clerks, holding out in the École Supérieure, was overwhelmed by Les Fusiliers Mont-Royal. The building was surrounded by a high wall and was only stormed at 1400. The attacking Canadians suffered heavily as their assault coincided with a rare air raid by the *Luftwaffe*. The Fusiliers recovered and pressed their advance. Half the German grenadiers surrendered when the building was fired, but the SS clerks died almost to a man. A half dozen, led by their burly corps commander in person, fought their way out of the trap to disappear into the ruins of the town.

On the outskirts they ran into an ambush of the Cameron Highlanders. Dietrich fell wounded as he led his men in a charge. The rest were cut down. As the Camerons checked the bodies, Corporal Alan MacGregor turned over the body of the leader. His eyes gleamed at the decoration at the throat of the older man. He reached down to take it, when the man's hand shot up to grab him by the wrist. He pulled away and had raised his rifle to smash the man's face with its butt when an officer took him by the shoulder. "We want this one."[29]

A Little Convincing, 12 August 1044

Patton chafed when he heard of the fall of Falaise. He may have been a tactless ally, but he had the combat instincts of the great captain that he was. If the Canadians were on the way now, he should be racing to meet them. But Bradley was hung up by the army group boundary line. He could be stubborn, especially when it concerned Montgomery whom he actively disliked. Let Montgomery initiate a boundary line change if he wanted the Americans to close the gap. He also appeared to be afraid that whatever Allied divisions tried to close the gap would be swamped as both German armies stampeded out of the trap. For a man who had boasted only days vefore of seizing an opportunity presented only once in a century, he now seemed to be counseling his fears too much.

Patton, on the other hand, could smell the opportunity—and the glory. And for him it was irresistible. A glance at the map showed that Falaise–Argentan–Trun formed a triangle with Trun to the east sitting on the hub of a vital road net. Simonds' two armored divisions were speeding to Trun, but it was a shorter distance to Trun from Argentan. Patton rang Bradley.

"Brad, this is the main chance! I can be in Trun before the British [he insisted on calling any formation commanded by Montgomery as British]. Haislip can do it, and we can bag two German armies."

Bradley seemed annoyed. "George, once the Germans find that we have forces in their rear the stampede out will swamp the few divisions we can deploy. I'd rather have a strong shoulder at Argentan than a broken neck at Trun."

"But Brad, this is the chance of a lifetime. Weren't you telling me that is just what you said to Morgenthau last week? Besides, the Krauts are so deep in the sack that the game will be up before they can get up a head of steam to break out. And even if they do try to rush out, they would have to get on the roads. I know the fly boys would be snapping their teeth in anticipation."

"I meant we could trap the Germans in a deeper envelopment on the Seine."

Patton put on his charming old boy manner. "Brad, the British are racing—there's a first time for everything—to close the gap. Now, if you're happy to let them win the war, that's fine. I just don't know how General Marshall and the folks back home will take it with all the laurels going to the Limeys. Montgomery will be even more insufferable, if that's possible."

Bradley paused. "Well, George, what can you send to Trun?"

"I can send the 90th [Infantry Division] right away. And as soon as I can find that French bastard Leclerc [and his 2d French Armored Division], I can send him too. All I have to do is convince him that Paris can wait. I think the prospect of trapping two German armies will do it."[30]

"By the Throat," Trun, 13 August 1944

Three miles east of Trun on the morning of the 13th, the recon elements of Leclerc's division met the 10th Polish Brigade. Leclerc had been immediately sensible to the historic role Patton had given him and scrounged up a movie camera to make sure the event was properly recorded. He even found a cinematographer from among his men to operate it properly. And happily it took only one take, and the original spontaneous one at that, unlike when the enveloping arms of the two Soviet armies had closed the ring around Stalingrad and had to restage the event for the benefit of the propaganda arm.

It was an especially sweet moment for both the Poles and the French to be the instrument of revenge for their stricken peoples. For Leclerc there was an extra sweet dollop of satisfaction to French pride that none of "les Anglo-Saxons" were present. Even the Canadian II Corps liaison officer with the Poles was a Quebequois. The fact that the link-up had been accomplished almost without the Germans playing a role surrounded the moment with a sense of the surreal. Neither Simonds' two divisions nor Patton's two had encountered any significant German forces other than lines of communications, supply and signals units which either surrendered or fled. After the rounds of toasts they braced themselves for the German attempt to break out.

Von Kluge was staggered when word reached him that enemy armored divisions had cut off his army group at Trun. He had been concentrating on too many fires to see what was happening in his rear. The first fire was to extricate his Panzer divisions from the trap at Mortain. The newer fire was to shore up the collapse at Falaise and the disappearance of his *I SS Panzer Corps* commander, not to mention the remnants of his corps. Now the worst had happened. It was the damning fate that anyone who had served in Russia had come to dread like a recurring nightmare. And as the fires rushed at him, he had that madman to deal with. Frantic signals to *OKW* were met with silence. Hours later, the order came to break out. But events had, as usual not kept pace with Hitler's sense of reality.

Von Kluge realized that a break-out was impossible. Thanks to Hitler the Panzer forces, which would have to spearhead a break-out, were at the opposite end of the long west–east pocket. Von Kluge had only just begun to discuss with his army commanders the necessity to start moving the support troops out of the pocket in preparation for its evacuation by the combat troops. Now the entire force was trapped, over 150,000 men. To transfer the Panzers east for a break-out would require them to use the roads and travel quickly. To do so would invite a slaughter from the air. To do so more slowly to protect the troops would just give the Allies more time to thicken the blocking force until it was impenetrable. Von Kluge went through the motions and issued the orders for *Leibstandarte*, *Hitlerjugend*, and *2d SS Panzer Division* to lead the break-out attempt.

The pocket convulsed as the word spread that they were trapped in a giant *Kessel* ("cauldron"). The German Army had suffered enough such traps in Russia to have developed a self-defeating phobia. Hope evaporated as individual commanders took matters into their own hands. Some of those further east headed their men to the gaps in the envelopment. Many of them ran into British I Corps coming up on the flank of Simonds' two armored divisions. Others further west in the pocket simply surrendered. The commanders of the three SS Panzer divisions realized that they were 60 miles from Trun, an impossible distance to cover even had they had the fuel. The fighting around Mortain had reduced them to the state of weak battle groups. They were divisions in name only. In fact, almost all of the 20 or so so-called divisions at the front were only shadows of their intended strength.

At last a calm settled over von Kluge and in the early morning of 14 August as he sent a final message to Hitler.

> "My Führer,
>
> Make up your mind to end the war. The German people have borne such untold sufferings that it is time to put an end to this frightfulness. I have always admired your greatness, your conduct in the gigantic struggle and your iron will to maintain yourself and National Socialism. If fate is stronger than your will and your genius so is Providence. You have fought an honourable and great fight. History will prove that for you. Show yourself now also great enough to put an end to a hopeless struggle when necessary.
>
> I depart from you, my Führer, as one who stood nearer to you than you perhaps realized, in the consciousness that I did my duty to the utmost."[31]

He then shook hands with his aides and senior staff, excused himself and said he would take a walk in the woods. A wave of apprehension rippled over the faces of his officers. He had told them himself on several occasions that had he been in Field Marshal Paulus' place at Stalingrad, he would have chosen not to survive such a defeat.

He found a quiet place in the trees and took out his pistol. He looked at it for a moment and sighed. From the headquarters a voice was crying out, "Herr Feldmarschall, Herr Feldmarschall." He could hear boots thudding down the path. His aide found him. Von Kluge noted that he had never seen such a sense of relief on anyone's face. The young man blurted out, "A message from General Montgomery." He handed him the signal. Pistol still in his other hand, von Kluge read it.

> "Commander,
> German Army Group B
> Sir,
>
> In light of the hopeless condition of your command, I invite your surrender in order to spare the inevitable and useless loss of life of troops

who have fought with such determined valor. I propose to send representatives through the lines to negotiate the instrument of surrender. I will also send under his parole General Dietrich, whom we have captured at Falaise, to add his personal observations.

General B.L. Montgomery
Commander, Ground Forces
Allied Expeditionary Force"

Von Kluge holstered his pistol.

"Send a reply that I will agree to meet his representatives."[32]

That evening Major-General Francis de Guingand, Montgomery's trusted chief of staff, arrived as head of the Allied delegation. With him came Dietrich, his shoulder heavily bandaged. Von Kluge greeted him correctly but excused himself to speak to Dietrich. Ever the realist, Dietrich's forceful personality was all it took to push von Kluge into doing what his heart told him was the right thing. He emerged from the meeting to sit opposite de Guingand. He said simply, "Herr General, I will surrender my command."[33]

With that the war essentially ended. Over 150,000 Germans went into the bag without a further fight. The shock to the German armed forces was crippling. The Atlantic port garrisons surrendered one after another. German commanders in southern France and Italy entered into negotiations for surrender as well. Germany's collapse took only as long as needed for the Allied armies to motor across the Rhine. With the complete loss of both armies, there was nothing of substance to stop them. The German armies on the Eastern Front pulled back into Germany and surrendered to the Western Allies in Berlin. Hitler was handed over to the victors by his own generals who had roused themselves as the end approached to save what they could with a last miserable sacrifice.

As the endless German columns shuffled into their POW cages throughout Normandy, a few guards noted one whipcord lean man in the uniform of an SS general. He was calm and resigned. Siegfried no longer, cheated of his hero's ride into Valhalla with his young warriors, Kurt Meyer raised his arms as a gum-chewing, pimply-faced American teenager searched him.

The Reality

Operation Totalize's failure to meet its objectives to take Falaise quickly set in motion a train of events that were to allow the war to drag on into the next year. The ending of the Normandy Campaign resulted in the ruin but not the destruction of the German *Seventh* and *Fifth Panzer Armies*. The failure of Bradley and Montgomery to realize their opportunity and work together to close the gap at Falaise resulted in the escape of a great part of the support troops of these armies as well as enough survivors of the fighting formations to form the cadres of the rebuilt forces that would prolong the war into the following spring.

If a single point of failure can be identified it is the presence of Kurt Meyer and the remnants of his *Hitlerjugend Division* on 7 August when the Canadian II Corps launched Operation Totalize. The reason Meyer remained in the area and was not sent to join the Panzer concentration for Operation Lüttich was that the division that would replace *Leibstandarte* in the line, *89th Infantry Division*, had been delayed by Allied air attacks and lack of fuel. *Hitlerjugend* was a necessary reserve. I have tweaked history by finding just enough fuel to get the *89th* into the line in time, thus allowing *Hitlerjugend* to join the Panzer concentration for Lüttich.

In the actual battle, as in this alternative battle, the German defenders of the *89th Infantry Division* briefly held but then collapsed under the massive air and artillery bombardment and night attack. In reality, however, it was Meyer who reorganized the front, stiffened it with his own men who had been in reserve, and thickened the new front with *III Flak Corps'* murderous 88mm guns. Meyer was quick off the mark because he had planned for such an eventuality by assigning his own liaison officers to the *89th* to warn him of problems. Without Meyer and his teenage killers, it is probable that Totalize would have met or even exceeded its objective, taken Falaise, and linked up with Patton's troops before the middle of the month. It is unlikely von Kluge could have reacted quickly enough to have prevented the Canadians and Americans from stoutly tying up the sack.

Bibliography

Blumenson, Martin, *The Patton Papers 1940–1945*, Houghton-Mifflin, New York, 1974.

Boatner, Mark M., *The Biographical Dictionary of World War II*, Presidio Press, Novato, CA, 1996.

Bradley, Omar. N., *A General's Life: An Autobiography by General of the Army Omar N. Bradley*, Simon and Schuster, New York, 1983.

Bradley, Omar. N., *A Soldier's Story*, Henry Holt, New York, 1951.

D'Este, Carlo, *Decision in Normandy*, Collins, London, 1983.

Hastings, Max, *Overlord: D-Day & the Battle for Normandy*, Simon & Schuster, New York, 1983.

MacDonald, Charles B., *The American Armed Forces in the European Theater in World War II*, Oxford University Press, New York, 1969.

Man, John, *The D-Day Atlas: The Definitive Account of the Allied Invasion of Normandy*, Facts on File, New York, 1994.

Messenger, Charles, *Sepp Dietrich: Hitler's Gladiator*, Brassey's Defence Publishers, London, 1988.

Montgomery, Bernard Law, *The Memoirs of Field-Marshal the Viscount Montgomery of Alamein*, World Publishing, Cleveland, 1958.

Montgomery, Bernard Law, *Normandy to the Baltic*, Hutchinson, London, 1947.

Stacey, C.P., *The Victory Campaign: The Operations in North-West Europe 1944–1945*, Vol III, *Official History of the Canadian Army in the Second World War*, The Queen's Printer and Controller of the Stationery, Ottawa, 1960.

Notes

1. Hitler's concrete bunker was under repair at the time, and his meetings were temporarily transferred to the map hut. With its lighter construction and windows, the force of the explosion found enough external outlet to save Hitler and most of the rest of those attending the meeting on 20 July. Had the meeting been in the concrete bunker, the bomb would undoubtedly have done its job.
2. Hastings, *Overlord*, p. 278.
3. Man, *The D-Day Atlas*, p. 109.
4. *Ibid.*, p. 111.
5. The Third Army would not be officially activated until 1 August, but Patton was never one to keep to schedules.
6. "OB West – Study in Command," MS No. B-308, German Report Series, U.S. Army Military History Institute, quoted in D'Este, *Decision in Normandy*, pp. 414–5.
7. *Ibid.*, p. 414.
8. Boatner, *The Biographical Dictionary of World War II*, p. 283.
9. Stacey, *The Victory Campaign*, p. 206.
10. Messenger, *Sepp Dietrich*, p. 137.
11. *Ibid.*, p. 138.
*12. Otto von Kershmer, *With Hitler Before the End: A Staff Officer's Account*, Collins, London, 1953, p. 323.
13. Bradley, *A Soldier's Story*, p. 132.
14. Blumenson, *The Patton Papers*, p. 503. Patton's diary entry for 7 Aug 1944.
15. Bradley, *A Soldier's Story*, p. 375.
16. *Ibid.*
17. Stacey, *The Victory Campaign*, pp. 204–5.
18. *Ibid.*, pp. 207–8.
19. *Ibid.*, p. 208.
20. *Ibid.*
21. *Ibid.*, p. 209.
22. *Ibid.*, p. 211.
*23. Field Marshal the Duke of Alamein, *Victory in Normandy*, Wentworth and Crocker, London, 1948, p. 433. Montgomery's role in the Falaise operation was the deciding factor in the decision by the Palace and Government to approve a dukedom for him. Had the war gone on with its growing butcher's bill, undoubtedly his title would not have been quite so grand.
24. Stacey, *The Victory Campaign*, pp. 215–6. Amiens was the opening of the Allied counter-offensive in the late summer of 1918 that resulted in such breach in the German lines that General Ludendorff was stunned and called it the "black day of the German Army in the history of the war." Amiens was truly a victory of the British Empire – British, Canadian, and Australian corps all performed well.
25. Stacey, *The Victory Campaign*, p. 247.
26. Man, *The D-Day Atlas*, p. 126.
27. Bradley, *A Soldier's Story*, p. 376.
28. Blumenson, *The Patton Papers*, p. 508.
*29. Malcolm E. Stuart, *D-Day to Falaise: The Story of the Canadian Third Infantry Division*, Canadian Defence Services Press, Kingstown, 1954, p. 352.

*30. George S. Patton, Jr., *Breakout to Victory*, Collinwood Press, New York, 1946, p. 336.

31. Stacey, *The Victory Campaign*, p. 255.

*32. Max von Oldendorf, *Die Ende in die Normandie*, Priller Verlag, Frankfurt, 1958, p. 336. This memoir by von Kluge's aide has been an invaluable source for the campaign since the field marshal took his own life right after he signed the surrender.

*33. F.W. de Guingand, *The End of It All: The Final Days in Normandy*, Collins, London, 1949, p. 392.

3
PATTON AND THE NARROW THRUST
The Ardennes Route into Germany

James R. Arnold

Vehicle Collection Point, 2 Miles North of St Lô, 18 July 1944
The T-2 recovery vehicle delivered the day's first casualty, an M4 Sherman tank. After maintenance crews unchained the tow, Lieutenant Belton Cooper began his inspection. The first round from the German 75mm PAK41 anti-tank gun had struck the armor protecting the Sherman's transmission at its thickest point. The projectile penetrated 4.5 inches of heavy duty armored casting, "passed through about a foot of fifty-weight oil, severed a five-and-a-half-inch steel driveshaft, then passed through another eight to ten inches of oil and a one-inch armored back plate before entering the driver's compartment."[1] Fortunately, by then the shell had spent itself. It came to rest between the driver's legs beneath his seat. Because the shell was armor-piercing, no explosion took place.

Cooper climbed on top the turret to examine the damage from the other hit. He was careful to avoid glancing at the body of the tank gunner that was still inside. The second round had hit the turret where the armor varied in thickness between two and a half and three and a half inches. It had carved a gash three inches wide and ten inches long, penetrated the gunner's periscope, and killed him.

Cooper looked at the impact point carefully. The shell's angle of incidence could not have exceeded fifteen degrees. The observation alarmed the lieutenant. During ordnance training, he had been taught that thirty-eight degrees was the critical angle, below which a shell would normally ricochet. Cooper had personally seen gunnery trials prove this point. However, he reflected, those trials featured the low velocity 75mm guns that equipped the Shermans. The Germans, he concluded, were not following the ordnance trials.

He dismounted from the tank and signaled to the cleanup crew. When a tanker received the full effect of penetration, the body and particularly the head frequently exploded, scattering gore throughout the entire compartment. The cleanup crew would try to collect all the body parts into a single shelter half to turn over to the graves registration people. Then, they would set to work with soap and disinfectant. They had learned that if a faint odor of death remained, it made a new crew jumpy.

Bradley's Headquarters, August 8, 1944

General Omar Bradley spoke into the phone, "Monty, we have the Germans under control at Mortain. They've made a serious blunder there. They've stuck their heads into the noose. If we hurry we can encircle them from the south and north."[2] For nearly two months the Allies had been bogged down in Normandy's *bocage*. Finally, the Americans had broken clear near St Lô. George Patton's newly activated Third Army was rushing south along a narrow corridor. Forewarned by Ultra intelligence, the Americans had contained the German thrust into Patton's flank at Mortain.

Now Bradley proposed a radical change to the Allied plan: instead of driving east toward the Seine, Patton's Third Army would wheel 90 degrees and attack north toward Argentan to trap the German forces that continued to block the British advance. Argentan was within the zone of General Bernard Montgomery's 21st Army Group. Bradley knew that Montgomery was excessively touchy about any American incursion into his zone of operations so he phrased his request as delicately as possible.

After a long pause, Montgomery replied, "My Canadians attacked this morning in the direction of Falaise. If we can close the gap completely... we shall have put the enemy in the most awkward predicament."[3]

Bradley hung up the phone and turned to the Supreme Allied Commander, General Dwight Eisenhower. "Monty says to go ahead. Georgie isn't going to like it though."

Eisenhower's face reddened. "You tell Georgie it's my God-damn army and that he'll do as he is told."[4]

Bradley's orders found Patton's XV Corps rapidly approaching the great road hub of Le Mans. From Le Mans, several excellent highways headed east toward Paris and beyond. Patton believed that few formed German troops stood between XV Corps and the German border itself. His every instinct told him to exploit the situation by continuing the drive east. Reluctantly, he accepted Bradley's orders to turn the corps north toward Argentan.

That evening, Patton disgustedly wrote a friend, "We are attempting to encircle the Germans doughboy fashion, rather than cavalry fashion."[5]

On 9 August, Montgomery's Canadians bogged down well short of Falaise. Patton ordered General Wade Haislip's XV Corps to advance beyond Argentan to close the gap. On 13 August, Haislip's corps encountered surprising German resistance near Argentan. As Haislip regrouped to press his attack, orders came from Bradley to halt at Argentan. Bradley worried about

German threats against Haislip's exposed flanks. He also feared "a dangerous and uncontrollable maneuver" with the risk of losses to friendly fire if the Americans pressed ahead into the Canadian zone.[6] A mere 25 miles separated the two Allied forces.

Montgomery's Canadians never quite managed to close the gap. Still, the Germans lost 50,000 prisoners, 10,000 killed, 220 tanks, and 700 towed artillery pieces while trying to retreat through the Falaise–Argentan gap. An American officer described the scene:

> "There were… vehicles, wagons, tanks, guns, prime movers, sedans, rolling kitchens, etc, in various stages of destruction… I walked through a mile or more of lanes where the vehicles had been caught close packed… The Germans were trying to run and had no place to run… Under such conditions there are no supermen—all men become rabbits looking for a hole."[7]

George Patton raged about Montgomery's failure to seal the gap. It also deeply frustrated Bradley. He had told a visitor, "This is an opportunity that comes to a commander not more than once in a century."[8] He secretly suspected that his own caution had contributed to the outcome.

So, despite staggering losses, enough German veteran cadres escaped to provide the nucleus to build new units. Whether they would be given the time to do so depended upon what the Allies did next.

The Seine Trap

Even while ordering Patton to drive on Argentan, Bradley had envisioned a wider envelopment to the Seine River. As the situation unfolded, Bradley saw a second opportunity to trap the enemy. His subsequent orders placed Patton in an awkward position. Patton's four-corps army lay stretched across a wide front with ongoing combat operations taking place in four directions. While the XV Corps was at Argentan, the VIII Corps was mopping up in Brittany and, along with the XII Corps holding the open Allied southern flank along the Loire River. This left XX Corps facing east near Le Mans.

Patton rose to the challenge. To nervous officers worried about the German threat along the Loire, he replied, "Air will spot anything before it happens."[9] He quickly concentrated XII and XX Corps near Le Mans and sent them east toward Chartres and Orleans. His objective was to cut off the German units fleeing from the Falaise pocket and to secure the Paris–Orleans gap.

Patton recognized the value of trapping the Germans against the Seine. Yet to him this maneuver was too conservative. With the Germans on the run, he sensed a matchless opportunity to drive east toward Germany itself. Accordingly, he alerted his corps commanders to be ready for advances beyond his designated objectives.

Bradley, on the other hand, again exerted a restraining influence, worried about the increasing strain imposed on his supply and communications. Overlord planning called for a secure logistical base before beginning operations over the Seine. Accordingly, Bradley "restricted Patton to Dreux, Chartres, and Orleans so that he, Bradley, could there regroup his forces and readjust the army boundaries."[10]

The speed of Patton's thrust surprised Germans and Americans alike. Although there was intense, local resistance at Chartres, elsewhere German opposition proved weak. Furthermore, by 19 August, XV Corps had determined that there was no effective obstacle other than the river itself to prevent a Seine crossing. However, it was becoming clear that combat gains were exceeding the capacity of the Communications Zone (COM Z) to supply frontline units.

The Tyranny of Logistics

By the second week of August logistics had become the major constraint affecting Allied operations. During planning for Overlord, supply officers had carefully calculated logistical requirements. They based their calculations upon the anticipated Allied rate of advance. Until the breakout from Normandy, the Allies were about 30 days behind schedule. COM Z easily met all requirements during this phase.

Planners had assumed that the Germans would make a series of phased withdrawals behind major river lines. Instead, the Germans had tried to contain the Allies in Normandy. When that effort failed, the subsequent breakout and pursuit threw all calculations into a cocked hat. The lines of communication could not be developed at the speed with which Allied mechanized equipment raced ahead. Patton's men closed on the Seine 11 days ahead of schedule on D+79. According to Overlord planning, by D+90 only 12 U.S. divisions could be supported on the Seine. Not until D+120, planners believed, could those divisions stockpile enough to attack over the river.

To conserve gasoline and other supplies in order to complete his drive to the Seine, Patton had held the XII Corps in place at Orleans. On 19 August, 21 C-47s delivered 47 tons of rations near Le Mans. "Why so little?" Patton demanded.

"Most are being held in reserve to support possible airborne landings at Orleans and Chartres," replied his chief of staff.

"It makes no God-damn sense," Patton snorted. "If they brought us gas instead, we could capture those cities without calling for the paratroopers."

"General Bradley said much the same thing," Colonel Oscar Koch, Patton's G-2 (chief of intelligence), quietly added.

"He did?" Patton asked with surprise. "Well I'll be God-damned. Good for Brad. Now, if he can just stand up to Monty, maybe we can go ahead and finish this war."[11]

Broad Front or Narrow Thrust

Just how to "finish this war" was the subject of an intense meeting on 19 August that divided senior American generals from their British counterparts and thrusting, combat leaders from cautious logisticians. Overlord strategists had always held that Berlin was too far east to be a serious objective. Consequently, they chose the Ruhr industrial region as the target for the main offensive. Planners envisioned a drive from the lower Seine via Liège to the Ruhr. They proposed a secondary route from the upper Seine through Metz to the Saar Basin and on to Frankfurt-am-Main.

Against this background, Eisenhower opened the conference with the observation that the Germans had unexpectedly chosen to fight in Normandy and had lost over half a million men doing so. Given that circumstances were much different than anticipated, he asked,

> "Should we change our strategy? The Combined Chiefs of Staff have given me broad strategic latitude. My orders are to advance to the heart of Germany and destroy Germany's military forces. Gentlemen, how should we proceed?"[12]

Bradley presented the American view. He argued that events indeed warranted a change of strategy. Rather than a broad advance to the German border, Bradley advocated a single thrust. Patton's spearheads were already much farther east than Montgomery's forces. All Allied resources should support a Third Army advance on the axis Verdun–Metz.

General Montgomery strode to a lectern. His aides unfurled an enormous map and Monty began his lecture with a lengthy campaign review that focused on the exploits of his 21st Army Group. He then seized a pointer and turned to the map. "As you see gentlemen, there are four possible invasion routes into Germany." Omar Bradley stifled a yawn. "Get on with it man," he said inwardly. "Everything you are saying was laid out long ago in the Overlord briefing papers."

Montgomery did not hear his silent plea and continued his methodical presentation:

> "One: we can advance across Flanders. Two: via Amiens, Maubeuge, and Liège along the northern edge of the Ardennes. Three: through the Ardennes. Four: south of the Ardennes through Metz, the Saar, and Frankfurt. Now, we rule out Flanders because it is too easily flooded. We rule out the Ardennes, of course, because it is hilly woodland, quite impassable. That leaves either side of the Ardennes. The southern route through Metz does not lead to decisive objectives. No, we should, we must concentrate everything north of the Ardennes. The Channel protects our left flank. We capture Antwerp and Rotterdam to open ports to nourish the offensive. We overrun those nasty V-weapon launching sites. We also collect excellent airfield sites for our own use.
>
> Gentlemen, history does not lie: this is the historically most traveled route between France and Germany. It leads to decisive objectives in the Ruhr and then Berlin. A single, dagger-like thrust, led by one operation commander, one operational commander mind, and the war is won."[13]

Montgomery lowered his pointer and turned toward his audience. There was a smattering of applause from the British generals. The Americans met his bravura performance with stony silence.

Through clenched teeth Bradley hissed to his chief of staff, "He's lecturing us like a school master lectures his students."[14]

Montgomery's tone also annoyed Eisenhower. He did not let it interfere with his strategic judgment. The Supreme Commander doubted that Montgomery and his men were capable of a *Blitzkrieg*-like advance. Nothing to date hinted that the British could conduct anything beyond a slow-moving, set-piece attack. Furthermore, in Eisenhower's mind a single thrust was subject to canalization and concentrated German counterattacks.

Accordingly, Eisenhower ordered that Montgomery, assisted by the First U.S. Army, advance toward the Ruhr on the Amiens–Liège axis. Patton would conduct a secondary effort in the direction Verdun–Metz. That night Eisenhower wrote to George Marshall:

> "I cannot tell you how anxious I am to get the forces accumulated for starting the thrust east from Paris. I have no slightest doubts that we can quickly get to the former French-German boundary but there is no point in getting there until we are in a position to do something about it."[15]

The Pursuit Begins

The next six days witnessed impressive gains by all Allied forces. Montgomery's First Canadian Army advanced northeast to close with the remnants of the German *Seventh Army* which held a tenuous line south of the Seine. Courtney Hodges' First U.S. Army filled in on Montgomery's flank upstream. But it was Patton's soldiers who showed the most spectacular progress. Even while one of his corps battered its way into Brest far to the west, Patton's other three corps rapidly drove east. On 25 August Paris fell. By that time the Third Army had carved out three bridgeheads over the Seine south of Paris. The 4th Armored Division, led by the gifted General John Wood, reached Troyes, some 80 miles southeast of Paris. The Third Army was 150 miles from the German frontier, closer to Germany than the vast majority of the German Army in France.

The Third Army debouched over the Seine on 26 August. Four days later it crossed the Meuse. Herculean supply efforts and 500 tons per day of airlifted supplies had enabled it to advance this far, but now Third Army ground to a halt for lack of fuel. With supply priority given to Montgomery, only 32,000 of the 400,000 gallons of fuel Patton demanded were delivered. Patton vociferously complained to Bradley, "My men can eat their belts, but my tanks have gotta have gas."[16] That evening, while he waited for a response, he wrote in his diary, "We have, at this time, the greatest chance to win the war ever presented. If they let me move on with three corps, two up and one back... we can be in Germany in ten days."[17] Patton's major worry was that senior leaders, "blind moles" he called them, would not see the opportunity.

Eisenhower Chooses the Single Thrust

Eisenhower scanned the day's Supreme Headquarters Allied Expeditionary Force (SHAEF) G-2 (intelligence) summary: "Two and a half months of bitter fighting... have brought the end of the war in Europe within sight, almost within reach. The strength of the German Armies in the West has been shattered."[18] The rapid Allied advance opened Eisenhower's eyes to the enormity of the German collapse. Like a child in a candy store given permission to make several purchases, Eisenhower looked at the map and saw he could seize a variety of glittering objectives. But he also knew that because of logistical constraints he could not have them all. His inclination was to continue with the broad front advance as far as possible. He judged it both good strategy and a politically expedient compromise. Like all compromises, it would not completely satisfy anyone, but it allowed both the British and the Americans to continue to advance and relieved him of the burden of having to favor Montgomery or Bradley.

The Allied broad front advance might have continued all the way to the Siegfried Line, where it undoubtedly would have run out of steam for logistical reasons alone, had not two events occurred: Montgomery made an unacceptable demand that infuriated Eisenhower; and Patton proposed a new, war-winning strategy. In retrospect, neither event was a surprise.

On 1 September SHAEF became operational on the continent. At this time Eisenhower was scheduled to assume personal command of Allied ground forces. Montgomery had a different notion. Claiming that he was too busy to absent himself from his own headquarters, the newly-promoted field marshal imperiously requested a visit from Eisenhower. When Eisenhower arrived, Montgomery tried to dominate further by insisting that, in the interest of secrecy, Eisenhower's chief administrative officer, an American lieutenant general, vacate the premises. Meanwhile, Montgomery's own chief administrative officer was to remain. Thus, having prepared his battle, Montgomery began his attack.

He argued again in favor of "one really powerful and full-blooded thrust toward Berlin."[19] The drive should take place in the north and aim at the Ruhr. All Allied resources should support this effort.

Warming to his subject, Montgomery launched into a condescending lecture on strategy. He reviewed the campaign to date in a highly critical manner. To avoid additional blunders, he strongly urged Eisenhower to limit himself to the political and administrative aspects of command while the field marshal assumed tactical control for all ground operations. As Montgomery started into another recitation of high command blunders, Eisenhower reached out and placed his hand on the field marshal's knee, "Steady, Monty! You can't speak to me like that. I'm your boss."[20]

Later, Eisenhower recorded his feelings: "To my mind and to that of my staff the proposition was fantastic... The only effect of such a scheme would have been to place Montgomery in position to draw at will, in support of his own ideas, upon the strength of the entire command."[21]

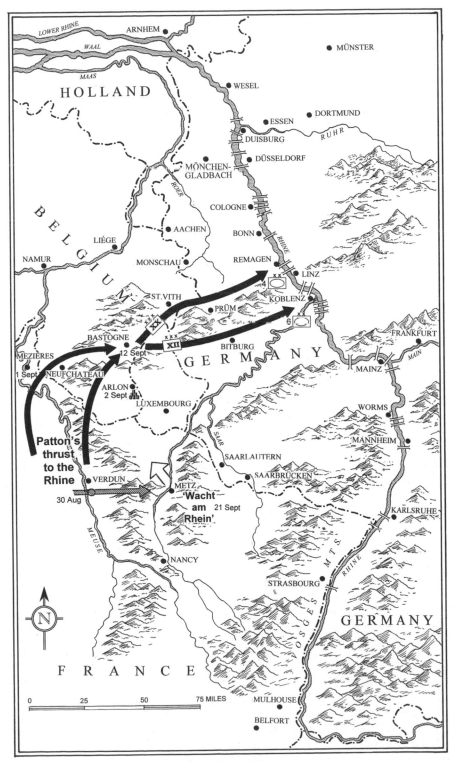

The Road into Germany

To allow emotions to cool, Eisenhower called for a break. While enjoying a cup of coffee and a cigarette, the latter something that Montgomery forbade in his presence, an aide summoned the Supreme Commander to the phone.

"What's up Brad?" Eisenhower asked.

"It's big, General. Too big to use an unsecured link. May I meet you somewhere?"

"When?"

"As soon as possible, General," Bradley replied.[22]

Through the Ardennes

Captain James E.B. Archer wiped his glasses and looked again through his binoculars. From his position atop the turret of his M5 Stuart light tank, he could plainly see the Meuse River bridges in the valley below. There were no signs of a German presence on the bridges.

Archer's troop belonged to a regiment of armored cavalry assigned to patrol the left flank of Patton's thrust toward Verdun and Metz. Possibly Archer's decision stemmed from the condescending attitude he too often experienced from the West Pointers. Perhaps it was his brief reflection on what Jeb Stuart, for whom the M5 was named, would have done. Archer raised his hand to signal the advance. His Virginia Military Institute ring caught the light of the early morning sun. The roar of mechanized equipment drowned out his piercing rebel yell as the cavalry thundered downslope into the streets of Mezières.

Had German Panzers been present, the Stuart's one and a half inch armor and puny 37mm main gun would have been no match. Instead, it seemed that the Germans had no idea that Americans were in the area. A pair of armored cars rolled into Mezières' main square where they found a German transport column parked, its drivers taking their ease at the nearby bistro. A burst of machine-gun fire scattered the Germans. Even Archer's dispatch rider, Staff Sergeant Hank Cupper, got into the fight. Cupper gunned his Harley-Davidson motorcycle into the square, dismounted with cigarette firmly clenched in his teeth, and emptied his Tommy gun into the bistro's front window. He charged into the building to find five German officers, including a general, cowering behind the bar. He marched them outside, grabbed the general by his collar, and returned with his chosen prisoner to the bar. Cupper sat down and gestured with his weapon for the general to serve him a drink.

Archer found him on his third beer. "Just interrogating the prisoners, Captain," Cupper explained.

"No time for that now!" Archer snapped.

Archer quickly scrawled a situation report and handed it over: "Deliver this to Colonel Spurrier. If he don't listen, take it to General Gibbs. Gibbs will know what to do. Go like hell!"[23]

In a cloud of burning rubber Cupper sped away while Archer detailed a few men to guard the prisoners and led the rest of the troop over the undefended Meuse bridge.

Archer's report quickly moved up the chain of command. By noon, Patton himself had learned that the Mezières' bridge was secure. Patton studied his maps. He knew that Metz, his assigned objective, might be a tough nut to crack. Its inner ring of 15 forts had been designed by Vauban. Germans had built an outer ring of 26 fortresses between 1871 and 1912. The Free French had supplied Patton's G-2 with information about the forts' condition as of 1940, but nobody knew how much the Germans had changed them.

Patton reflected that, if the Germans remained too disorganized and demoralized to garrison the Metz fortresses, a rapid advance might have taken them on the bounce. But, after a pursuit of some 500 miles in 26 days, his forward elements had ground to a halt for lack of gas. Given a breathing space, it was reasonable to think that the Germans had manned the forts. Furthermore, in his heart of hearts, Patton knew that an advance through Metz did not lead to decisive objectives.

Which led him to reconsider Bradley's account of the high command's 19 August meeting. Montgomery had repeated the analysis of the Overlord planners and dismissed the Ardennes because it was impassable. Yet those same planners had said it would not be feasible to support 12 divisions over the Seine until D+120 while in fact at D+90 there were already 16 divisions being supported 150 miles beyond the Seine.

Patton placed his finger on Mezières and traced a route along the main highway to Neufchâteau and Bastogne. His pulse quickened. Bastogne was obviously a key road hub. "If we capture Bastogne," Patton reflected, "we can make a two-prong advance. One directly east toward Bitburg, the other through St Vith to Prüm." Patton measured the distance from Bastogne to Koblenz on the Rhine and whistled. Then he picked up the phone to call Bradley.

"So George proposes redirecting his advance through the Ardennes," Bradley told Eisenhower.

"And what do you think, Brad?"

"It might not work, but if it doesn't we haven't really lost anything. We've been talking about taking a break to get COM Z forward anyway. But if it works, we could shorten the war by months and save a whole lot of casualties."

"The planners say the Ardennes is impassable."

Bradley laughed. "I said the same thing to George and you know what he said? 'Hell! The Boche found it plenty passable in 1940.'"

Bradley saw a grin spread across Eisenhower's face. It was a marked contrast to the weary, discouraged look when the Supreme Commander had first shown up. "Damn!" thought Bradley. "He may just buy this."

"What about Monty?" Eisenhower inquired.

"As you know, our original planning called for 21st Army Group to work along the French coast and open up the ports up to Antwerp. That's not a long distance. He won't need a lot of fuel. If all goes well he'll have Antwerp open about the time we reach the Rhine."

"A single, full-blooded thrust," Eisenhower said, mimicking Montgomery's distinctive accent, "through the Ardennes." A serious tone returned to the Supreme Commander's voice. "Make it happen Brad."[24]

The German Response

The extent of the German disaster was stunning. Since 6 June the German Army in the West had lost almost 300,000 men. Another 230,000 occupied coastal fortresses in France and were thus unavailable to defend the Reich. The army had sent about 2,300 tanks and assault guns against the Western Allies. No more than 120 had returned to the east bank of the Seine. Hitler's trusted fireman, Field Marshal Walther Model, told Hitler that the 11 mobile divisions that had made it across the Seine averaged five to ten tanks each. The 16 infantry divisions that reached the Seine's east bank had only their small arms. They might be rebuilt into four divisions providing they received heavy weapons.

Still, there was some hope for recovery. Back in July Hitler had ordered a series of steps that by 1 September were beginning to bear fruit. Two of the 18 new divisions that Hitler had ordered formed were now available on the Western Front. By the middle of September, the first of 100 fortress battalions would be available as replacement units. Twenty-five new reserve divisions, to be called *Volksgrenadier* divisions, had begun to form. Six would become available in September.

Hitler had seen that he could never match Allied numerical superiority in tanks. Therefore, he turned to quality over quantity and demanded that for every new Panzer IV, one Panzer V Panther must also be built. In spite of Allied bombing, German industry responded. A total of 358 Panthers were built in August along with 279 Panzer IVs and 97 Tigers. The West received priority for new tanks. Rather than reinforce depleted units, the tanks went to ten new Panzer brigades, numbered 101 to 110, that were formed from cadres of various wrecked Eastern Front units. Lastly, the veteran *3d* and *15th Panzergrenadier Division*s moved from Italy to France.

German strategists had no doubt about where to deploy these fresh forces. Patton's Third Army presented the greatest risk. Accordingly, during the first days of September a new formation, the *First Army*, took up position along the Moselle River. The *First Army* was by far the strongest German formation in the West. Its commander was a distinguished Panzer veteran from the Eastern Front, General der Panzertruppen Otto von Knobelsdorff. Knobelsdorff's assignment was to stop Patton's drive on Metz.

Elsewhere, the Allies were too far from the West Wall to worry about immediately. One advantage of fighting closer to home was that the roads to the front were not so long and therefore not so vulnerable to Allied fighter-bombers. To assist the build-up of forces facing Patton, the Germans established three major supply depots at road hubs that could nourish the front but were safely out of the way of Patton's advance. One was at Belfort near the Swiss border, a second around Nancy and Toul, and a third in Arlon, bordering the Ardennes in Luxembourg.

Patton Attacks

Patton explained his intentions to Eisenhower and his staff:

> "So my plan is to keep up the pressure toward Metz to convince the Germans that Metz is our objective. Meanwhile, I switch Walker and Eddy north. Under strict radio-silence they drive like hell to Bastogne, which the armored cavalry report is undefended. The Germans will have no idea that Third Army is in Luxembourg until they see us at the German border."[25]

Eisenhower and his lieutenants carefully studied Third Army's proposed 90-degree wheel into the Ardennes. "How soon will you be able to attack, George?" Bradley asked.

"Now," Patton snapped.

"You mean today?"

"I mean as soon as you've finished with us here."

Eisenhower frowned. "Don't be fatuous, George."[26]

Part of Patton's confidence came from his knowledge that his frontline was farther along than SHAEF realized. Even before Bradley authorized a drive into the Ardennes, Patton had begun shifting his strength in that direction. He called it his "rock soup" strategy, a time-tested approach to persuade cautious superiors to support a bold attack. As he later related to his personal staff, a tramp went to a house and asked for boiling water to make rock soup. The owner was interested and gave him the water in which the tramp placed two polished rocks. He then asked for some potatoes and carrots to flavor the water and eventually ended up securing some meat. In similar fashion, Patton pretended to order a reconnaissance, then reinforced the reconnaissance, and hoped finally to receive permission to attack.

Also, Patton had deliberately omitted to share with Bradley, Eisenhower or the cautious SHAEF accountants, news of a minor American coup that occurred on 30 August. On that day, Combat Command A (CCA), 6th Armored Division, captured intact a huge German aviation fuel depot near Verdun. The fuel was lower grade than American fuel. However, as Patton cheerfully observed, even poor gas in a hot engine would suffice to propel the vehicle forward.

The actual movement to Bastogne proved to be the easiest part of the operation. By now General O. P. Weyland's XIX Tactical Air Command had followed the methods developed by his predecessor "Pete" Quesada to provide a near seamless air-ground liaison. The lead tank in each armored column carried an experienced pilot who communicated via the standard fighter-bomber SCR-522 radio to relays of fighter-bombers flying armored column cover. Weyland explained the essence of the air-ground tactical cooperation:

"Our success is built on mutual respect and comradeship between the air and ground... You can talk to any of my boys about that... My boys like the way the Third Army fights. My kids feel that this is their army."[27]

Logistics again promised to be more of an obstacle than German resistance. Reorienting Third Army from a drive toward Metz to a drive through the Ardennes thoroughly scrambled lines of communication and traffic flow. With his reputation on the line, Patton worked like a man possessed, hounding his subordinates for greater speed, instructing a corps commander to do as he had done in the First World War and drain the fuel from some of his vehicles in order to allow the balance to continue.

Patton's G-2 found the general acting as military policeman to unsnarl a mechanized column at a congested crossroads. Koch interrupted Patton's profanity-laced traffic directions. "I've got good news. Wood's boys just moved through Arlon where they found a depot that dwarfs what 6th Armored secured. Wood says it's like a giant department store; food, booze, and lots of fuel."

"Hot damn!" Patton replied. "Now we can really get moving."[28]

High ranking logisticians regarded Patton's thrust as a hare-brained scheme that was logistically impossible. COM Z's commander, the imperious General J.C.H. Lee, chose this time to take several invaluable quartermaster truck (GTR) companies and use 25,000 gallons of fuel to move his large headquarters to Paris. Here he and his officers selected billets in the finest hotels.

Only Bradley's constant prodding forced a reluctant COM Z into supporting Patton. The result was an American masterpiece of improvisation: the Red Ball Express. Three newly arrived U.S. divisions were immobilized and stripped of their organic transport. Likewise, heavy and anti-aircraft artillery units, engineers, chemical warfare elements, and all less essential formations throughout Third and First Armies shed their transport to create additional *ad hoc* GTR companies. They were added to the regular GTR companies to deliver supplies along a loop system of one-way highways reserved exclusively for the supply services. Day and night, thousands of Red Ball Express drivers drove full out to deliver ammunition and fuel to Patton.

Simultaneously, Eisenhower wisely canceled all planned airborne operations. Most C-47 transports had been held in reserve to support a series of planned drops ahead of the advancing ground forces.[29] Released from this duty, they began an aerial shuttle that helped keep Patton moving. Even Air Marshal Tedder did his part. He overcame strenuous objections from the strategic bomber generals and managed to persuade them to use some of their planes as emergency transports.

There were hitches of course. Somehow, by the end of August the American forces had contrived to lose over half of the 22,000,000 jerrycans they had received. This impaired the entire fuel delivery system. During their advance to the Meuse, Patton's men had delighted in shooting up captured French locomotives and rolling stock. Now their absence also reduced the flow of supplies. Montgomery ruefully had to report that 21st Army Group needed to borrow American trucks because some 1,400 newly-delivered British lorries had broken down due to faulty pistons. When the replacement engines arrived, their pistons also failed.

But overall, the ability of the supply services to support Patton's offensive through the Ardennes surprised and pleased Eisenhower and his staff. It caused Montgomery intense vexation.

Wacht am Rhein

The Third Army's advance to Bastogne during the first week of September caught the Germans hopelessly off balance. Virtually all available mobile reserves had been sent to the Upper Moselle to block Patton's thrust toward Metz. Field Marshals von Rundstedt and Model had gambled that the rest of the Siegfried Line would not be attacked until it could be manned by the fruits of Hitler's desperate improvizations. The clacking teleprinter at Rundstedt's headquarters delivered Model's judgment of the gamble's outcome:

"The enemy enjoys almost complete freedom of movement as far as the West Wall, which is held… by only seven or eight battalions on a front of 120 kilometres."

Model concluded that in the absence of substantial reinforcements, which he very well knew did not exist:

"The strategic breach for which the enemy has been striving… will be opened automatically, this time on the German frontier."[30]

Rundstedt and his staff examined their alternatives. If Patton continued east from Bastogne, and there was no reason to think that he would do otherwise, there was nothing to check him short of the Rhine. Because of the crippling fuel shortage and the overwhelming Allied air superiority, even the mechanized units in the German *First Army* were incapable of long route marches. Instead, they would have to move by time-consuming rail transfer.

The only solution was for the *First Army* to attack Patton's long right flank. Limited fuel would constrain the attack, but the Americans would not know this. Rundstedt imagined his counterpart examining his map. The German intelligence dossier did not rate Eisenhower as an aggressive or even a competent strategist. Eisenhower's map would depict Patton's forces bulging eastward with long, exposed flanks. Eisenhower would have to worry that the Panzers were attacking to sever Patton's lines of communication and thereby isolate and annihilate him. After all, an attack against the shoulders of a bulge was the textbook solution. But did Eisenhower know this?

Von Rundstedt leafed through the pages of Eisenhower's dossier. He had little combat command experience. His background was essentially that of a staff officer. Von Rundstedt concluded that Eisenhower must be aware of the textbook solution.

Hitler approved of the attack and helpfully suggested a code-name for the offensive: Wacht am Rhein.

From Bastogne to the Rhine

Patton arrived at the crossroads town of Bastogne on 8 September to plan the advance to the Rhine. Everywhere was evidence of the overwhelming Allied air superiority. Planes were stacked in layers overhead. At low altitude, C-47s flew graceful circuits over the open fields west of Bastogne to deliver ammunition by parachute. An F-5 (P-38) from the 10th Photo Reconnaissance Group darted through a gap to swoop down and drop a canister containing film of the Rhine bridges at Remagen and Koblenz. Above the transports were rocket-armed P-47s flying east on armed reconnaissance and armored column cover. At higher altitudes waves of light and medium bombers fanned out to interdict roads and rail lines leading to Patton's objectives. And higher still flew watchful pilots in their P-51 Mustangs to provide protection should the *Luftwaffe* try to interfere.

During the campaign across France, Patton had changed the composition of his corps depending upon circumstances. At Bastogne, he did so again. He wanted veteran armored divisions commanded by the two officers he most trusted to lead the way to the Rhine. Accordingly, he ordered the officer who had so ably conducted the *Blitzkrieg* through Brittany, John P. Wood, to take his 4th Armored to St Vith and then on through the Losheim Gap. Patton instructed General Robert Grow, his G3 (operations officer) before the war, to drive straight east with his 6th Armored and not stop until he crossed the Rhine at Koblenz. Grow later recalled, "It was what we had spent years studying and training for." Grow was delighted to have "received a cavalry mission from a cavalryman."[31]

Patton's bold proposal alarmed the commander of the XII Corps, General Manton Eddy. Eddy worried about a German thrust against his exposed southern flank. The farther east he drove, the longer the flank would become, and, in Eddy's view, the greater the danger. Patton dismissed Eddy's concerns: "Manton, if I had worried about flanks, we'd all still be sitting in the hedgerows in Normandy."[32]

Patton chose his words to buck up a nervous subordinate. In fact, as he later explained to his intelligence chief, the open flank was a calculated risk. But in Patton's view, the risk was acceptable because the Germans were still on the run and thus unable to coordinate an effective counter-offensive.

Still, Patton did not plan a reckless, heads-down charge to the Rhine. He ordered his two spearhead corps, Eddy's XII and General Walton Walker's XX Corps, to advance in depth with one division echeloned behind the other. "That will," he explained, "give you striking power and at the same time cover your flanks."[33]

The German Counter-Offensive

Throughout the war, generals on both sides, whether in Russia, Africa, or France, had searched for the right tactical offensive mix. They all appreciated that mechanized units were ideal to exploit a breakthrough. The difficulty was in selecting which arm, infantry or armor, to create the breakthrough. The Panzer specialist, Knobelsdorff, had risen to prominence in Russia because he seemed to have a sure tactical touch.

Because he confronted only a light screening force and had the advantage of surprise, Knobelsdorff chose the newly equipped *106th Panzer Brigade* to create his breakthrough. Unlike most of the brigades in this series, the *106th* featured two Panzer battalions along with a Panzergrenadier battalion and an engineer company. In addition to the brigade's 48 Panzer IVs and 48 Panthers, Knobelsdorff added a Tiger detachment. He figured that the mighty Tigers would crush any American strongpoints. However, he knew that once the battle became fluid, the ponderous, fuel-guzzling Tigers would not be able to keep pace.

Knobelsdorff reinforced the *106th*'s Panzergrenadiers with an assault demonstration unit from the Saarbrücken infantry school. To provide extra élan and to serve as shock troops, he attached a class of 16- and 17-year-old students from nearby NCO training schools. Knobelsdorff planned for the veteran *3d* and *15th Panzergrenadier Divisions* to pass through the breach the *106th* created and then fan out along every available road to create havoc in Patton's rear.

On 10 September, Knobelsdorff's thoroughly professional plan collapsed on contact. Because of the need for haste, preparation for the attack had been conducted by wireless. As had been the case when Hitler ordered the Mortain counterattack, Ultra decrypts alerted the defenders well in advance. Patton's veteran 79th Infantry Division lured the inexperienced youths from the NCO training school into an artillery trap. The result was a slaughter. The American field artillery then set to the task of separating the Panzergrenadiers from their armor.

The Panzers rolled forward without support. In places it was the old story with the pitiful American 57mm anti-tank guns making little impression against the Panthers, let alone the Tigers. The German tanks had to be tackled at close quarters by brave GIs wielding bazookas and satchel charges. The GIs knew that the bazooka was a virtual suicide weapon yet there was no lack of volunteers. Isolated German tanks broke clear and had to be hunted down by Shermans from the tank battalions that backstopped the infantry. The tankers accepted the grim calculus that it took five Shermans to stop one Tiger and that four of the Shermans would probably be knocked out.

Since the breakout from Normandy, Belton Cooper's tank repair teams had little work beyond routine maintenance. The German offensive brought the resumption of tank-versus-tank fighting and again revealed the Sherman's deadly design flaws. The tank's nine-cylinder, air-cooled radial engine had been manufactured for the air force. Pre-war economy measures had forced this unsuitable engine upon the fledging tank corps. When a driver started the engine, it usually backfired noisily thus revealing the tank's position and often bringing a deluge of hostile fire.

Cooper examined one M4 which had been hit by a high explosive artillery round that struck the glacis plate just above the bolted seam that secured it in place. The impact had ripped out the bolts along a 14-inch span, dented the plate inward, and allowed the blast to enter the fighting compartment. In the absence of human remains, the graves registration team relied upon company records to identify the dead.

When pitted against the heavier German tanks, armor-piercing rounds routinely penentrated the Sherman's armor. If they did not richochet around the fighting compartment to destroy all they touched, they still typically produced a shower of incandescent particles that killed instantly on contact. Alternatively, the particles shorted out electrical cables that, in turn, ignited oil and gas vapors along with the paint, seats, and insulation. It all happened so fast that crew members seldom had time to to pull the master lever to release the carbon dioxide fire extinguisher. As surviving crew members scrambled to escape, the exploding gasoline and ammunition vented through the open cupola to create heat so intense that it annealed the hardness of the armor leaving the tank beyond repair. The only advantage, a maintenance technician sardonically reflected, was that few tanks survived long enough to require the onerous 100-hour engine overhal.

As Cooper's team conducted its grim labor, overhead the morning mists lifted. Ground controllers vectored flight after flight of rocket-firing Thunderbolts from the overhead "taxi ranks" against the stalled German armor. Before nightfall, Hitler's last gamble, Wacht am Rhein, had been decisively defeated.

Thirty minutes after sunrise the next day, lead elements of the U.S. 4th Armored Division rolled past startled German security forces and over the Rhine at Remagen. Five hours later, the 6th Armored secured the Rhine bridge at Koblenz. Neither bridge had been prepared for demolition. After a diligent search, combat engineers declared the bridges open for traffic and Patton's follow-on infantry poured into the bridgeheads.

At his plush headquarters in the opulent Hôtel de Place in Paris, J.C.H. 'Jesus Christ Himself' Lee was putting the finishing touches to his staff lecture. His topic concerned the utter impossibility of supporting the Third Army over the Meuse. Lee knew that Eisenhower's chief logistician, General Harold Bull, would be in the audience and he wanted to make a forceful presentation. If he could convince just a few officers, Lee told himself, then he could save the Allies from a colossal blunder.

A knock on his door interrupted Lee. An aide delivered the news that Patton had swept over the Rhine. Lee dismissed him with a curt nod. He glanced at his watch: five minutes until Bull arrived. He studied the map in silence before returning to his draft. With red pen he substituted Rhine for Meuse and headed out to the marble corridor leading to the lecture room.

On the Channel coast, Field Marshal Montgomery received the news of Patton's triumph later the same day. He, too, had been reviewing a draft text, his account of the campaigns of 21st Army Group in Europe. Its provisional title was 'From Normandy to the Baltic.' The Field Marshal stared hard for a moment, recovered, and with characteristic precise hand, scratched out Baltic and substituted North Sea.

The Reality

Often the plot of an alternative history requires a historical leader to see something that in reality he overlooked. Such is not the case with my story. In fact, the senior Allied army commanders recognized that after the Falaise Gap they held in their hands a historic opportunity. From that time onward, the wisdom of Eisenhower's choice of the broad front has been debated.

Critics abound. Basil Liddell Hart, whose theory of war was closely studied by some German masters of the *Blitzkrieg*, interviewed German generals after the war. His conclusion was straightforward: "The war could easily have been ended in September 1944."[34] Von Rundstedt's chief of staff Siegfried Westphal concurred. Westphal observed that none of the Rhine bridges was prepared for demolition until weeks after von Rundstedt's re appointment on 5 September. "Until the middle of October," Westphal wrote, "the enemy could have broken through at any point he liked with ease, and would then have been able to cross the Rhine and thrust deep into Germany almost unhindered."[35] Westphal particularly identified the Ardennes as a vulnerable area.

The costs of failure are also clear: two-thirds of the 750,000 Allied casualties suffered in Western Europe came after the September check; millions of men and women died in the subsequent fighting elsewhere and in the concentration camps. Berlin and Prague were available to the Western Allies before the Russians. Thus, the borders of the Cold War could have been established much farther east with incalculable consequences.

Eisenhower and his faithful lieutenant, Omar Bradley, defended the decision in their post-war writings. It is easy to dismiss some of their rationale. Eisenhower wrote that he believed that the Germans could readily counterattack to seal off a narrow thrust. But Montgomery proposed a 40-division advance, which is a far cry from a 'narrow thrust.' Even Patton's proposed advance with three armored and six infantry divisions hardly constituted a narrow thrust. More importantly, in the weeks following their Falaise debacle, the Germans simply did not have enough mobile units to stage a significant counter-attack. As long as the Allies advanced on a broad front, the Germans could barely check them with small, local counterattacks. If the Allies delivered a powerful, concentrated attack, the Germans had no answer.

Bradley loyally supported his chief in his own book where he observed that: "Inside Germany, beyond the Rhine, there was still a German army. We were to be reminded of that... on December 16 in the Ardennes."[36] This is a spurious argument. The "army" that attacked in December did not exist in September.

The debate comes down to what Martin van Creveld has called "the war of the accountants." Everyone agrees that there were ample amounts of supplies in France. The problem was moving them to the front. So, van Creveld, like the Overlord planners, entered the realm of logistical algebra, calculating sums like average distance from ports to front, load capacity of quartermaster truck companies, and daily divisional requirements. Fortunately, as van Creveld noted, Patton would have none of it. He only saw his G-4 (chief of logistics) twice during the European campaign, once when he assumed active command and again in the war's last week.

It is also worth noting that Allied logisticians planned on the basis of a division requiring 650–700 tons per day. In contrast, German logisticians planned their early war offensives on a much reduced divisional requirement. Moreover, the Allies in France possessed far more motor transport than any contemporaries and, in contrast to the Germans in Russia, enjoyed a modern road net and a friendly population to provide assistance.

A pursuit, like the one Patton conducted, makes far lesser logistical demands than a set-piece battle. It fundamentally reduces, as Patton fully appreciated, to gas and ammo. Even ammunition requirements are low because the advancing forces seldom face organized resistance and, when they do, they can usually bypass it. The Third Army also had "flying artillery" provided by its accompanying fighter-bomber umbrella.

Eisenhower's "broad front" plan of advance to the Rhine was designed to crack the resistance of an unbeaten enemy. The situation confronting the Supreme Commander after Falaise was entirely different and called for a pursuit without pause. The problem Liddell Hart identified is that at this time of "supreme opportunity," the top Allied planners "were not prepared, mentally or materially, to exploit it by a rapid long-range thrust."[37] An Allied Guderian or Rommel, and Patton himself, would have seized the moment.

Patton called the decision to transfer logistical support from Third Army to Montgomery, "the momentous error of the war." Given Patton's character, this might appear merely to be anti-British carping. But consider another of Patton's reflections regarding this decision: "One does not plan and then try to make circumstances fit those plans. One tries to make plans fit the circumstances. I think the difference between success and failure in high command depends upon the ability, or lack of it, to do just that."[38]

If one agrees with this assertion, then Eisenhower, to whom the comment refers, stands guilty of prosecuting a flawed strategy at a time when greatness beckoned.

Bibliography

Allen, Robert, *Lucky Forward: The History of Patton's Third U.S. Army*, Vanguard
    Press, New York, 1947.
Blumenson, Martin, *Breakout and Pursuit*, Office of the Chief of Military History,
    Department of the Army, Washington, D.C., 1961.
Bradley, Omar N., *A Soldier's Story*, Henry Holt, New York, 1951.
Breuer, William B., *Death of a Nazi Army: The Falaise Pocket*, Scarborough House,
    1985.
Cooper, Belton Y., *Death Traps: The Survival of an American Armored Division in World
    War II*, Presidio Press, Novato, CA, 1998. A damning indictment of U.S. tank
    design by a veteran who saw the Sherman's flaws exposed.
Creveld, Martin L. van, *Supplying War*, Cambridge University Press, Cambridge,
    1977.
Eisenhower, Dwight D., *Crusade in Europe*, Doubleday, Garden City, NY, 1948.
Greenfield, Kent Roberts, ed.,*Command Decisions*, Harcourt, Brace and Company,
    New York, 1959. Note especially the esay by Roland G. Ruppenthal, "Logistics
    and the Broad-Front Strategy." Ruppenthal also wrote *Logistical Support of the
    Armies* in 1950 for the Army 'Green Book' series.
Liddell Hart, B.H., *History of the Second World War*, G.P. Putnam's, New York, 1970.
Liddell Hart, B.H., *The Other Side of the Hill: Germany's Generals, Their Rise and Fall,
    With Their Own Account of Military Events*, Cassell, London, 1951. Note that this is
    much expanded from the 1948 edition, published in the U.S. under the title *The
    German Generals Speak*.
Patton, George S. Jr., *War as I Knew It*, Houghton Mifflin Company, Boston, 1947.
Spires, David N., *Air Power for Patton's Army: The XIX Tactical Air Command in the
    Second World War*, Air Force History and Museums Program, Washington, D.C.,
    2002.
Toland, John, *Battle: The Story of the Bulge*, Random House, New York, 1959.
Westphal, Siegfried, *The German Army in the West*, Cassell, London, 1951.
    Westphal served as Rundstedt's Chief of Staff upon the latter's re-appointment
    on 5 September, 1944.
Wilmot, Chester, *The Struggle for Europe*, Harper, New York, 1952.

Notes

  1. Cooper, *Death Traps*, p. 19.
 *2. Ralph R. Reinertsen, *Inside Bradley's Headquarters*, The Ralph Press, New
    Canaan, CT, 1952, p. 219.
  3. Martin Blumenson, "General Bradley's Decision at Argentan," in *Command
    Decisions*, p. 308.
 *4. Reinertsen, *Inside Bradley's Headquarters*, p. 221.
  5. Breuer, *Death of a Nazi Army*, pp. 226–7.
  6. Bradley, *A Soldier's Story*, p. 377.
  7. Blumenson, *Breakout and Pursuit*, p. 558.
  8. Bradley, *A Soldier's Story*, p. 375.
 *9. George Mangano, *Patton and Napoleon: Who Was the Better General?*, Napoleon
    Books, Lexington, VA, 2001, p. 716.
 10. Blumenson, *Breakout and Pursuit*, p. 565.
*11. Cited in Mangano, *Patton and Napoleon*, p. 855.

*12. The conversation is cited by Basil Liddell Hart in "The Indirect Approach to the West Wall," *Journal of Military History*, Vol. 12, No 2., August 1948, p. 87. The analysis of invasion corridors is according to Overlord planning documents.

*13. Field Marshal The Viscount Montgomery of Alamein, *Normandy to the North Sea*, Houghton Mifflin, Boston, 1948, p. 193.

*14. Reinertsen, *Inside Bradley's Headquarters*, p. 240.

*15. Blumenson, *Breakout and Pursuit*, pp. 659–60.

16. Wilmot, *The Struggle for Europe*, p. 473.

17. Blumenson, *The Patton Papers*, Vol. 2, p. 523.

18. *Ibid.*, p. 255.

19. *Ibid.*, p. 277.

20. Wilmot, *The Struggle for Europe*, p. 489.

21. Eisenhower, *Crusade in Europe*, pp. 284–5.

*22. Reinertsen, *Inside Bradley's Headquarters*, p. 263.

*23. O.W. McCleod, *With the Gear in the Rear: The Wartime Experiences of a Supply Clerk,* Burro Station Press, Lexington, VA, 1998, p. 155. This slender volume is a gold mine of stories collected by an ambitious would-be author who sensed that the exploits of his frontline comrades would be necessary to enliven an otherwise mundane memoir of clerical duty at regimental headquarters.

*24. Reinertsen, *Inside Bradley's Headquarters*, p. 280.

*25. Mangano, *Patton and Napoleon*, vol. 2, p. 254.

26. Toland, *Battle: The Story of the Bulge*, p. 131.

27. Spires, *Air Power for Patton's Army*, p. 183.

*28. Mangano, *Patton and Napoleon*, vol. 2, p. 344.

29. In reality there was a six-day suspension of air supply to the advancing units at this period because the transports were assigned to the planned drop of airborne forces near Tournai, south of Brussels.

30. Model to von Rundstedt, 8 September, 1944 in Wilmot, *Struggle for Europe*, p. 482.

31. Blumenson, *Breakout and Pursuit*, p. 370.

32. Allen, *Lucky Forward*, p. 117.

33. *Ibid.*

34. Liddell Hart, *History of the Second World War*, p. 557.

35. Westphal, *The Germany Army in the West*, p. 174.

36. Bradley, *A Soldier's Story*, p. 400.

37. Liddell Hart, *History of the Second World War*, p. 567.

38. Patton, *War as I Knew It*, p. 116.

4

A BACK DOOR INTO GERMANY
Monty Bounces The Rhine

Andrew Uffindell

The Rhine at Arnhem

The Lower Rhine glittered in the sunlight as it writhed its way through the Dutch countryside like a golden snake. In the skies above, seven Horsa gliders cast off their tow ropes and began a gentle descent towards the peaceful city of Arnhem. It was 12:15 p.m. on Sunday, 17 September 1944 and one of the boldest airborne assaults of the war was underway. On board the gliders were A and B Companies of the 1st Battalion of the Border Regiment, tasked with seizing three vital bridges over the river in a lightning attack. Each glider carried a platoon of 26 men. Four platoons constituted a company so eight gliders had taken off from England, but one, containing 13 Platoon from B Company, had been forced to land shortly afterwards near Hatfield.

Brigadier George Chatterton, the commander of the Glider Pilot Regiment, was flying the first glider. He had personally advocated this *coup-de-main* and had volunteered to lead it. At first, the Royal Air Force had objected that heavy anti-aircraft fire could be expected near the bridges and that the land south of the river was too soft and criss-crossed with drainage ditches for gliders to land safely. But Chatterton had identified areas near the two bridges where small-scale landings should be possible and had even been prepared to ditch his lightweight gliders in the Lower Rhine itself, close to the river bank, if the R.A.F. had persisted in its opposition.[1] 'We must land right beside those bridges and take them with a thunderclap,' he had insisted. 'A *coup-de-main* is vital. We must accept the dangers, or call off the entire operation.'

Chatterton could distinctly see the bridges ahead of him. The most important was the Arnhem road bridge, code-named Waterloo, with its large arc of girders forming a single span. Half a mile to the northwest was a pontoon bridge, code-named Putney, with a gap where the Germans had removed some pontoons and brought them to the south bank. Finally, the railroad bridge, Charing X, stood south of the town of Oosterbeek, 2½ miles west of the road bridge.

The Horsas had been released a few miles southwest of Arnhem, rather than directly over the German flak positions near the bridges. They had cast off at 4,500 feet and glided northeastwards in two groups, dropping 400 feet a minute. The noise of the tug aircraft had died away, leaving an eerie silence. The Horsas glided for seven minutes and then, after reaching an altitude of 1,500 feet, began a steeper dive to pass swiftly through the worst of the anti-aircraft fire. Five men of A Company were killed or injured when a flak burst tore a hole in the side of their glider. But the fire was not as heavy as had been anticipated and did not inflict further casualties. After a couple of minutes, the gliders levelled out, ready to touch down.

Major Tom Armstrong, commanding B Company, landed his platoons at both ends of the railroad bridge, two on the meadows to the north of the river and the third at the southern end. The gliders hurtled along the ground for up to 100 yards before coming to a halt. Armstrong's men immediately burst out and charged for the bridge, firing at the terrified German troops responsible for guarding it. By using gliders rather than dropping by parachute, the British were able to land troops precisely on target and in units that were immediately ready to fight without having to take time to assemble. The Germans had a demolition party of 11 conscripts billeted in houses at the southern end. These men had little chance to blow the bridge and, faced with landings at either end, were more concerned with saving themselves. Hobnailed boots rang on the metal plates of the bridge as Armstrong's men ran to cut demolition wires and throw explosives into the river. Within six minutes, the bridge was secure.

Meanwhile, A Company under Major Thomas Montgomery had attacked the road bridge. Three of its gliders landed south of the river: one in the fields and two on the ramp of the roadway leading up to the bridge, which made an excellent landing strip. The north bank was covered with the houses of Arnhem, but the fourth glider under Brigadier Chatterton swooped over the rooftops and circled clockwise round the twin spires of St Walburgis Basilica to touch down on the northern exit ramp at 85 miles per hour. The Dutch inhabitants of the nearby houses watched in awe as the Horsa with its massive wingspan of 88 feet ran up the sloping road before coming to a halt with a splintering crash as its wingtips were torn off by the first of four sets of lampposts leading up to the bridge span. There was a moment of stunned silence and then German soldiers opened fire from one of the two short towers that contained staircases linking the ramp of the bridge to the streets below.[2] The Borderers poured out of the Horsa and shot back amid the screams of their injured comrades. Within minutes, men from the other platoons charged over the bridge from the south bank covered by smoke bombs. The German garrison, about 20 veterans of the First World War, surrendered after their tower was struck by a PIAT round.[3]

Major Montgomery sent a platoon to seize the nearby pontoon bridge, but any German troops stationed there had already fled. By 1240 p.m, all three bridges at Arnhem were in British hands and the greatest airborne operation in history had secured its first stunning success.[4] Already, a platoon of pathfinders was parachuting from four Stirling planes to mark out drop zones south of the river. Twenty minutes later, the air was filled with a thunderous roar as the first of 143 C-47 Dakota transport aircraft flew overhead, bringing the 1st Parachute Brigade to reinforce the Borders' companies holding the bridges. Each plane carried a stick of 19 paratroopers who jumped through a door in the side of the fuselage. Hundreds of parachutes suddenly filled the hitherto empty sky and floated earthwards. Successive waves of parachutists followed for 15 minutes, dropping closer and closer to the bridges. From a distance, it seemed to be snowing.

Breakout from Normandy

The airborne attack on Arnhem had its origins in the spectacular Allied triumph in Normandy following the D-Day invasion of 6 June 1944. By the end of August, the Allied Expeditionary Forces, under the supreme command of General Dwight D. Eisenhower, had broken out of their bridgehead and dealt the German Army a crushing defeat. After liberating Paris, they thrust right across northern France towards the German border and the Low Countries. The Germans had suffered massive losses of men and equipment and by the end of August had little with which to oppose the Allied advance.

But the Allies found their logistics increasingly strained, as they still depended on supplies drawn from the Normandy beaches up to 250 miles away. The French railroad system, bombed by the Allies and wrecked by the defeated Germans, was inoperable and the Allies lacked enough road or air transport to bring sufficient supplies to the front. They could not continue their rapid advance all along the front without capturing and clearing Antwerp, or another major port, in the Low Countries. But at the same time, they were keen to keep going and bounce their way across the River Rhine before the Germans could recover and consolidate a defensive line along this formidable barrier.

The remarkable charge across France lulled many Allied commanders into believing that they had practically won the war and that they could afford to take risks. General Sir Bernard Law Montgomery, the British commander of the 21st Army Group in the north, was determined to play the lead role in winning the war by the end of the year. In Normandy, he had commanded all the forces on the ground, but Eisenhower took direct control of the land campaign on 1 September. Montgomery was now only one of three army group commanders, the other two being the American lieutenant generals Omar N. Bradley (12th Army Group) and Jacob L. Devers (6th Army Group, from the south of France).

Montgomery resented his reduced position and failed to recognise its inevitability now that the Americans had significantly more troops in Northwest Europe than the British. He criticised Eisenhower's strategy of advancing on a broad front, which he saw as being unlikely to produce decisive results anywhere, and demanded that the other Allied armies further south be halted in order to give him sufficient supplies to make one major thrust into northern Germany. Montgomery wanted to destroy Germany's ability to continue the war by seizing the Ruhr, its industrial heartland, and opening the road to Berlin. Not since Wellington had occupied Paris after Waterloo in 1815 had a British commander led an army into the capital of a defeated European enemy.

But Eisenhower knew that it was politically unacceptable at home to halt the American armies in favour of Montgomery. He was also concerned at the potential for Montgomery's single thrust on Berlin to create an exposed salient vulnerable to counter-attack, and doubted if Montgomery's proposal could be supported logistically. Furthermore, Montgomery had a reputation for caution and slowness and it did not make sense to halt the flamboyant and aggressive Lieutenant General George S. Patton Jr., whose Third U.S. Army (part of Bradley's 12th Army Group) was advancing on Germany's other important industrial area, the Saar, 150 miles further south.

The argument grew increasingly intense. Exploiting the Germans' disarray, Montgomery raced through Belgium and on 4 September seized Antwerp and its intact dockyards. The port could not be used until the Germans had been cleared from the banks of the Western Scheldt estuary for the 60 miles between Antwerp and the sea. But, with his eyes fixed on the Rhine, Montgomery failed to see the urgency of clearing the Scheldt before resistance solidified, or of cutting the line of retreat of the German *Fifteenth Army*, which he had pinned against the southern bank of the Western Scheldt. As a result, 65,000 German troops were gradually ferried at night across the Western Scheldt to the South Beveland Peninsula. They were then able to escape eastwards to the mainland of Holland, where they could help block the Allied advance.

The Germans began to stabilise the front with whatever forces they could collect or improvise. General Kurt Student rushed a collection of parachutists, soldiers, policemen and over- and under-aged men by train to Holland to form the First Paratroop Army. When Montgomery resumed his advance through northern Belgium on 7 September, after a two-day halt, he encountered stiffer resistance. On the 11th, after seizing a bridge over the Meuse–Escaut Canal, two miles south of the Dutch border, he halted. The other Allied armies also encountered increased opposition in their sectors further south.

Montgomery now produced an audacious plan, Operation Market-Garden, to restart the stalled Allied advance and force Eisenhower to give him priority in supplies. He proposed a massive airborne operation, combined with a ground offensive, to seize crossings over a series of waterways through central Holland and bounce his way over the Rhine at the city of Arnhem. From there, he hoped to burst out into the North German Plain, where he could exploit the superior numbers of Allied tanks on favourable terrain. The plan had the additional benefit of cutting off, in western Holland, the launch sites of the German V2 rockets, the first of which landed on London on 8 September.

Eisenhower approved the plan, for he was keen to secure a bridge over the Rhine and outflank the Siegfried Line, a belt of fortifications on the German frontier, even more than he was to open the port of Antwerp. He intended the operation to have the limited objective of bouncing the Rhine. But Montgomery hoped that success would force Eisenhower to support him for a subsequent and more ambitious drive.

Operation Market-Garden

Eisenhower had placed the First Allied Airborne Army at Montgomery's disposal. This included the U.S. 82d ('All American') and 101st ('Screaming Eagles') Divisions; and the British 1st Airborne Division, which had an attached Polish brigade. Montgomery's audacious plan consisted of two parts. The first, called 'Market', involved laying a carpet of 39,000 airborne troops along a 64-mile stretch of highway leading north from the Meuse– Escaut Canal to the Lower Rhine at Arnhem. The airborne soldiers were to seize bridges over six major waterways: the Wilhelmina Canal; the Zuid Willemsvaart Canal; the River Maas at Grave; the Maas–Waal Canal; the River Waal (the main course of the Rhine) at Nijmegen; and the Lower Rhine at Arnhem. The 101st Airborne Division would be responsible for the most southerly crossings; the 82d for those between Grave and Nijmegen; and the 1st Airborne for those at Arnhem.

Then, in the second, or 'Garden', part of Montgomery's plan, the XXX Corps of the British Second Army, with 100,000 men and 20,000 vehicles under Lieutenant-General Brian Horrocks, would break through the crust of the German defenses along the Meuse–Escaut Canal and then charge down the main road to reach Arnhem in, Montgomery estimated, 48 hours. The thrust would be spearheaded by the Guards Armoured Division and supported on either flank by the VIII and XII Corps, which would enlarge the salient.

Montgomery ordered Lieutenant General Lewis H. Brereton, commander of the First Allied Airborne Army, to plan 'Market'. Brereton chose his deputy, Lieutenant-General Frederick Browning, to command it.[5] One problem soon became clear to them: the Allies lacked sufficient aircraft to land the whole of the airborne force in a single lift. Furthermore, Major General Paul L. Williams, the commander of IX Troop Carrier Command, refused requests for more than one lift per day. He claimed that two lifts would unduly strain his air and ground crews and allow insufficient time for servicing the aircraft in between lifts, especially as his largely inexperienced pilots were, he argued, unfit for night flying. As a result, it would take three days to deliver all the airborne troops. Yet German anti-aircraft fire would inevitably increase over time and poor weather could delay later lifts, leaving the initial force dangerously exposed.

Objective: Arnhem

The northernmost drop, that of the 1st Airborne Division under Major-General Roy Urquhart at Arnhem, was the most dangerous. Of the three airborne divisions, Urquhart's would have to hold out the longest. But he found himself handicapped by Williams' refusal to deliver the whole of the division and its attached Polish brigade on the first day by flying two lifts one after the other.[6]

Urquhart also found that he had been allocated landing and drop zones six to eight miles west of Arnhem. Instead, he wanted to put his men down as close as possible to the bridges to seize them by surprise and avoid having to fight his way through on the ground. But Air Vice-Marshal L.N. Hollinghurst, the commander of No. 38 Group of the R.A.F. and the man responsible for planning the delivery of Urquhart's division, objected to landing troops near the bridges. Hollinghurst was concerned that his tug and transport planes would be exposed to anti-aircraft fire if they flew near the bridges. The planes would be flying slowly and at low altitude while delivering the airborne troops and would then have to pass over Deelen airfield five miles north of Arnhem as they returned home. Reports from bomber missions over Germany had reported heavy flak around both Deelen and the bridges. In fact, as reconnaissance photographs established, the Germans had since removed much of the flak from Deelen and many of the remaining positions around Arnhem could be knocked out by preliminary air attacks.

Hollinghurst, supported by reports from the Dutch Resistance, also argued, wrongly as it turned out, that the polder land south of the Lower Rhine was unsuited to glider or paratroop landings. Hollinghurst believed that gliders ran the risk of running into ditches or being quickly brought to a halt and turning over on to their backs as their noses dug into the soft ground.

Fortunately, at an early stage Browning consulted the experienced Major-General Richard Gale, who had led the British 6th Airborne Division in Normandy. Gale stated that in Urquhart's place, he would insist "to the point of resignation" on at least one parachute brigade being landed near the bridges. He also pointed out that Eisenhower had personally overruled objections from Air Chief Marshal Sir Trafford Leigh-Mallory during the preparations for the invasion of Normandy. Leigh-Mallory had protested that the American airborne forces would lose 50–75 percent of their strength during the D-Day landings. This proved to be a wildly inflated estimate.

Urquhart and Browning accepted that the south bank of the Lower Rhine was unsuitable for large-scale glider landings. But with Brereton's support they overcame Hollinghurst's objections to delivering a *coup-de-main* force in eight gliders to seize the Arnhem bridges. They also insisted on dropping 1st Parachute Brigade under Brigadier-General Gerald Lathbury south of the river, after the *coup-de-main* force had been able to take out any flak positions near the bridges. Once on the ground, Lathbury would lead his men over the river to occupy the city of Arnhem.

Meanwhile, another of Urquhart's units, the 1st Airlanding Brigade under Brigadier-General Philip Hicks, would land in gliders on the heaths six miles west of Arnhem, between the villages of Wolfheze and Heelsum. The division's remaining glider-borne units would arrive on the second day and Hicks would then march his brigade to join Lathbury at the Arnhem bridges.

The second day would also see Brigadier-General John Hackett's 4th Parachute Brigade dropping south of Arnhem as reinforcements. A final lift on the third day would deliver Major-General Stanislaw Sosabowski's Polish 1st Independent Parachute Brigade to the same drop zones south of the river. Sosabowski's artillery and other glider-borne elements would land either on the heathland near Wolfheze if that was still practicable, or on an alternative location to be fixed by Urquhart.

Intelligence sources, including reports from the Dutch Resistance and aerial reconnaissance photographs, indicated the presence of German armor in the Arnhem area. Early in September, the severely depleted *II SS Panzer Corps* had arrived in Holland to refit following its mauling in Normandy and by coincidence was based north and east of Arnhem. Similarly, Field Marshal Model, commander of *Army Group B* (holding the sector opposite Montgomery's 21st Army Group), established his headquarters in the town of Oosterbeek, three miles to the west.

Browning correctly decided to proceed with the operation despite the reported presence of German armor. The reports, like so many others, might be misleading. The aerial photographs did not confirm how many tanks were present, or whether they were all serviceable.[7] In any case, it was too late to make major changes to the plan and postponement or cancellation would have dealt a catastrophic blow to morale. But Browning was wrong in not alerting Urquhart for fear of unnerving him and his men. The 1st Airborne Division would have been willing to go anyway and Urquhart could have taken more anti-tank weapons and adjusted his plans for the battle on the ground.

Sunday, 17 September

Allied fighters and bombers attacked German barracks and flak positions on the morning of 17 September. The Germans had become so used to air raids in the previous weeks that they did not suspect the imminent airborne onslaught.

Over England the sky filled with planes and gliders, which assembled and headed out over the North Sea for Holland. By 12:40 p.m., the glider-borne A and B Companies of 1st Borders had seized the Arnhem bridges intact. Four Stirling IV aircraft dropped a platoon of pathfinders south of the river to identify two drop zones and prepare smoke canisters to help indicate the wind direction.

As scheduled, the 2,283 men of the 1st Parachute Brigade began dropping at 1:00 p.m.. At least two soldiers dropped into the river itself and were drowned by the weight of their equipment. Others landed actually on the road bridge, including one who accidentally came down on the metal girders of the

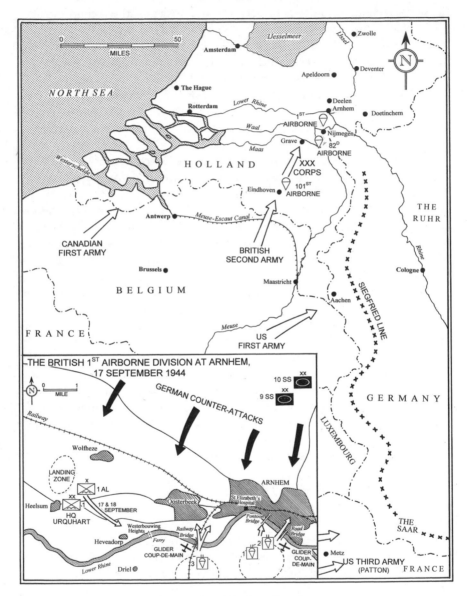

Operation Market-Garden

great arched span and had to be rescued as he dangled 50 feet above the roadway. A few men landed on or next to the houses on the north bank.

The Dakota transport aircraft delivering the brigade had to fly at only 80–90 knots and as low as 600 feet to drop their parachutists and were therefore vulnerable to anti-aircraft fire. Several of them were hit by flak. One received a direct hit and exploded in mid-air, scattering debris over the city. Another, trailing black smoke from a stricken engine, made an emergency landing north of Arnhem. Then two more went down. One lost a wing to a flak burst and crashed into a row of houses, blocking one of the boulevards that allowed access to the northern ramp of the road bridge. The other plane fell from the sky in flames. Soldiers of 1st Borders stationed on the road bridge ran for their lives as the plane hurtled towards them. "My God, she's going to hit the bridge!" a corporal shouted in anguish from a rooftop on the north bank. For several heart-stopping moments, it seemed the bridge would either be smashed or engulfed in flames, spelling disaster for the operation. But, at the last minute, the stricken plane banked slightly, screamed immediately over the span and then plunged into the Lower Rhine, throwing up a massive plume of water.

Despite the losses in transport aircraft, the overwhelming majority of the men of 1st Parachute Brigade landed safely on the south bank and assembled in their units within 40 minutes. The 3d Battalion of the Parachute Regiment reinforced the Borders' company at the railroad bridge and pushed into the town of Oosterbeek half a mile to the north. The paras encountered about 270 Panzergrenadiers from SS Captain Sepp Krafft's depot and reserve battalion, who were training in the nearby woods.

Meanwhile, Lieutenant-Colonel John Frost led the 2d Battalion of the Parachute Regiment over the road bridge, blowing his hunting horn as a recognition sign for his men. He found the Borders holding the houses at the northern end of the bridge against a counter-attack by a reinforced company of infantry from the *9th SS Panzer Division*. Frost drove the Germans back and secured the neighbourhood.

The German commandant of Arnhem, Major-General Friedrich Kussin, took charge of the battle to contain the British. He began receiving reinforcements towards 2:00 p.m., in time to block the 1st Battalion of the Parachute Regiment, which had leapfrogged past the 2d Battalion and was pushing through Arnhem, intent on occupying the high ground to the north. Despite this check, the 1st Parachute Brigade had managed to carve out a united perimeter encompassing most of Oosterbeek and a large part of Arnhem.

After beginning to move against the bridges, the Germans were confronted by reports of massed glider landings six miles west of Arnhem. This was the 1st Airlanding Brigade arriving on the heathland near Wolfheze. The first gliders touched down at 1:25 p.m. and the landings continued for 40 minutes. Accompanying the brigade was Urquhart with his headquarters, along with

Major Freddie Gough's Reconnaissance Squadron, the glider-borne vehicles and heavy equipment of 1st Parachute Brigade, and artillery units.

By 4:10 p.m., the 1st Airlanding Brigade had assembled on the heath. The Reconnaissance Squadron set out to locate German positions and link up with the 1st Parachute Brigade at the bridges. Already, Urquhart had found that his radio sets were unable to pick up signals beyond a couple of miles. He could not contact Lathbury to find out the situation in Arnhem, but knew that he had to reinforce his lightly-armed paratroopers as soon as possible. He therefore sent him the bulk of the available artillery and the 1st Parachute Brigade's equipment. Escorted by the Reconnaissance Squadron and by C and D Companies of 1st Borders, these units moved four miles southeastwards through Oosterbeek to the railroad bridge.

The rest of Hicks' brigade (the 7th King's Own Scottish Borderers and two companies of the 2d South Staffordshires) would remain on the heathland overnight to guard the landing zones for the second glider lift, due at 10:00 a.m. the next day. This would bring the outstanding two companies of the 2d South Staffordshires; those gliders that had been forced by malfunctions to land soon after take-off in England; and some remaining artillery and divisional units.

Intervention of the II SS Panzer Corps

The immediate danger to the Arnhem landings lay with the *II SS Panzer Corps* under General Willi Bittrich. The corps had two divisions, each with a much-reduced combat strength of 2,500–3,000 troops and a few vehicles. In order to refit, the *9th SS Panzer Division "Hohenstaufen"* had been ordered to hand its vehicles over to the *10th SS Panzer Division "Frundsberg"* and entrain for Germany. The *10th* would then be brought up to strength near Arnhem. Naturally, the *9th* had kept as many of its vehicles as possible by claiming they were unserviceable; when the British struck at Arnhem, these vehicles were on trains ready to leave for Germany. The *9th*'s fighting units were dispersed in quick reaction units of company strength along the main roads leading north and northeast from Arnhem. About ten of these units lay within ten miles of the road bridge and could reach it in about 30 minutes by vehicle or two hours on foot.[8] Fortunately, the *9th* would not be able to use its vehicles in its counter-attacks until it had unloaded them from the trains and prepared them for battle.

The *10th SS Panzer Division* was stationed further east, between the *9th* and the German border.

The Germans were surprised by the initial assault on the bridges. Field Marshal Model was informed that airborne troops had landed near the Arnhem bridges while he was lunching at his headquarters in the Tafelberg Hotel in Oosterbeek. He immediately raced to Bittrich's headquarters at Doetinchem, 15 miles east of Arnhem. There, he received reports of a separate landing on the heathland six miles to the west of Arnhem. This confused the situation: Model could not be sure whether the units on the heaths intended to march on the bridges; stay put pending the arrival of further airborne lifts; or attack potential secondary objectives, such as Deelen airfield, where reinforcements could be flown in.

Model realised that the priority was for Bittrich's *II SS Panzer Corps* to regain the Arnhem road bridge, to enable the Germans to drive south and seize the bridge at Nijmegen and thus prevent Montgomery's ground offensive from crossing the Waal. With the British tanks checked in the south, the isolated airborne forces at Arnhem would inevitably be crushed. "It is on the Waal that we will win the Battle of Arnhem," insisted Model with a thump of the table.

Already, he had sent orders to General Friedrich Christiansen, the commander of the German occupation forces in Holland, to support Bittrich with whatever units he could assemble. Additional reinforcements, including flak batteries and Tiger tanks, would come from Germany and occupied Denmark.

Units from the *9th SS Panzer Division* reached Arnhem either on foot, on bicycles or in carts or vehicles. As they arrived, they found themselves pitched into a fierce battle with only a limited grasp of the situation. Two truck-loads of infantry were massacred after driving headlong into streets held by the British. Disjointed actions flared up around the city and then died away.

At 6:00 p.m., the German threat became more serious. SS Captain Viktor Gräbner's reconnaissance battalion from the *9th SS Panzer Division* arrived from the north with 30 armored cars and half-tracks, intent on seizing the Arnhem road bridge. The 1st Parachute Brigade had no anti-tank guns; these had yet to arrive from the heathland. But access to the bridge was partly blocked by the wreckage of the crashed Dakota and the rubble of destroyed houses. With the help of local people the British had felled trees and used some captured German vehicles to create makeshift roadblocks. At the bridge itself, Chatterton's glider on the roadway was soon set ablaze in the exchange of fire. Gräbner had hoped to break through by charging across the bridge at speed. Instead, he was forced slowly to negotiate the obstacles and found his vehicles picked off one by one by grenades and PIATs, while his men were shot down as soon as they left cover. Gräbner himself died during this disastrous attack and the wreckage of his battalion now completely blocked the northern ramp.

Bittrich ordered SS Lieutenant-Colonel Walter Harzer to reduce the British at Arnhem with the *9th SS Panzer Division*, while the *10th* under SS Brigadier-General Heinz Harmel tried to reinforce the German units posted at Nijmegen. The *10th*'s leading battalion, under SS Captain Karl-Heinz Euling, reached Arnhem that evening, but found the bridge still firmly in British hands. Euling became tied down in the fighting and it was not until the following day that Harmel began to move his other units to the southeast, intent on bypassing Arnhem and ferrying his men across the Lower Rhine at Pannerden to reach Nijmegen. Harmel knew that it would be a slow and tedious process, but without the bridge at Arnhem he had no choice.

Monday, 18 September

The failure of Urquhart's radio equipment left him cut off at Arnhem and unable to communicate with his superior, Lieutenant-General Browning, who had landed near Nijmegen with the U.S. 82d Airborne. But during the night, Lieutenant-Commander Arnoldus Wolters, a Dutch liaison officer attached to Urquhart's headquarters, managed to contact the Allied forces further south by using a clandestine telephone network run by the local Resistance. Using similar means, including the separate telephone system that connected electric power stations, Wolters began collecting intelligence of German movements from Dutch patriots.[9]

But good intelligence alone could not win the battle and the second day began rather badly for Urquhart and his men. At dawn, the German forces struck between Oosterbeek and Arnhem, seizing the St Elizabeth Hospital and penetrating to the north bank of the Lower Rhine, thus splitting Urquhart's position into two bridgeheads based on the road and railroad bridges. Lathbury, the commander of the 1st Parachute Brigade, was severely wounded during this attack.

Bad weather delayed the arrival of Urquhart's reinforcements on the second lift. It was only at 2:06 p.m. that Hackett's 4th Parachute Brigade began to drop south of the river. Brandishing his walking stick, Hackett immediately led his men across the road bridge into Arnhem and took command of that bridgehead.

Meanwhile, the gliders had landed successfully on the heathland, which was protected by Hicks' men. Since Model was intent on regaining the vital road bridge, he had concentrated most of his available forces at Arnhem. As a result, Hicks was able to contain those units sent against him. He then evacuated the landing zones and fought his way through to the railroad bridgehead.

Initially, Urquhart had hoped to retain the landing zones on the heathland pending the arrival of the gliders carrying the heavy equipment of the Polish Parachute Brigade on the 19th. (The men of the brigade were to parachute south of the river.) But the unexpected strength and speed of the German reaction made it imperative to rush all of Hicks' troops to the bridges. In any case, it had now been established that the Poles' gliders could be safely landed south of the river. Urquhart contacted Horrocks by telephone, asking for the landing zone to be changed. He also arranged for a new supply drop zone south of the railroad bridge.

Urquhart considered abandoning one of the two bridgeheads to concentrate the whole of his resources on the defense of the other and prevent his division from being crushed piecemeal. But he soon decided against it. His most important objective was the road bridge, but as the Germans held most of Arnhem, the XXX Corps on its arrival would have problems expanding the airborne perimeter without the second bridgehead based on the railroad line being in British hands as well.

An abandoned Sherman Tank of the British 7th Armoured Division with a *Kubelwagen* of the *12th SS Panzer Division* parked next to it. In the period after D-Day the Germans were able to defeat the 7th Armoured Division's attempt to re-create its deep advances of 1940.

General Bernard Law Montgomery. The British and Canadian planning and execution for D-Day was "Monty's" to an extent rare in the Second World War.

Above right: Lieutenant-General Guy Grenville Simonds, commander Canadian II Corps.

Above left: Simonds' innovation for Operation Totalize—the "Kangaroo"—
an M7 Priest self-propelled gun transformed into an armored personnel carrier.

Left: Josef "Sepp" Dietrich, commander of *I SS Panzer Corps,*
inspects some of his men.

Above: Patton drove his Third Army into Germany before the leaves had fallen. Tanks of the 6th Armored Division are shown crossing a small tributary of the Rhine near Koblenz.

Above left: Canadian tanks and infantry in the hard fighting for Falaise on 12 August 1944.

Left: A knocked-out Sherman tank during the fighting in the Ardennes, 1944

Above: SS Panzergrenadiers in action. The unexpected presence of the *9th* and *10th SS Panzer Divisions* in the vicinity of Arnhem was a potential disaster for the lightly equipped British 1st Airborne Division. *(U.S. Army)*

Above right: The replacement road bridge over the Lower Rhine at Arnhem. In 1974 it was named after Brigadier-General John Hackett, the commander of the British 4th Para Brigade.

Right: The American "Brains Trust": Generals Bradley, Eisenhower and Patton in the bomb-damaged streets of Bastogne.

Above: A confused sequence of orders left the 101st Airborne Division's acting commander, Brigadier General Anthony McAuliffe, unaware that his men were due in Bastogne, not Werbomont. *(U.S. Army)*

Above left: Men of the 101st's 327th Glider Infantry Regiment set up a machine-gun position after the retreat from Bastogne. (U.S. Army)

Left: Troopers of the 101st retreat from Mande St Etienne after the failed attempt to relieve Bastogne. (U.S. Army)

Top: British Churchill Crocodile flamethrower tank from
XXX Corps in action. *(U.S. Army)*

Above: Canadian infantry take a well-earned break outside Namur.

Above left: Officers of the *Sixth SS Panzer Army* on the road to Malmedy. Despite the
fearsome and well-deserved reputation of the *SS*, it was the *German Army's
Fifth Panzer Army* that would come closest to success. *(U.S. Army)*

Left: Canadian Sherman Firefly tanks of 4th Armoured Brigade in the counterattack
that stopped the German attempt to seize Namur.

Main picture: British Sherman Firefly, armed with a high-velocity 76mm gun, on the Meuse. *(U.S. Army)*

Left: (L to R) Maj Gen Collins, Field Marshal Montgomery and Maj Gen Ridgway worked together well to defeat the German offensive in the Ardennes. *(U.S. Army)*

Below: U.S. tank destroyer moves up in support of the 82nd Airborne Division during the *Herbstnebel* campaign of December 1944.

A knocked-out German Mark IV tank destroyed in the battle of Luxembourg City.
(U.S. Army)

American paratroops finish off a Tiger II tank with bazooka fire as other U.S. troops watch from a road embankment in the village of La Glière, during the *Herbstnebel* campaign. Note the destroyed Panther tank behind the American soldiers.

Panther tanks arriving by rail to reinforce *Seventh Army* in its bid to stop George Patton. *(U.S. Army)*

General der Panzertruppen Erhard Raus, one of the finest Panzer commanders of the *German Army*.

General George Patton. After the Ardennes disaster he was made overall Allied Ground Forces commander. *(U.S. Army)*

(*From left*) Vice-President Henry Wallace, President Franklin Roosevelt, and
Senator Harry Truman in the 1944 presidential campaign.

Some of the German troops who won the Battle of the Ardennes,
setting off political convulsions in London and Washington. *(U.S. Army)*

Tuesday, 19 September

Everything now depended on the prompt arrival of Horrocks' XXX Corps. Urquhart had hoped that it would reach him by the evening of the 18th. But its spearhead, the Guards Armoured Division, reached the River Maas at Grave, 18 miles south of Arnhem, only at 8:20 a.m. on the 19th. Even as he advanced, Horrocks found himself forced to defend the long, narrow salient that he had created. German forces to both west and east tried desperately to cut his supplies by severing the main road, which was soon dubbed 'Hell's Highway' by the U.S. 101st Airborne.

Urquhart knew that powerful German reinforcements were heading for Arnhem. But the last of his own reinforcements, the Polish Parachute Brigade, was prevented from taking off by bad weather in England. This was fortunate for the Poles, as the Germans had increased the intensity of their anti-aircraft fire by bringing up additional flak units. They also had 300 *Luftwaffe* planes based across the border in Germany, just ten minutes away in flying time.

Inside Arnhem, Hackett held a bridgehead over a mile wide at the base, on the Lower Rhine, and extending up to half a mile northwards into the city. He had the 2d and 3d Battalions of the Parachute Regiment of the 1st Parachute Brigade, in addition to his own 4th Parachute Brigade. He had artillery, including 6-pounder anti-tank guns, and brilliantly conducted the defense of his perimeter, even as the Germans began systematically destroying the buildings held by his men, using artillery and tank fire and blasting or burning the defenders out with grenades or flamethrowers. British snipers enjoyed superb vantage points in the tower of St Eusebius Church, until it was smashed by German shells.

Further west, Hicks had a larger perimeter around the railroad bridge. Its base was a triangle of flat, open ground enclosed by a bend of the Lower Rhine to the southwest and southeast and, to the north, by the houses of Oosterbeek and the outskirts of Arnhem. Hicks held most of Oosterbeek and part of the western suburbs of Arnhem, but was acutely conscious that if he lost his grip on these built-up areas, his men would be cruelly exposed as they fell back across the half mile of exposed meadows to the Lower Rhine. Fortunately, the Germans were concentrating their attacks against the more important road bridge. To defend his bridgehead, Hicks had available the 1st Battalion of the Parachute Regiment; the men of the Glider Pilot Regiment; artillery units; and his own 1st Airlanding Brigade.

The Germans hoped to seal the fate of the 1st Airborne Division by blocking the Allied ground offensive at Nijmegen, ten miles to the south. The U.S. 82d Airborne Division was responsible for this sector and its commander, Brigadier General James M. Gavin, had hoped to seize the road and rail bridges at Nijmegen soon after landing on 17 September. But his division also had to take bridges further south over the Maas–Waal Canal and hold the Groesbeek Heights to the southeast against counter-attacks expected from the Reichswald Forest across the German border. The Groesbeek Heights, as the only relatively high ground in the area, dominated the 82d's other objectives and had to take priority. Gavin simply lacked enough men in the first lift to take all his objectives immediately.

Hence it was only at 10:00 p.m. on the 17th that two companies of the 1st Battalion of the 508th Parachute Infantry Regiment reached Nijmegen. Fortunately, the British seizure of the Arnhem bridges had prevented the *10th SS Panzer Division* from moving across the road bridge and driving south to Nijmegen. As a result, the men of the 1/508th found the Nijmegen bridges defended by a single German battlegroup of 750 men, including police reservists and other rear area units. The two American companies were reinforced by a third and, skilfully exploiting the darkness, penetrated the German positions. By dawn, they had gained the railroad bridge, but were unable to reach the other, road, crossing in the face of fire from the 88mm and 20mm guns deployed to protect it.

Later on the 18th, SS Brigadier-General Harmel began ferrying his *10th SS Panzer Division* across the Lower Rhine eight miles southeast of Arnhem. This took a long time, but some units, including a handful of tanks and tank destroyers, reached Nijmegen on the 18th and 19th. The 1/508th came under increased pressure and eventually had to be reinforced by the 3d Battalion. The Americans clung on in an epic, last-ditch battle at both ends of the railroad bridge[10] and were saved from complete destruction by the arrival of the Guards Armoured Division at noon on the 19th.

That evening, after fighting their way through Nijmegen, four Sherman tanks clanked on to the 1,960 foot-long road bridge and were soon fiercely engaged with the Germans. Two tanks were knocked out at the centre of the bridge. Then bright flashes appeared at the bridge supports and the roadway suddenly sagged and collapsed into the Waal as the sound of explosions thundered across the battlefield.

Acting on his own initiative, Harmel had prepared the bridge for demolition and blown it just in time. Fortunately, the American paratroopers were already converting their railroad bridge into a roadway and this work continued through the night. Horrocks halted, intending to break through the remaining German units north of Nijmegen the next day. He was now only ten miles from the beleaguered British airborne division at Arnhem.

Wednesday, 20 September

The Betuwe, the flat, marshy ground north of Nijmegen, favoured the defense. Tanks would have to advance along a single causeway raised above the surrounding flat polder land, leaving them exposed to German fire and unable to manoeuvre. Secondary roads to either flank were simply embankments paved with bricks and unsuitable for heavy traffic.

Ideally, more infantry were needed to support the attack. Horrocks had ordered the 43d (Wessex) Division up from the rear early on the 19th. But the 43d had made such slow progress up the traffic-clogged highroad that its leading brigade would reach the northern side of Nijmegen only in the late afternoon of the 20th. Browning therefore suggested dropping the Polish

Parachute Brigade of nearly 1,700 men directly into the Nijmegen area. But bad weather in England continued to prevent the brigade from taking off until it was no longer needed.

Thus, it was left to the Irish Guards Battlegroup of the Guards Armoured Division to attack out of the Nijmegen bridgehead at 1:00 p.m. on the 20th. Half-a-mile to the north, the Irish lost three Shermans to German anti-tank guns and came to an abrupt halt.

Despite this setback, Urquhart was already receiving artillery support from the XXX Corps' guns. Urquhart's signallers had managed to establish radio communications with the 64th Medium Regiment, which was sited 11 miles away on the south bank of the River Waal near Nijmegen. The 64th's shells stabilised the critical situation in the bridgeheads. The fire, directed by observers at Arnhem and Oosterbeek with pinpoint accuracy, repeatedly broke up German attacks, although the number of rounds had to be rationed given the difficulty in bringing supplies up Hell's Highway.

The German commanders were now seriously alarmed. More units of the *10th SS Panzer Division* were being ferried across the Lower Rhine to the Betuwe, but were unlikely to establish a sufficiently strong position in time to block the XXX Corps permanently. Only by recapturing the vital Arnhem road bridge could Model foil the British and he knew that this was unlikely to happen within 24 hours.

The Irish Guards were temporarily checked on the highroad. They were unable to summon air support, as the radio sets in their R.A.F. contact car were not working. Instead, they had to halt their tanks while their accompanying infantry tried to work their way round the German flank and clear the way for a renewed advance. This took time, for the guardsmen found themselves pinned down by mortar fire.

Meanwhile, at 3:00 p.m., the armored cars of the 2d Household Cavalry Regiment slipped past the Germans by using sideroads well to the west. They turned off the highroad immediately north of Nijmegen, followed the bank of the River Waal northwestwards for seven miles and then headed north for the Lower Rhine. At 5:30 p.m., they linked up with Urquhart at the railroad bridge and ensured that he could now communicate with ease with XXX Corps through their radios.

The Irish Guards finally broke through the last of the German opposition on the highroad with the help of the leading elements of the 43d Division. They now dashed northwards for the final leg of their 64-mile advance. At 10:30 p.m., the leading troop of tanks roared over the Arnhem road bridge and linked up with Hackett's ecstatic men.

Consolidating the Bridgehead

Horrocks had secured Market-Garden's most important objective, but realised that for the moment it was a bridge to nowhere. Ironically, the airborne troops' success in holding the road bridge made it impossible for Horrocks to advance off the ramp. It would take a day to clear the exit ramp of the tangled and burnt-out wreckage of German vehicles and the skeleton of Brigadier Chatterton's glider. An armored bulldozer was brought up on the morning of 21 September, only to be put out of action almost immediately by a German 88mm gun. It became clear that the clearance work would have to wait until the Germans had been driven back from the nearby ruins by infantry. Supporting artillery fire was available, but ammunition restricted.

Even after the exit ramp had been cleared, tanks would have problems advancing through streets half-blocked with rubble and infested with German infantrymen armed with *Panzerfausts*, effective, hand-held anti-tank weapons. The British commanders were acutely conscious of their country's shortage of manpower and were appalled at the thought of the heavy casualties that would result from driving the Germans from the devastated city. In discussing Arnhem, they increasingly referred to the bloody battles for Caen and Stalingrad.

To secure their bridgehead, the British would not only have to take Arnhem, but also establish a firm foothold on the high ground to the north. This terrain was only about 330 feet high, but dominated Arnhem and the flat countryside to the south over which Horrocks would have to deploy his corps.

Convinced of the futility of trying to mount his main attack through Arnhem from the road bridge, Horrocks concentrated on the railroad bridgehead. Here, engineers were able to convert the bridge to a roadway in 24 hours. It was wide enough for only a single lane of vehicles, but enabled Horrocks to pass a brigade of the 43d Division and a squadron of tanks from the 8th Armoured Brigade over to Oosterbeek on the night of 22 September.[11]

Horrocks confounded German expectations by initially attacking westwards from Oosterbeek instead of fighting his way eastwards towards Arnhem to reunite his two bridgeheads. His initial aim was to seize the ferry across the Lower Rhine between Driel and Heveadorp. This lay over a mile west of the railroad bridge and so far had been ignored by both sides, whose attention was fixed by the bridges further east. Horrocks seized the Westerbouwing Heights on the north bank, which commanded the crossing.

The Polish Parachute Brigade finally dropped south of the river and used the ferry to reinforce the units on the far side. Engineers built a Bailey bridge at the same spot to carry tanks, ammunition trucks, and ambulances. The whole of the 43d Division was deployed in the bridgehead and attacked northwards from the area of the Westerbouwing Heights on the 26th.

Supplies were flowing more freely up Hell's Highway now that supporting formations were strengthening and widening the salient. The Germans tried desperately to destroy the Arnhem bridges, using jet aircraft and even a glider packed with explosives. On the night of 28–29 September, a team of frogmen slipped under a boom and swam down the Lower Rhine during a diversionary air raid. The frogmen brought explosive charges, whose timer mechanisms would automatically be activated when placed upright. Fortunately, the Germans were spotted at the pontoon bridge and shot. Shortly afterwards, explosions tore apart the pontoons and put the road bridge out of action for 24 hours.

The Allies began to regain air superiority over Holland. Their tactical air forces had not been permitted to operate during the airborne landings or supply drops, for fear of hitting friendly forces. Their planes had often been grounded by the weather and even when they were flying, their communications with Allied ground forces had been faulty. The Allies now addressed these problems and established more advanced fighter bases, including one at Oud Keent, some two miles west of Grave.

When Horrocks' offensive stalled in the face of fierce resistance, Montgomery also demanded the support of heavy bombers, despite the disappointing results of this tactic during the fighting in Normandy. On 9 October, 300 bombers pulverised the northern half of Arnhem and the German positions in the countryside further west. The citizens had already been forced to leave their homes by the Germans, but the British troops in the city lost over 100 men when bombs fell short. The rubble and bomb craters so impeded the attack that it was four days before the Germans were finally driven from Arnhem, largely by the threat of being cut off by units advancing from Oosterbeek. Montgomery's failure to achieve a breakthrough despite the bombing provoked recriminations as bitter as those surrounding Operation Goodwood in Normandy. The air chiefs believed that their true role lay in trying to bomb Germany into submission and alleged that the use of tactical bombing sapped the British Army's willingness to attack vigorously without it.

Despite the limited impact of the bombing, Horrocks' offensive finally took the high ground overlooking Arnhem on 16 October and overran the airfield at Deelen, five miles north of the city. The airportable 52d (Lowland) Division had been held in readiness to be flown in transport planes to the airfield, along with valuable supplies. The 52d had proved during an exercise that 36 aircraft could be landed, unloaded and flown off again every hour, using a single airstrip.[12] But the airfield had been so wrecked in the fighting as to be useless until heavily repaired. Nor could it be used safely with German anti-aircraft guns so near. Horrocks now became bogged down with the onset of heavy rain and overcast skies and, with his troops exhausted, could advance no further.

In any case, Eisenhower was concerned at the delay in opening a supply route into Antwerp and also at the diverging lines of advance of the British Second Army at Arnhem and the First U.S. Army at Aachen, 90 miles to the south. He therefore ordered Montgomery to cancel any plans for a resumption of the offensive in the foreseeable future. Montgomery was bitterly disappointed, but had lost his credibility and was increasingly sidelined.

It became clear that Operation Market-Garden had over-extended the Second Army and left it vulnerable to counter-attacks by German forces seeking to cut its communications across the Betuwe immediately south of the Arnhem bridgehead. Its predicament was reduced in November, when the Ninth U.S. Army entered the line immediately to the south, in the previously weak sector between Second Army and the First U.S. Army. American pressure around Aachen successfully diverted German forces from Arnhem. The battle for the Arnhem bridgehead was finally over and major fighting would not resume there for four months.

The Fallout

Montgomery had hoped to secure a backdoor into the open plains of northern Germany. But Operation Market-Garden had failed to achieve its final objectives: Horrocks had not reached the IJsselmeer, 30 miles north of Arnhem, to isolate western Holland; or gained bridgeheads over the River IJssel, the start line for any subsequent eastward offensive against the Ruhr or Berlin.

Even if Montgomery had managed to reach the IJsselmeer from Arnhem, the Germans in western Holland would not simply have surrendered. Their counter-attacks might have cut the XXX Corps off from the rest of the over-stretched Second Army. Failing that, they could have left units to hold the Scheldt and other key areas such as Rotterdam, while their surplus troops escaped across the IJsselmeer at night, either by boat or along the Afsluitdijk, the 300-foot wide dyke at its northern end.

Moreover, Montgomery's bridgehead over the Rhine was in the wrong place. An attack on Wesel, 37 miles to the southeast, would have gained a more direct route into Germany's heartland, over easier terrain and without over-extending the Second Army northwards.

Operation Market-Garden also precipitated a humanitarian catastrophe in Holland. In retaliation for a Dutch railroad strike in support of the Allied attack, Artur Seyss-Inquart, the Nazi High Commissioner in Holland, banned the transport of food supplies from the farmlands to the heavily populated western areas of the country. By the time the ban was lifted six weeks later, the situation was critical. The Dutch transport infrastructure had collapsed and the canals would be unusable once they froze over. Fifteen thousand Dutch civilians would starve or freeze to death during the winter. The exiled Dutch Prime Minister, Pieter S. Gerbrandy, vainly wrote to Eisenhower to protest against the delay in liberating Holland: "The Dutch Government cannot accept the fact that merely corpses will be liberated."

Such considerations, and the bitter controversy over the bombing of Arnhem, undermined Montgomery's position at a crucial moment in his ongoing dispute with Eisenhower over Allied strategy. Eisenhower saw the blunting of Market-Garden as a vindication of his broad front advance. He lost patience with Montgomery's outspoken criticism and his demands for absolute priority on resources for an early resumption of the offensive at Arnhem. He referred the dispute to the Allied Chiefs of Staff, insisting that they either back him or sack him. Churchill was alarmed at the damage caused by this escalating dispute and knew that an outcry would ensue in Britain if Montgomery was fired. He therefore flew to Paris on 20 October with the Chief of the Imperial General Staff, Field Marshal Sir Alan Brooke, to meet both Eisenhower and his troublesome subordinate. The problem was resolved most tragically when the plane bringing Montgomery back from the front crashed near Chantilly, killing all on board.

Alexander Takes Command

Churchill immediately sent for his favourite general, Field Marshal Sir Harold Alexander, the commander of the Fifteenth Army Group fighting its way through Italy. Alexander may have lacked Montgomery's ruthlessness and sureness of touch in strategy, but was a superb tactician and, like Eisenhower, a diplomat with a knack of enabling strong-willed subordinates to work together. In Italy, he had successfully commanded troops from eleven allies[13] and men as independent-minded as Lieutenant General Mark Clark.

At the beginning of September, Churchill had informally told Alexander that he would be promoted to supreme command of the Mediterranean Theater. Churchill now wanted Alexander not simply to take over 21st Army Group, but also to act as Eisenhower's ground force commander.[14] Montgomery had long argued that Eisenhower lacked both the time and experience to co-ordinate the operations of the Allied armies while also dealing with the wider political aspects of his role as supreme commander.

Eisenhower also initially favoured Alexander's appointment, but after consulting with his superiors in Washington, General George C. Marshall and President Franklin D. Roosevelt, he insisted that he would continue to give orders directly to his army group commanders. Alexander was therefore limited to command of 21st Army Group, which was strengthened by the permanent addition of the Ninth U.S. Army.

Eisenhower summoned a conference of his senior subordinates at Versailles a week after Churchill's visit. He explained that all the Allied armies would close to the Rhine before any major offensive was launched on the east bank. But he promised Alexander that his 21st Army Group would then be entrusted with the main Allied push into Germany. At this conference, Alexander's charm and reputation did much to restore good relations between the Allies. Alexander's immediate concern was to open Antwerp and eliminate the western flank of the Second Army's salient by pushing the Canadian First Army up the Dutch coast. The Canadians had begun operations along the Scheldt at the start of October, but needed to be able to concentrate their forces and to have more logistical support if they were to make significant progress over the difficult, flooded ground. It was not until after the Arnhem bridgehead was secure that the Second Army could take over any of the Canadians' sector. Thus, the Allied success in securing the bridges at Arnhem delayed the opening of Antwerp and may even have prolonged the war.[15] The first supply ships did not reach Antwerp until 7 December.

The Battle of the Bulge

On 16 December, Hitler launched a major offensive in the Ardennes, a heavily-wooded and hilly area in southeastern Belgium. The Allies were taken by surprise, having doubted Germany's ability to return to the offensive. Nor did they expect an attack through the Ardennes, which they were using as a rest area for units recovering from actions elsewhere. The First U.S. Army, whose sector included the Ardennes, was over-stretched, having been pulled northwards as a result of Operation Market-Garden.

The German spearheads penetrated to the River Meuse before being checked in the streets of Dinant. Alexander took temporary command of all Allied forces on the northern side of the salient and restored American confidence with his unflappable calm. He spent most of his time visiting units at the front and established a legendary reputation among the American rank-and-file for his courage under fire. By the end of January 1945, the Germans had been thrown back after their spearheads had been cut off by counter-attacks mounted by Alexander and Patton from north and south of the salient. They had lost 125,000 men, 800 tanks and 1,000 aircraft and had exhausted their reserves. Now they were left exposed to the inevitable resumption of the Allied offensives, particularly on the Eastern Front, where the Russians would unleash a massive onslaught in Poland on 12 January in response to Anglo-American appeals for a diversion.

1945: The End of the War

During the winter, the Germans blew gaps in the dykes to flood large tracts of the Betuwe immediately south of the Arnhem bridgehead. They also flooded as much of the countryside along the River IJssel as they could and eventually destroyed the Arnhem road bridge by bombarding it with V2 rockets. This reduced the attractiveness of Arnhem as a jumping-off area for a major offensive east of the Rhine and increased Eisenhower's resolve to secure additional bridgeheads further south for the American armies.

The Germans on the Western Front concentrated most of their surviving Panzer forces in the north, to block Alexander's anticipated thrust on Berlin. This was one reason why Eisenhower insisted on Alexander's advance from Arnhem being co-ordinated with American crossings of the Rhine further south. The Allies could not risk an assault crossing of the Rhine until late March, as before that date ice floating down the river could wreck pontoon bridges. The Rhine was also slightly less prone to flooding by the end of March. Thus, Alexander's offensive would have to wait until the Allies had cleared the Germans from the whole of the west bank of the Rhine.

By the middle of March, the Allies had closed to the Rhine. The operations had been difficult, but had cost the Germans a further 90,000 casualties and 250,000 prisoners, besides much equipment. The Germans had also lost the use of the Rhine itself, which was a vital transport artery.

Alexander ordered the Canadian First Army to launch an offensive northwards from Arnhem on 12 March. The Canadians reached the IJsselmeer within a week, isolating western Holland. The Germans now blew up dykes and flooded large areas as a defense against both ground attack and airborne assaults. This made thousands of civilians homeless and contaminated valuable farmland with salt water. The Allies secured a local truce in western Holland, halting their attacks there in exchange for German agreement to allow Operation Manna, the dropping of food supplies from Allied planes.

The Canadian gains provided a jumping-off point for the subsequent offensive by the XXX Corps of the Second Army. This began on 20 March with an assault crossing of the River IJssel, seconded by airborne landings. The XXX Corps then pushed southeastwards along the eastern bank of the Rhine towards the Ruhr. Its advance allowed bridges to be thrown over the Rhine at Wesel for the U.S. Ninth Army to make an unopposed crossing. The bridges at Wesel also shortened communications, ready for Alexander's drive across northern Germany.

The Germans were now too weak to guard the whole course of the Rhine adequately. The American and French armies easily established bridgeheads in the south and thrust across Germany. Eisenhower had intended to make his main thrust under Alexander in the north, where the terrain was less hilly, but the speed of the American gains in the south led him to broaden the emphasis of his advance. He was also overly-concerned by wild rumors that the Nazis planned to form a redoubt in the Alps on his southern flank.

Berlin

Alexander helped surround the Ruhr, where 325,000 German soldiers of the trapped *Army Group B* surrendered on 10 April. His next objective was Berlin. By the 12th, the Ninth U.S. Army managed to secure a bridgehead over the River Elbe at Tangermünde, 55 miles west of the city. The 5th Armored Division continued to race eastwards without waiting for orders and met minimal resistance. Thousands of German soldiers surrendered enthusiastically, relieved that they had escaped the clutches of the Russians.

Eisenhower by this stage had downgraded the significance of Berlin. At the Yalta Conference that February, the Allied leaders had placed it well within the Soviet occupation zone. (The city itself would be divided between the Soviets and the Western Allies.) This did not mean that the Western Allies could not seize it, but Eisenhower was reluctant to suffer casualties for ground that he would have to evacuate later. He decided to halt the Ninth Army, but was informed that American spearheads were already in the outskirts of Berlin and had overrun the airfields.

Berlin's defenses were weak and undermanned. Sporadic resistance was crushed. The once-famous zoo still contained about 600 animals. Terrified by the fighting around them, some managed to escape when shells blasted holes through cages and enclosures and they began to roam the cratered Tiergarten. Pongo the gorilla was shot dead after valiantly jumping on a German soldier from one of the surviving trees and stealing his helmet,[16] while the mystery surrounding the disappearance of Hitler's personal secretary, Martin Bormann, as he tried to escape from the doomed city was solved when a Berliner testified that he had seen him eaten by a lion. Hitler's architect and Minister of Armaments, Albert Speer, was found hanged from one of his own ornamental lamp-posts, but it remains unclear whether he committed suicide or was lynched by a vengeful mob.[17]

The Berliners had never been strongly in support of the Nazis. They also feared the Russian armies, which had advanced through East Prussia and Poland and had reached the River Oder, just 50 miles to the east. Josef Goebbels, Hitler's Propaganda Minister, had blundered in publicising the atrocities allegedly committed by the Soviet soldiers. The Berliners were so terrified at the fate they could expect from the Russians that they welcomed the Americans as saviors.

The Russians launched their expected offensive from the Oder on 15 April, aghast that they had been beaten to Berlin. Their onslaught encountered fierce resistance and caused the German commanders in Berlin to order their men to surrender to the Americans. Hitler and his remaining followers were arrested in their bunker under the Chancellery on 18 April and handed over to the American authorities.

On the morning of the 19th, Berliners awoke to see the Stars and Stripes, the banner of freedom, flying from the roof of the ruined Reichstag.

The Reality

In reality, Operation Market-Garden failed to secure a bridgehead over the Lower Rhine at Arnhem. Montgomery later admitted that he should have insisted on at least one parachute brigade being dropped near the Arnhem bridges. Browning did consult Major-General Gale about the planned landings at Arnhem, but felt that it was too late to make major changes. Urquhart had wanted to land his division nearer the bridges, but was unable to persuade the R.A.F. to agree. Instead, 1st Parachute Brigade was expected to march to the bridges from the landing and drop zones on the heathland six to eight miles west of Arnhem.

The 2d Battalion of the Parachute Regiment under Lieutenant-Colonel Frost reached and secured the northern end of the road bridge and, with other detachments, held out heroically until the morning of the 21st. The rest of Urquhart's men were unable to break through stiff German resistance to reinforce Frost. Instead, they fell back and established a defensive perimeter three miles west of Arnhem at Oosterbeek. The survivors were evacuated across the Lower Rhine on the night of 25–26 September. Arnhem had proved to be "a bridge too far."

Market-Garden could have won a meaningful victory only if the Germans had offered minimal opposition; or if the plan had been drastically revised, for example with two lifts of airborne troops being delivered on the first day. But such sweeping revisions were unlikely given the over-confidence that resulted from the decisive Allied victory in Normandy.

Bibliography

Badsey, Stephen, *Arnhem 1944: Operation 'Market Garden'*, Osprey, London, 1993.

Blair, Clay, *Ridgway's Paratroopers: The American Airborne in World War II*, U.S. Naval Institute, Annapolis, Maryland, 2002.

Blake, George, *Mountain and Flood: The History of the 52d (Lowland) Division 1939–1946*, Jackson, Son & Co, Glasgow, 1950.

Bradley, Omar N., & Blair, Clay, *A General's Life: An Autobiography*, Sidgwick & Jackson, London, 1983.

Brereton, Lewis H., *The Brereton Diaries: The War in the Air in the Pacific, Middle East and Europe 3 October 1941 – 8 May 1945*, William Morrow, New York, 1946.

Cowley, Robert, *More What If?: Eminent Historians Imagine What Might Have Been*, Macmillan, London, 2002.

Creveld, Martin van, *Supplying War: Logistics from Wallenstein to Patton*, Cambridge University Press, Cambridge, 1977.

D'Este, Carlo, *A Genius for War: A Life of General George S. Patton*, Harper Collins, London, 1995.

Eastwood, Stuart; Gray, Charles; & Green, Alan, *When Dragons Flew: An Illustrated History of the 1st Battalion The Border Regiment 1939–45*, Silver Link, Peterborough, 1994.

Essame, H., *The 43rd Wessex Division at War 1944–1945*, London, 1952; *The Battle for Germany*, Batsford, London, 1969; and (with E. Belfield) *The North-West Europe Campaign 1944–1945*, Gale & Polden, Aldershot, 1962.

Farrar-Hockley, Anthony, *Airborne Carpet: Operation Market Garden*, Macdonald, London, 1970.

Foot, M.R.D., *SOE in the Low Countries*, St Ermins, London, 2001.

Fraser, Sir David, *Wars and Shadows: Memoirs of General Sir David Fraser*, Allen Lane, London, 2002.

Frost, John, *A Drop too Many*, Buchan & Enright, London,1982.

Gavin, James M., *On to Berlin: Battles of an Airborne Commander 1943–1946*, Viking, New York, 1978.

Greenfield, Kent Roberts, ed., *Command Decisions*, Methuen, London, 1960.

Hackett, John, *I was a Stranger*, Chatto & Windus, London, 1977.

Hamilton, Nigel, *Monty: Master of the Battlefield*, Hamish Hamilton, London, 1983; *Monty: The Field Marshal 1944–1976*, Hamish Hamilton, London, 1986.

Hibbert, Christopher, *Arnhem*, reissued Windrush Press, London, 1998.

Horrocks, Sir Brian, *A Full Life*, Leo Cooper, London, 1974; and (with E. Belfield) *Corps Commander*, Sidgwick & Jackson, London, 1977.

Kershaw, Robert, *'It Never Snows in September': The German View of Market-Garden and the Battle of Arnhem, September 1944*, Ian Allan, Shepperton, 1994.

Maass, Walter B., *The Netherlands at War: 1940–1945*, Abelard-Schumann, London, 1970.

McKee, Alexander, *The Race for the Rhine Bridges 1940, 1944, 1945*, Souvenir Press, London, 1971.

Middlebrook, Martin, *Arnhem 1944: The Airborne Battle, 17–26 September*, Viking, London, 1994.

Nicolson, Nigel, *Alex: The Life of Field Marshal Earl Alexander of Tunis*, Weidenfeld & Nicolson, London, 1973.

Perret, Geoffrey, *Winged Victory: The Army Air Forces in World War II*, Random House, New York, 1993.

Reynolds, Michael, *Sons of the Reich: The History of II SS Panzer Corps in Normandy, Arnhem, the Ardennes and on the Eastern Front*, Spellmount, Staplehurst, 2002.

Ryan, Cornelius, *A Bridge Too Far*, Coronet Books, London, 1974.

St Croix, Philip de, ed., *Airborne Operations*, Salamander Books, London, 1978.

Soffer, Jonathan M., *General Matthew B. Ridgway: From Progressivism to Reaganism, 1895–1993*, Praeger, London, 1998.

Strawson, John, *If By Chance, Macmillan,* London, 2003.

Tedder, Sir Arthur, *With Prejudice: The War Memoirs of Marshal of the Royal Air Force Lord Tedder G.C.B.,* Cassell, London, 1966.

Urquhart, Major-General R.E., *Arnhem*, Cassell, London, 1958.

Waddy, John, *A Tour of the Arnhem Battlefields*, Leo Cooper, Barnsley, 1999.

Warren, John C., *Airborne Operations in World War II, European Theater*, U.S.A.F. Historical Studies, No. 97, Air University Press, Maxwell A.F.B., 1956.

Weigley, Russell F., *Eisenhower's Lieutenants: The Campaign of France and Germany 1944–1945*, Sidgwick & Jackson, London, 1981.

Whiting, Charles, *A Bridge at Arnhem*, White Lion, London, 1976.

Notes

1. McKee, *The Race for the Rhine Bridges*. Chatterton's own glider had landed in the sea during the invasion of Sicily the previous year. During Operation Market-Garden, several gliders successfully ditched in the North Sea after they accidentally came down.
2. The Germans were inside a wooden structure, on the top of the tower, containing a 20mm flak gun. See Reynolds, *Sons of the Reich*.
3. Projector, Infantry, Anti-Tank. The hand-held PIAT had a range of 115 yards and its 2½-pound bomb could be used against strongpoints as well as tanks.
*4. Cornelius Ryan, *A Bridge To Glory*, Coronet Books, London, 1974, p. 98
5. Browning's appointment has been criticised. He had never commanded airborne troops in action, unlike his American rival, Lieutenant General Matthew B. Ridgway, a veteran of the airborne operations in Sicily and Normandy and unquestionably a better candidate for the job. But could even Ridgway have secured revisions to the 'Market' plan, given the lack of time, widespread over-confidence and opposition from the air force commanders?
6. Blair, *Ridgway's Paratroopers*, pp. 344–5
7. Similarly, Lieutenant-General William Slim decided, correctly, to proceed with the Chindit operation to support Lieutenant General Joseph Stilwell's offensive in northern Burma in March 1944. This was despite Wingate's recommendation that it be cancelled after aerial photographs revealed that the Japanese had placed logs across one of the intended landing zones.
8. Kershaw, *It Never Snows in September*.
9. Foot, *SOE in the Low Countries*, pp. 392–3
*10. Stephen Ambrose, *Death or Glory: The Epic Defence of the Nijmegen Railway Bridge*, Greenhill, London, 1993.
11. Essame, *The 43rd Wessex Division at War*, p. 123
12. Blake, *Mountain and Flood: The History of the 52nd (Lowland) Division*, p. 62
13. These troops were British, American, French, New Zealand, Indian, Canadian, South African, Italian, Polish, Brazilian and Greek.

14. An alternative was for Alexander to replace Air Chief Marshal Sir Arthur Tedder as Eisenhower's deputy, but with the additional responsibility for overseeing the ground campaign. Another British general would then be appointed to command 21st Army Group. See Nigel Nicolson, *Alex*, pp. 273–4.

*15. Historians have vigorously debated this question. Two key points are clear. Firstly, the existence of the Arnhem bridgehead did not necessarily accelerate the fall of Berlin, given that Eisenhower insisted on closing to the Rhine before exploiting the bridgehead. Secondly, regardless of when Antwerp was opened, the allies could not have mounted an assault crossing of the Rhine before the middle of March 1945, given the likelihood of flooding and the vulnerability of pontoon bridges to ice floating down the river. Thus, securing the bridgehead at Arnhem is unlikely to have altered the timing of the end of the war drastically. But even a couple of days could have been enough to alter the outcome of the race to reach Berlin before the Russians. For an assessment of how events could have unfolded if Montgomery had not secured the Arnhem bridges, see Andrew Uffindell, "Disaster at Arnhem: Montgomery fails to bounce the Rhine, September 1944," in Peter Tsouras ed., *The Battle of the Bulge: An Alternative History*, Greenhill, London, 2004.

*16. Dr Bruno Tippelskirchen, *Gorillas: An Illustrated History*, Bamboo Publications, London, 1976.

*17. Cornelius Ryan, *The Last Battle: The American Liberation of Berlin*, Coronet Books, London, 1966, p. 256.

5
THE RACE TO BASTOGNE
Nuts!

Christopher Anderson

Watch on the Rhine

The parties ended early on the evening of 17 December 1944. Throughout the old French cavalry barracks at Mourmelon, France, that were serving as the temporary home of the war-weary 101st Airborne Division, staff and regimental officers emptied their glasses and hurried to divisional headquarters for an unexpected meeting with acting division commander Brigadier General Anthony C. McAuliffe.[1]

When everyone had gathered, McAuliffe told the officers that he had just received news from XVIII Airborne Corps that the Germans had launched a massive offensive in the Ardennes sector and that the division had been ordered to head north to plug a hole in the American lines. McAuliffe's news was greeted with looks of wonder and confusion. After all, the division was less than three weeks off the line following 72 brutal days of combat in Holland and was in no condition to rush back into the fray. The men were tired and badly in need of a rest; replacements had to be integrated into their new units; missing and worn equipment had to be repaired or replaced and many of the division's personnel—including its commander Major General Maxwell D. Taylor—were away on leave. Never one to mince words, the plainspoken McAuliffe told his dismayed officers, "All I know of the situation is that there has been a breakthrough and we have to get up there."[2]

Thirty-eight hours earlier, on the morning of 16 December, three German armies of more than a quarter-million men had come crashing through thinly-held American lines in the Ardennes. Now, as McAuliffe and his surprised officers began making arrangements to hurry to the front, the Germans were rushing across eastern Belgium headed for their ultimate objective of Antwerp.

Since the Allies' successful breakout from the Normandy beachhead and the dash across France in the summer of 1944, German commanders had been trying desperately to come up with some means of at least slowing the American and British juggernaut long enough to restore the situation in the

West and regain the initiative. Nothing seemed to work. In July, as Allied armies were bursting out of Normandy, Adolf Hitler's chief of staff, a panicked Field Marshal Wilhelm Keitel, had asked Commander-in-Chief West, Field Marshal Gerd von Rundstedt, "What shall we do?" "Make peace, you fool," von Rundstedt snapped, "What else can you do?"[3]

Fired by the *Führer* for his "lack of nerve," von Rundstedt must have followed the unfolding disaster in France with grim satisfaction. Paris was liberated on 25 August, and Brussels and Antwerp on 4 September. Hoping to reinvigorate the defenders of Germany's western border, Hitler reappointed von Rundstedt to command. By the first week in September, however, Allied forces in the West had still liberated most of France as well as large swathes of Belgium and Holland. In the south, German forces had barely escaped from Greece, and Field Marshal Harold Alexander had advanced into the Po Valley. Finally, along the Eastern Front, Red Army forces had advanced into Yugoslavia and were threatening East Prussia.

Stunned by their own success, Allied leaders were becoming increasingly convinced of the inevitability of victory. The optimism infected even the highest levels of command. Supreme Commander, Allied Expeditionary Force, General Dwight D. Eisenhower had bet Field Marshal Bernard L. Montgomery £5 that the war would be over by Christmas, and U.S. Army Chief of Staff George C. Marshall had sent a letter to senior U.S. commanders on the subject of transferring American forces in Europe to the Pacific since, "cessation of hostilities in the war against Germany may occur at any time."[4]

Victory, however, was not certain. The farther the Allies advanced from Normandy, the longer their supply lines became. With German garrisons still holding out in the Channel ports, Anglo-American forces had to rely on improvized facilities in Normandy to supply more than 95 divisions as well as care for millions of recently liberated civilians. Inevitably, the pace of the advance slowed and, in September, it ground to a halt. One writer later quipped that, "the Germans were losing the war faster than the Allies could win."[5]

On 16 September, the *Führer* met with senior officers for his daily briefing at the Wolf's Lair in East Prussia. The situation, as outlined by Hitler's close confidant, General Alfred Jodl, was not good. Although the Allied advance had slowed, British forces were well into Holland, and in the south, the First and Ninth U.S. Armies had reached the Siegfried Line and would soon be threatening the German city of Aachen. With Germany itself about to be attacked, all the officers present expected to discuss what could be done to prepare the final defense of the Reich. They were shocked, therefore, when, following Jodl's briefing Hitler announced, "I have just made a momentous decision. I shall go over to the counterattack here—out of the Ardennes—with the objective Antwerp."[6]

A week later, a draft outline of an offensive plan had been prepared, and after that, another meeting was held at the Wolf's Lair to review the details of the all or nothing offensive dubbed *Wacht am Rhein* (Watch on the Rhine). By combing Germany for available replacements and calling upon every remaining resource, the Germans were able to concentrate three armies of more than a quarter-million men for the attack, which would be launched out of the Ardennes—the weakest point of the Allies' over-stretched lines— toward Antwerp and Brussels. The *Führer* hoped that a successful drive to the vital Dutch port city and the Belgian capital would so derail the Allied advance in the west that, at best, it would rupture the alliance between Britain and the United States. At the very least, a successful offensive would sufficiently disrupt Eisenhower's timetable that Germany would have time to focus its attention on the advancing Soviets.[7] From meetings with the Japanese ambassador in August, Hitler was also aware that, despite his reverses on the Russian Front, the bloodletting his forces had inflicted on the Red Army had made the possibility of a negotiated settlement with Josef Stalin not altogether impossible. Although incredibly risky given the forces arrayed against Germany, a successful offensive in the West held out the very real possibility of preventing the total collapse of the Third Reich.[8]

In the north, General Josef "Sepp" Dietrich's *Sixth Panzer Army* would drive for the Meuse. After taking Liège, the SS general would advance on the Albert Canal and then on Antwerp. In the center, General Hasso von Manteuffel's *Fifth Panzer Army* would cross the Our River, seize the heights of the Schnee Eifel, cross the Clerf River, and seize the important crossroads towns of St Vith and Bastogne before advancing to Brussels and then Antwerp. In the south, Lieutenant General Erich Brandenberger's *Seventh Army* would advance westward to the junction of the Meuse and Semois Rivers and protect the German advance from American attacks in the south. The *Führer* intended that his forces would have secured their crossings of the Meuse within two days. If successful, Eisenhower's "broad front" would be burst open with the primarily British 21st Army Group cut off from the Americans in the south and trapped at Antwerp.

To ensure surprise, Hitler ordered the most extreme measures taken to guarantee secrecy. Von Rundstedt was only informed of the plan on 21 October. The *Führer*'s precautions worked.[9] Despite overwhelming air superiority and access to Ultra intelligence, Allied leaders were unaware of the scope and intentions of the massive German build-up. In the three months prior to the start of the offensive, the Germans were able to move 12 armored and 29 infantry divisions, 1,420 tanks and assault guns, 15,000 tons of ammunition and five million gallons of fuel to jump-off positions underneath the noses of the complacent Americans in the Ardennes. By 15 December, everything was in order. Hitler's last great offensive would begin at 5:30 the next morning.[10]

As soon as he had received his orders, General Manteuffel, a veteran of armored warfare in both Russia and Africa, had set to work devising a plan of attack. He knew that speed was vital if he were to be able to seize St Vith and Bastogne quickly and move toward Namur. The first obstacle in his path was the Our River, which had to be secured in order to allow the Panzers to continue their advance to the west.

Fortunately for Manteuffel, Major General Troy H. Middleton's VIII Corps, which consisted of three weak American infantry divisions, an armored division, and a cavalry group, was responsible for holding more than 80 miles of ground. In the north, in front of the Our, the green 106th Infantry Division manned scattered posts along the Schnee Eifel. Never before in combat, the 106th had been sent to the Ardennes to acclimatize its men to conditions at the front. It had been on the front line for less than a week. South of the 106th was the 28th Infantry Division in positions along "Skyline Drive"—high ground that sat between the Our and Clerf rivers. In combat since the Normandy breakout, the 28th had been badly battered in the fighting in the Hürtgen Forest and had been sent to the Ardennes to rest and refit. Finally, south of the 28th were the veteran, but exhausted, 4th Infantry and 9th Armored divisions. The 14th Cavalry Group covered the crucial Loshcim Gap between the VIII Corps and the V Corps to the north.

Manteuffel assigned the mission of clearing the Schnee Eifel to the two Volksgrenadier divisions of General Walther Lucht's *LXVI Corps*. After clearing away the 106th, Lucht would then cross the Our and seize St Vith. The *Fifth Panzer Army*'s two remaining corps—the *LVIII* under General Walter Krüger and the *XLVII* commanded by General Heinrich von Lüttwitz—would be responsible for eliminating the 28th. In the north, Krüger's *116th Panzer* and *560th Volksgrenadier Divisions* would cross the Our at Ouren and strike the 28th Division's 112th Infantry Regiment.

Perhaps sensing the importance of the strategically important town of Bastogne to the planned advance, Manteuffel gave the three divisions of Lüttwitz's corps the important task of crossing the Our at Dasburg and Gemund before advancing on Clerf and from there on to Bastogne and Namur.

Lüttwitz's corps was among Manteuffel's most potent. It consisted of the veteran *2d Panzer Division* with 85 tanks under the command of Colonel Meinrad von Lauchert; *Panzer Lehr*, commanded by former *Afrika Korps* chief of staff Major General Fritz Bayerlein, with 57 tanks, additional assault guns, and a reinforced reconnaissance battalion; and Major General Heinz Kokott's *26th Volksgrenadier Division*. It would be the responsibility of Kokott's infantrymen to secure the crossings of the Our and Clerf rivers to allow for the passage of Lüttwitz's two armored divisions. As Lüttwitz's corps raced westward, Kokott's division would seize Bastogne while the Panzers continued on toward the Meuse.[11]

With preparations and plans completed, in the final hours before the attack was to commence officers filled their men in on what was expected of them. Field Marshal von Rundstedt had a message read to his men:

"Soldiers of the West Front, your great hour has arrived. Large attacking armies have started against the Anglo-Americans. I do not have to tell you anything more than that. You feel it yourself. We gamble everything! You carry with you the holy obligation to give everything to achieve things beyond human possibilities for our Fatherland and *Führer*!"[12]

While some simply scoffed at the notion of being able to throw back the Americans, many believed von Rundstedt's message and saw the attack as the long-awaited counteroffensive that would restore the *Wehrmacht* to the glory days of 1939–40. One young *SS* soldier waiting behind the Siegfried Line wrote his sister a quick note:

> "I write during one of the great hours before we attack... full of expectation for what the next days will bring. Everyone who has been here the last two days and nights (especially nights), who has witnessed hour after hour the assembly of our crack divisions, who has heard the constant rattling of Panzers, knows that something is up... we attack and will throw the enemy from our homeland. That is a holy task."

As an afterthought, after sealing the envelope he scribbled on the back, "Ruth! Ruth! Ruth! We March!"[13]

In the hours before dawn, Manteuffel brought men as close to the American lines as he dared. Kokott was even able to send almost an entire regiment across the Our without being discovered. Nowhere were the Germans more than a couple of miles from the American positions.

On the March

Just seconds before clocks chimed half-past five on the morning of 16 December, an American sentry in Hosingen reported by radio that he could see dozens of flickering lights flashing from German lines. Before he could receive an acknowledgement, the American positions around him—and all along the front from Monschau to Luxembourg—were saturated by German artillery fire. Almost before the startled GIs could man their weapons, thousands of German soldiers had come out of the fog and were overrunning their positions.

The task for the advancing *Landsers*[14] of the *Fifth Panzer Army* was made easier by the fact that the Americans did not occupy a continuous line of defense. With so much ground to cover, Middleton had been forced to position his available manpower in villages and at key crossroads along the front. While this defensive arrangement often caused delays to advancing German troops, it also left wide gaps between U.S. units that Manteuffel's men could exploit. Within hours of the attack, these isolated defensive positions were islands in a sea of field-gray clad opponents.

In the north, the two divisions of Lucht's *LXVI Corps*, brushed aside the 14th Cavalry Group and were soon in the process of trapping and destroying two regiments of the 106th Infantry Division on the Schnee Eiffel before continuing on to St Vith. Krüger's corps drove toward Ouren. Further south still, General Lüttwitz's *XLVII Panzer Corps* was quickly across the Our River and had soon broken open the 28th Division's defensive line. While some of the veterans of the 28th put up a more determined resistance, particularly at Hosingen and Marnach, there was little that one depleted infantry division could do against overwhelming numbers of Germans flushed with victory. By mid-afternoon on the first day of the attack, engineers had bridged the Our in two places, and the Panzers could cross the river and begin their westward drive. By nightfall, the remnants of the 28th Division's 110th Infantry Regiment in Clervaux were the only VIII Corps troops east of the Clerf and the tanks of the *2d Panzer* and *Panzer Lehr* were in position to cross the river early the next morning and proceed with the drive on Bastogne.

SHAEF Reacts

Miles away from the disaster unfolding in the Ardennes, Supreme Commander Dwight Eisenhower was enjoying a relaxing day. He had just learned of his promotion to five-star rank—and was attending the wedding of his aid, Mickey McKeough—when he received word of the German breakthrough. So startling had the attack been that many at Supreme Headquarters Allied Expeditionary Force refused to accept the scope of what was happening. Eisenhower knew, however, that some help would have to be quickly sent to Middleton.

Eisenhower moved swiftly to reinforce the rapidly expanding hole in his front. He told the 12th Army Group commander, Lieutenant General Omar N. Bradley, to have Third Army commander, George S. Patton, release the 10th Armored Division and move it north toward Luxembourg City where it could support Middleton. When Bradley told his old friend that Patton would probably object to such a demand, an understandably irritable Eisenhower snapped, "Tell him Ike is running this damn war!"[15] As expected, when he received this order, the mercurial Patton protested bitterly but he soon had the 10th on the road. Other divisions were also sent to reinforce the northern shoulder of the breakthrough in an effort to keep the German penetration as narrow as possible. Still, Eisenhower had little to offer the hard-pressed VIII Corps' commander. The Allied front was stretched and relied on a pencil thin supply line. Many of the reserves available to the supreme commander were still in England waiting for sufficient transport to send them to Europe. All that remained quickly available to Eisenhower was the XVIII Airborne Corps' 82d and 101st Airborne Divisions, which he was reluctant to release immediately.

Beyond the Clerf

Meanwhile, all along the Clerf, Lüttwitz's men were well positioned to renew their attack toward Bastogne early on the 17th along two main axes of advance. In the north, the *2d Panzer Division* would continue to pass through Clervaux and head toward the N12, one of the main roads leading into Bastogne. Once on the road, Lauchert could continue his movement toward the Meuse or, if the situation demanded, lend support to the drive to capture

Bastogne. In the south, *Panzer Lehr* and the *26th Volksgrenadiers* would advance on secondary roads through Hosingen, Drauffelt and Neiderwampach before picking up the N12 near Longvilly, and from there, seize Bastogne.

At dawn, American infantrymen in Clervaux were having their first encounters with German troops. The attacking Volksgrenadiers were soon joined by tanks, which added considerable punch to their advance. In a repeat performance of the day before, brave, but isolated, groups of Americans tried valiantly to stop the German flood. There were even attempts to counterattack Lüttwitz's rapidly advancing units. Early in the morning, an attack by the hard-pressed 110th Infantry Regiment's 2d Battalion toward Marnach ran into the entire *2d Panzer Division* and in the totally one-sided encounter the battalion was destroyed. Elsewhere, a column of Stuart light tanks tangled with German 88mm anti-tank guns with predictable results.

By 6:00 p.m. German tanks were roaming freely in Clervaux, destroying what remained of the town's garrison, although there was a mixed bag of headquarters personnel and stragglers holding out in the town's medieval castle. At 6:25 Colonel Hurley Fuller had to call 28th Division commander, Major General Norman D. Cota, with the news that he was abandoning Clervaux. Although the defenders of the town's castle were able to slow German vehicles passing through Clervaux, they could do little to stop them. The Germans were now a mere 15 miles from Bastogne.

The second day of the attack had gone well. Although the Germans had yet to reach Bastogne itself, they had torn open the VIII Corps' front, all but destroyed two infantry divisions and inflicted crippling casualties on many smaller units. More important, perhaps, was the fact that cold, isolated and scared groups of GIs encountering Panzers and well-equipped Panzer-grenadiers were wondering what, if anything, could be done to stop the Germans. By nightfall on the 17th, Lüttwitz's *XLVII Panzer Corps* was across the Clerf, the last major natural obstacle in front of Bastogne. To the north, General Lucht's *LXVI Corps* had isolated the remnants of two U.S. infantry regiments on the Schnee Eifel and moved within striking distance of St Vith, the other major road hub in the Ardennes.[16]

Further to the north, Dietrich's *Sixth Panzer Army* had crashed into the 99th Infantry Division and, although the Americans put up a series of courageous delaying actions, they could do little to prevent the Germans from moving westward. Leading *Sixth Panzer Army*'s advance was *Kampfgruppe Peiper*, commanded by the hard-driving SS Panzer commander Colonel Jochen Peiper. This group had, after some initial delays, advanced all the way to Stavelot, seizing the vital bridge over the Amblève River at Stavelot before stopping for the night. Peiper's tanks were now only 50 miles from the Meuse.

Only in the south was the German advance not proceeding as well as had been expected. General Brandenberger's force lacked the armored punch of the two armies attacking further to the north and, therefore, was unable to overcome 4th Infantry Division positions with the same ease as Dietrich and Manteuffel. Nevertheless, as his mission was to protect the southern shoulder

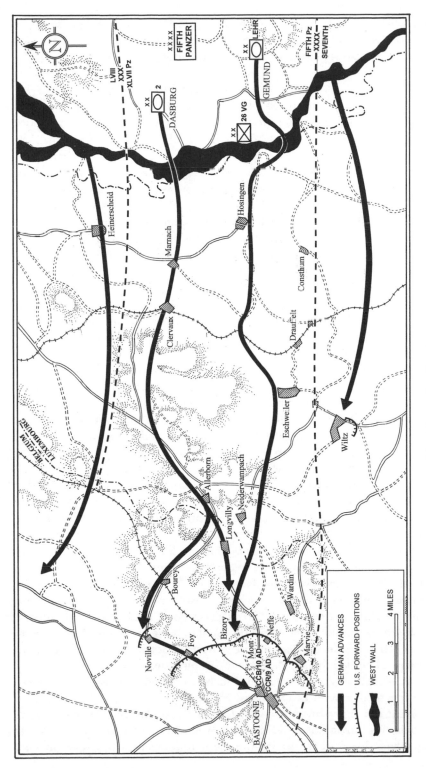

The Race for Bastogne

of the advance, it was hoped that the *Fifth* and *Sixth Panzer Armies* would be over the Meuse and on their way to Antwerp by the time General Patton's Third Army could mount an effective counterattack.

The Race for Bastogne

At VIII Corps headquarters, Middleton was looking for some way to throw additional roadblocks up in front of the Germans who, he knew, would soon be moving down the road toward Bastogne. He also knew that if the town fell, the Germans would hold the key to an intricate road network that would make it difficult, if not impossible, to restore his shattered front. All that remained to the VIII Corps' commander, however, was Colonel Joseph H. Gilbreth's Combat Command R (CCR) of the 9th Armored Division, three engineer battalions, and a handful of miscellaneous headquarters troops.

Aware that he had little other choice, Middleton deployed these men along roadblocks to the northeast, east and southeast of town. The two principal roadblocks were placed along the N12, the main road leading from Clervaux into Bastogne. These blocking positions were manned by CCR. Gilbreth placed his first blocking position at the Antoniushof road junction, the second a few miles behind near the village of Allerborn. Middleton knew that Gilbreth and the others had little hope of stopping the Germans, but he hoped that their inevitable sacrifice would buy him enough time for reserves to reach the town.

Following a most welcome telephone call at midnight on the 17th, the harried VIII Corps commander received the word, through First Army commander Courtney M. Hodges, that Eisenhower had finally agreed to release his two elite airborne divisions. The 82d and 101st would soon be headed his way. He was also expecting the 10th Armored to reach him in due course. Although the news was welcome, he knew that the two airborne divisions would be traveling from Reims, more than 100 miles away, and that it would not be until the 19th that he could expect any of the badly needed men to reach him in Bastogne in sufficient numbers to make a difference.

While the two airborne divisions prepared to move, the men along Middleton's hard-pressed front would be fighting for their lives. At first light on the 18th, his roadblocks came under attack from elements of *2d Panzer*. While the Americans gave as good as they got, destroying several tanks as the Germans stumbled on their positions in the early morning light, the outcome was never really in question. By 11:00 Task Force Rose at the Antoniushof roadblock was surrounded on three sides and fighting for its life. As Task Force Rose began to break up, German reinforcements were moving around the position and headed toward the second roadblock near Allenborn.

After a brief pause to reorganize, Lauchert ordered his division to proceed down the road toward Longvilly, where he knew he could then begin his movement to the northwest and head for the Meuse. Meanwhile, in the south, Bayerlein was moving toward his goal as well. Although progress was slowed by less than ideal road conditions and the traffic jams caused by two divisions fighting for the use of one bridgehead and a handful of roads, *Panzer Lehr* and the *26th Volksgrenadiers* were able to move forward. By 6:00 p.m., Bayerlein's lead column had reached the tiny crossroads hamlet of Niederwampach, only six miles from the square at Bastogne.

Two hours earlier, however, as Bayerlein's men were closing in on Niederwampach, Middleton was greatly cheered by the arrival of Colonel Roberts and his CCB of the 10th Armored Division. The reinforcements could not have arrived at a better time. After a day of heavy fighting, the Germans were at the Feit'sche crossroads, less than ten miles from VIII Corps headquarters. Middleton told Roberts to break up his combat command into three teams and send these mixed armored and infantry commands to the east of Bastogne to form yet one more line of defense.

After receiving his instructions from the corps commander, Roberts made his way to his headquarters at the Hôtel Lebrun, just off the main square at Bastogne, to issue orders to the commanders of his three combat teams. The first force that was dispatched was Team Cherry, commanded by Lieutenant Colonel Henry T. Cherry. Team Cherry was sent toward Longvilly. Next was Team O'Hara, commanded by Lieutenant Colonel James O'Hara, which was sent down the Luxembourg road to Wardin and finally, Major William Desobry's Team Desobry was sent north from the city toward the little town of Noville. Perhaps Roberts sensed from his earlier discussions with Middleton that the battle that would decide the fate of Bastogne was about to be fought. Desobry was close to Roberts, and the CCB commander took the 26-year-old major aside to tell him:

> "You are young, and by tomorrow morning you will probably be nervous. By midmorning the idea will probably come to you that it would probably be better to withdraw from Noville. When you begin to think that, remember that I told you it would be best not to withdraw until I order you to do so."[17]

Team Cherry was already on the road as Major Desobry was receiving his final words of encouragement from Roberts. Cherry moved through Bastogne quickly on the N12 toward Longvilly. Along the way, he established his headquarters in the Château Neffe, just outside the small village of the same name, and ordered the bulk of his team on to Longvilly. The forward elements of the team arrived around midnight and ran into remnants of CCR, which had fallen back toward the town after their battering at the hands of Lauchert's *2d Panzer*.

Unfortunately for this isolated force, the intervention of a Belgian civilian had placed a large force of Bayerlein's *Panzer Lehr* in Mageret, which cut Cherry off from the bulk of his command. After reaching Niederwampach with a small armored force that had moved ahead of the rest of the division, Bayerlein had been faced with how best to reach Bastogne quickly. The most apparent option was to strike north toward Longvilly, pick up the N12 and head into Bastogne from there. Another possibility was to move south until reaching the N34 and then against Bastogne from that direction. Bayerlein, however, was uncomfortable with both of these choices. While both routes would provide a good solid surface for his vehicles, the potential further delay in reaching them would throw him even further off of his timetable. Also, he knew that, if he headed toward Longvilly, he ran the risk of again becoming entangled with advancing elements of the *26th Volksgrenadier Division*.

As he studied his maps, Bayerlein saw a third possibility. There was a country road that led from Niederwampach to Mageret. Although the road was not ideal for vehicles, if he moved along it quickly enough, he would be able to pick up the N12 at Mageret, even closer to Bastogne. A hurried conversation with a local civilian convinced him that the road was firm enough to support his tanks and Bayerlein soon moved out. The *Panzer Lehr* commander quickly discovered, however, that the Belgian had lied to him. The road soon turned into a muddy path and there was considerable delay in moving his tanks along this route.

As Bayerlein struggled along the road, Lauchert was finishing off what remained of CCR's roadblock at Allerborn. At around 8:00 a.m., Panther and Tiger tanks of the *2d Panzer Division*, some of them equipped with infrared sights, began the destruction of Task Force Harper, CCR's last remaining roadblock. The fight lasted a couple of hours, but Lauchert's tanks were soon continuing their advance toward Longvilly with the remnants of the American task force retreating ahead of them.

By midnight on the 18th, much of Lüttwitz's force was astride the N12 and German commanders at every level were deciding what move they would make next. Upon reaching Mageret, a villager told Bayerlein that a force of 40 or more American tanks had passed through the village earlier that evening headed for Longvilly. If this were true, it would mean that his isolated column could be cut off from the rest of the division. The former *Afrika Korps* chief of staff briefly considered turning toward Longvilly to counter this threat, but then decided against it. He knew that the rest of his division, as well as elements of the *26th Volksgrenadiers*, were nearby if necessary. In addition, he surmised that the gunfire he had heard on the advance from Niederwampach earlier that evening had to be from *2d Panzer* and he felt confident that any force in Longvilly could be dealt with by Lauchert. Besides, he had already been misled once by a local civilian and he was disinclined to let this happen again.

For his part, after he had removed the roadblock at Allerborn, Lauchert had contacted Lüttwitz and told him that, according to the original plan, he would turn right on the Bourcy road and begin his movement to the northwest. Lüttwitz, however, had other ideas. The *XLVII Panzer Corps* commander knew from intercepted radio transmissions that Eisenhower had released the two airborne divisions on the 17th. Although he did not know exactly where they were at that moment, he was confident that they were headed his way. As much as he wanted to allow Lauchert to move toward the Meuse, he knew that possession of Bastogne was necessary in order to maintain the momentum and strength of his advance. Although it would further delay his progress, Lüttwitz finally decided that he would order Lauchert and Kokott to consolidate their now disorganized commands in preparation for an all-out attack on Bastogne early the next morning. Meanwhile, Bayerlein would continue down the road toward Bastogne, clearing as much of the way as possible.

After seizing the town, Lauchert could leave the 26th to defend it against any American reinforcements while his two Panzer divisions joined with Manteuffel's other corps and Dietrich's Sixth Panzer Army in their drive to the Meuse. As the fighting on the 18th died down, the big question for Lüttwitz was when the 82d and 101st would arrive.

Where Is the Cavalry?

It was also a question being asked with some urgency by many at VIII Corps headquarters. Almost as soon as he had seen Roberts to the door to begin moving his combat teams to their blocking positions, Middleton had been asking about the whereabouts of McAuliffe and the 101st. Calls to higher headquarters had confirmed that the two divisions had left their camps near Reims earlier that morning, but, as of yet, none of the airborne troops had arrived. Later that evening Major General James Gavin, acting commander of XVIII Airborne Corps, turned up at Middleton's headquarters to explain that both divisions had left Reims that morning and were, even then, moving toward the threatened sector. In order to counter the threat farther north, Gavin said, the 82d Airborne Division would now move to Werbomont and be assigned to V Corps, while the 101st would proceed to Middleton's assistance at Bastogne. As the situation deteriorated east of town, however, Middleton still had not heard any concrete news of when the expected reinforcements would arrive. His confusion was further compounded when, at around 8:30 p.m., XVIII Airborne Corps commander, Major General Matthew B. Ridgway arrived with the news that his corps headquarters would be established at Bastogne and that both divisions would remain under his command.

Ridgway was startled to be told that he had no troops in Bastogne to command. The corps commander was dumbfounded. He knew that both divisions had left their assembly areas near Reims, and he had followed along for some distance in column before he got off the main road in order to speed ahead.

Middleton and Ridgway were still trying to sort out the confusion of exactly who was in command of what, when, not long after midnight, the VIII Corps commander was informed that defensive positions on the eastern edge of the town were coming under fire and that the large monastery below the high ground at Mardasson had been hit by German mortar rounds.

Now desperate to find his men, Ridgway left Middleton's headquarters building and headed toward Werbomont, while other officers began making frantic phone calls to try and locate the missing—and badly needed—airborne troops.

The fire was coming from Bayerlein's column. Rather than wait for morning, *Panzer Lehr*'s commander had decided to keep moving toward Bastogne. While he did not necessarily believe he could seize the town with the force available to him, he believed that his presence that close to Bastogne would unsettle the American defenders and give the rest of Lüttwitz's corps the initiative when they began their attack in the morning.[18]

As shells rained down on the monastery and Middleton began to order what remained of his headquarters away to safety, the long-lost 101st Airborne Division was trying to get itself untangled from a tremendous traffic jam 25 miles away from where it was most needed.

Communications Failure

The traffic jam, and the confusion about what, exactly, was expected of the 101st was, in part, due to the suddenness of the German attack. Believing as they did that all was quiet along the Western Front, many of the XVIII Airborne Corps' senior commanders were away on a variety of official functions while many of the men were enjoying well-earned leave following the division's extended time on the line in Holland when the German attack began on the morning of the 16th.

Ridgway was away in England providing a post-mortem on the recently concluded Holland operation with the 101st's assistant division commander, Brigadier General Gerald J. Higgins when the German offensive began. The 101st's commander, Major General Maxwell Taylor, was in Washington. Although they rushed to get back to France as soon as they received word of the German attack, the inevitable delay threw what remained of the divisional staffs into some confusion. Ridgway's absence meant that the corps command was temporarily in the hands of Major General James M. Gavin, the 82d's young commander.

Fortunately Gavin, the youngest division commander in the U.S. Army, was up to the task. Hodges had requested that Gavin move his corps to the Ardennes beginning at dawn on the 18th. At Hodges' order, the first division to leave Reims would head toward Bastogne, while the second would travel further north to Werbomont. Because the 82d had been longer out of combat since Holland and had more time to prepare for its next operation the "All Americans" were told to move out first. As soon as the 101st was ready, it would proceed to Werbomont. After issuing orders to his two divisions, Gavin headed out for First Army headquarters at Spa, Belgium, to get further instructions while his subordinate commanders made the necessary arrangements for the move.

Gavin traveled through the night and reached Spa early the next morning. He finally spoke with Hodges at 9:00 a.m. on the 19th and learned that the situation facing V Corps in the north was almost as bad as it was opposite the VIII. As Manteuffel's *Fifth Panzer Army* was racing toward Bastogne and St

Vith, Dietrich's *Sixth Panzer Army*, with its powerful *SS* Panzer divisions was approaching Werbomont. Since the 82d was at the head of the column, it was decided that Gavin's own division would move on toward Werbomont while the 101st would now move toward Middleton's rapidly crumbling position in and around Bastogne.

Unfortunately, in the confusion that had engulfed Allied headquarters since the German offensive began, word of this change in plans did not reach the 101st's staff in Mourmelon. After receiving the initial call from Gavin's staff at 10:30 on the evening of the 17th and informing General McAuliffe of the orders from corps, Colonel Ned Moore, the 101st's chief of staff had thrown himself into the task of preparing his division for its movement to Werbomont.

McAuliffe was just as busy. A thousand small things had to be accomplished quickly if the division was going to be ready to meet the trucks that would take them the 137 miles to Werbomont. Throughout Mourmelon, officers alerted what men were available and tried, as best they could, to outfit them with the supplies necessary for a winter campaign. Robert Bowen, a sergeant in the 401st Glider Infantry Regiment, remembered how the men of his company greeted the news:

> "The leaders of C Company assembled in the orderly room. It wasn't a happy gathering. Instead of passes to Paris, we were facing a trip back to the front. Memories were still fresh from the loss of friends in Normandy and Holland. Emotionally and physically, most of us were drained. Months of little sleep, a diet of C and K rations and the gradual diminution of our platoons had had their effect. We were not looking forward to more of the same."[19]

Further away in Paris, the word went out to military police authorities in the city that anyone seen wearing a Screaming Eagle or All American patch was to be gathered at assembly points and hurried to Mourmelon. Private Charles Brown had just sat down with some friends in a Paris bar after paying for an evening of drinks in advance when the MPs came and dragged him along. Despite the size of the city, the MPs were thorough, and soon the unfortunate troopers who had had their leaves unexpectedly cancelled were on their way back to camp. Some, remembered Sergeant Donald R. Castona, were still not fit for duty when they reached Mourmelon:

> "I was in charge of quarters on December 18 when we got the news that there had been a German breakthrough some place and we were being sent up to help stop the attack. The officer of the day, First Lieutenant Kenneth Holmes, told me to go around and get the guys ready to go. A lot of our guys had been on pass to Paris and got back to Mourmelon a lot the worse for wear. We had to pour some of them on the trucks when we left."[20]

Leave, however, they did. Despite the poor condition of some of the men and a dreadful shortage of ammunition and adequate winter clothing, the 101st was ready to move on the morning of the 18th. General McAuliffe was the first to leave. The acting division commander departed with an advance party at 12:25. The group would race ahead of the division and get to Werbomont as quickly as possible, where the officers would make the necessary arrangements to receive the division while McAuliffe, hopefully, would meet with XVIII Airborne Corps officers who could give him a better idea of what was happening. Although all of the officers knew that time was of the essence, they could have no idea of how critical the situation in front of Bastogne was. Before he left, McAuliffe left instructions with Moore that as soon as Brigadier General Higgins, or any other divisional officer, arrived at Mourmelon, they were to make their way to Werbomont as quickly as possible.

An hour and a half later, the rest of the division, 11,840 men, pulled out of Mourmelon and headed to the front. It was, by all accounts a miserable ride. Troopers were crammed into open-topped cattle trucks that provided little in the way of comfort or warmth. Captain Wallace Swanson remembered: "We were loaded on trucks, probably 50 or more men to a big semi-trailer with high sideboards and we were standing up—no room to lie down—might be able to push enough to let a few men get some rest." Still, the men soon had some idea of the necessity of such a hurried move. "The situation was so urgent," Swanson continued, "that we traveled all night with headlights blazing. Had the weather broken and the German air force spotted us, the results would have been devastating."[21]

An hour after McAuliffe's departure, General Ridgway arrived in Mourmelon and went directly to the division's command post. Unable to locate any officer who knew what was happening—Moore and the remaining divisional staff officers were around Mourmelon seeing to the departure of the division—Ridgway called XVIII Airborne Corps headquarters and was told that the 101st was to proceed to Bastogne while the 82d would move ahead to Werbomont.

Angry at having been caught unawares in England when the German offensive started and anxious to rejoin his troops, Ridgway hurried to his waiting staff car and was soon headed for Bastogne, where he hoped to discuss the situation with Middleton. As he pulled away, he saw Higgins, who had left England with him and was now trying to find the rest of his division. Quickly halting his car, Ridgway told Higgins of the change in plans and hurried up the road to Bastogne.

After listening to the corps commander, Higgins hurried off to find a jeep and rush to meet McAuliffe. As he pulled away, he saw Moore and thought about stopping, but seeing how busy he was decided he would speak to him when everyone got to Bastogne.

While Ridgway, Higgins, and others were trying to sort out what was happening, McAuliffe and the advance party were racing ahead toward

Werbomont. As the small party neared Herbaimont, just nine miles from Bastogne, McAuliffe briefly considered taking a detour to Bastogne to get some news from Middleton on exactly what was happening. Given the urgency of getting his men into the line, however, McAuliffe decided to continue on to his assigned rendezvous at Werbomont. Once he had everything in order there, he thought, he could quickly return to Bastogne to meet with Middleton.

It was just after eight o'clock in the evening when McAuliffe, stiff and sore from his long drive, pulled into Werbomont. Upon his arrival, the general was surprised to see vehicles with 82d Airborne Division markings throughout the town. He was even more surprised to run into Gavin, who excitedly informed him that, at that very moment, he (McAuliffe) was supposed to be in Bastogne, where his division was to be placed into the line.

McAuliffe told Gavin that the last instructions he had received had ordered him to bring his division to Werbomont. After several frantic calls, McAuliffe was able to reach Middleton. The VIII Corps commander told him that he needed to get his men into Bastogne as quickly as he could. Forgetting his exhaustion, McAuliffe quickly gathered together his advance party and headed off to find his division.

Just outside of town, McAuliffe ran into Colonel T.L. Sherburne, the acting divisional artillery commander, who was at the head of the column. It was around 9:00. McAuliffe told Sherburne what had happened and then proceeded to rush down the column with the news that Bastogne, not Werbomont was the destination.

It took the rest of the evening for McAuliffe and his staff to get the snarled traffic around Sprimont turned around and get the restored column headed in the direction of Bastogne. It was dawn the next morning before the forward vehicles of the column reached Mande St Etienne, on the outskirts of Bastogne, and they could see the city shrouded in a cloud of smoke from the shower of artillery shells hammering the town. McAuliffe stood there as the import sank in. His jaw set hard, as he spat out, "Nuts!" The Americans had lost the race for Bastogne.

The End in Bastogne

Following a short, but violent, artillery barrage, three German divisions attacked the town at dawn on the 19th. In the north, Lucht's *2d Panzer Division* attacked Team Desobry in Noville. The young team leader held out for a little over an hour before he found himself attacked on three sides and his route of retreat through Foy being threatened. Desperate to save what remained of his command, Desobry called Roberts in Bastogne and asked for permission to withdraw. Hoping to hold the perimeter long enough for the 101st to reach the town, Roberts denied the request and Team Desobry died in place. By mid-afternoon, the handful of survivors were retreating down the Foy Noville road when they were caught by elements of the *26th Volksgrenadiers* which had moved behind them during the fight for Noville and cut the road. Badly wounded during the retreat, Desobry was captured outside of Foy.[22]

Further south, Team Cherry met a similar fate. A combined armored and infantry assault against Longvilly pushed Team Cherry out of the town. As the column retreated, it ran into a roadblock established by Bayerlein at Mageret. One of the first German artillery rounds knocked out the lead vehicles in the column and soon traffic was blocked between the two villages. Unfortunately, with soft ground to one side and high ground to the other, Cherry's vehicles could not move off the road. As frantic American officers tried to get their vehicles moving again and smash their way through Mageret, German tanks and infantry reached the road and the slaughter began. With nowhere for the trapped vehicles to go, the destruction of Team Cherry was completed quickly. After clearing the road, the Germans proceeded down the N12 toward Bastogne and reached Bayerlein and his small force on the heights of Mardasson by early afternoon. From the heights the Germans had a commanding view of the town.

German artillery spotters quickly saw the vehicle park opposite the barracks that had been serving as Middleton's headquarters and were soon bringing fire down on the vehicles and nearby buildings. When Middleton called Hodges to report on the situation, the First Army commander could hear the shells hitting the barracks. Reluctantly, he ordered Middleton to get what remained of his headquarters out of the city as soon as possible. The last order Middleton issued from Bastogne was to instruct Team O'Hara to move southwest as quickly as it could and try to join American forces west of the city.

The stoves were still warm in Middleton's abandoned headquarters when the Germans entered the town. The commanders of Lüttwitz's three divisions were soon in communication with their chief to give him the good news. With Bastogne now in his hands, Lüttwitz felt secure in sending his armored columns toward the Meuse. After a hasty consultation with Manteuffel, Lüttwitz issued orders that his two Panzer divisions would continue their advance on the morning of the 20th, while Kokott's Volksgrenadiers prepared to guard the southern shoulder of the advance.

Fortunately for the exhausted 101st, Lüttwitz's men became disorganized as they moved into Bastogne and consolidated their hold on the town. The respite gave McAuliffe time to pull his men back to the northwest and link up with the 82d.[23]

Reactions at the Top

News of the fall of Bastogne reached General Eisenhower as he was preparing to meet with Patton, Bradley and other senior Allied leaders in Verdun. Not only had Bastogne fallen, but the two regiments of the 106th Division that had been cut off on the Schnee Eifel in the early days of the offensive had surrendered as well. It also seemed unlikely that St Vith would be able to hold out for much longer. It was clear that the First Army front was finished.

Anxious Allied commanders now looked to Eisenhower for some plan to restore the situation.

After much debate, Eisenhower concluded that the only alternative was to fall back. It was imperative that the Germans not be allowed to cross the Meuse and the only way for Eisenhower to restore his broad front was to retreat. He knew that such a move would likely prevent any further major Allied advance until at least the late spring of 1945 but by then, he hoped, the supply situation would be improved and this would give him more flexibility in renewing the offensive against the Germans.[24]

The Supreme Commander knew that retreating would surrender the initiative to Hitler and that he ran the risk of a costly stalemate all along the front, but he saw little alternative. Reluctantly, Eisenhower concluded that it would be best to withdraw his remaining forces to the western bank of the Meuse and attempt to hold the Germans there. After issuing the necessary orders, Eisenhower looked at his shoulders and wondered if Army Chief of Staff, George C. Marshall, and President Franklin D. Roosevelt would soon be reconsidering his promotion to five-star rank.

Beginning the next day, while the remnants of First Army conducted a fighting withdrawal, Ninth Army strengthened its positions on the west bank of the Meuse. In Germany, news of the advance was greeted with joy. Perhaps, at last, the victory that the *Führer* had promised for so long had begun. Propaganda Minister Josef Goebbels ordered that radio stations throughout the Reich broadcast the news:

> "The speedy collapse of every organized Allied defense has considerably eased our tasks... We have all been asking ourselves why is the *Führer* so silent. Perhaps he is ill? Now we can tell you. The *Führer* is enjoying excellent health, but he has been preparing this new offensive down to the minutest details. His silence had been worth it. The enemy received a shock. We must force the enemy to throw in the sponge. He must realize that the battle no longer pays!"[25]

An elated Field Marshal Walther Model contacted Field Marshal von Rundstedt and discussed their next move. The two knew that much of their success thus far had been due to the suddenness of their attack and the poor weather. The "Hitler Weather," which had prevented the Allies from making use of their overwhelming superiority in the air, would not last forever and in the respite afforded by the cloud covered skies over Western Europe, the two field marshals knew they had to make what advances they could.

Beginning on the 20th, the *Fifth* and *Sixth Panzer Armies* continued their advance to the northwest, swinging in a giant wheel with Aachen as the pivot point. Coming up against the shattered remains of the First U.S. Army, the two German armies made steady progress toward the Meuse, seizing the bulk of the First Army's massive fuel dump outside of La Gleize after jittery Belgian guards had abandoned it. As they advanced, the Allies continued their retreat, abandoning Aachen and clearing all Allied forces from Germany by the end of the year.

Much to the relief of Eisenhower and other Allied commanders, the weather began to clear in the last week of December and soon Allied airpower was slowing the German advance to a crawl. New Year's Day saw fierce battles along the Meuse, particularly for the cities of Liège and Namur. It was becoming increasingly clear, however, that neither side had the strength to bring the struggle for the Meuse line to a decision. The Germans, flushed with victory and reinforced by much of the *"Führer* Reserve," had punished the Anglo-Americans and served notice that the *Wehrmacht* was far from finished. Lacking airpower, however, they were unable to maintain the momentum of their attack. The Allies, although they had suffered a grievous blow, were still blessed with overwhelming materiel might that, in the coming year, could be used to resume the offensive. With all hope of decisive victory in the West in 1944 at an end, Hitler's only hope drastically to alter the strategic situation was for a reversal of fortunes in the East.

All Quiet on the Western Front

Reaction among Allied leaders to the disaster in the Ardennes was understandably panicked. In response to cries of incompetence from members of Congress and the media President Roosevelt began pressing Marshall to replace Eisenhower. Although reluctant to remove the SHAEF commander, Marshall was finding it increasingly difficult to protect his protégé from the demands of the President to take some action. The Chief of Staff knew that he could resist only so long as Roosevelt did not order him to make such a change. In London, the cries for Eisenhower's removal were even louder. The events of December seemed to support the assertions of Chief of the Imperial General Staff, Field Marshal Alan Brooke, and 21st Army Group Commander, Field Marshal Bernard L. Montgomery, that all Eisenhower's broad front strategy would do would be to ensure that the war would go on even longer than necessary. Surely, Brooke and Montgomery reasoned, the time had come to remove Eisenhower and place someone in command who would use all of the Allies' available resources to launch a powerful thrust directly into Germany.

For his part, British Prime Minister Winston Churchill was eager to do whatever he could to bring the war to a speedy conclusion. Britain had been at war since 1939 and was running out of men. Churchill knew that the island kingdom that had stood alone against the might of the Axis during the dark days of 1940–41 simply did not have the manpower to continue the war into 1946 or beyond.[26]

Both Churchill and Roosevelt knew that, if the acrimony among their military leaders continued, the coalition that they had worked so hard to build would be in jeopardy of coming apart. In an act of desperation, Churchill, with Roosevelt's consent, sent a personal letter to Soviet Premier Josef Stalin and pleaded for assistance. "The battle in the west is very heavy," Churchill explained, "I shall be grateful if you can tell me whether we can count on a major Russian offensive during January. I regard this matter as urgent."[27]

When he received the letter, Stalin was dumbfounded. How could it be, he wondered, that the British and Americans, with all of the material wealth they possessed, had been defeated so soundly? Was it that the British and Americans were simply unwilling to pay the price of defeating the Germans once and for all? Stalin had long mistrusted the Western Allies' intentions and now this defeat, coupled with the failure of the operation in Holland in September, had brought Eisenhower's methodical approach to the Reich to a halt. Now Stalin had received this request from Churchill asking that Soviet armies throw themselves at the Germans in the hope that it would give the Americans and British a chance to save themselves in the West. It was beginning to seem as though the British and Americans were willing to fight the Germans until every last Russian was dead.

Stalin, of course, cared little for the losses his armies endured on their advance westward. What he was concerned with, however, was that he have the strength to secure his ambitions in Eastern Europe and that he remain in power. After careful consultations with his closest advisors, the Soviet Premier responded to Churchill's request by saying that the weather and conditions of his armies prevented him from launching an attack before the spring.

Following close on the heels of his letter to Churchill, Stalin had Foreign Minister Vyacheslav Molotov make contact with the Japanese ambassador to Russia with a message to be passed to the Germans (Japan and the Soviets were not at war). Stalin, Molotov told the Emperor's representative, would consider a halt of his westward advance if Germany would withdraw to its 1939 borders.[28]

When he received word of Stalin's offer, Hitler at first discounted it, but then began to reconsider. A temporary truce with Stalin would allow him to commit additional resources to the war in the West and at the same time complete the development of weapons such as jet aircraft and ballistic missiles that could prove decisive. The *Führer* had no intention of becoming a great friend of Soviet Russia but, as had been demonstrated in the past, a temporary agreement with the Soviets could be beneficial.

An agreement between the two dictators was soon arrived at, and at the end of January, Roosevelt and Churchill were shocked when they received a letter from Stalin informing them that, "for the good of his long-suffering people," he had decided to halt his armies at Germany's eastern borders.

With little other option open to them, Churchill and Roosevelt asked their military chiefs what could be done. Marshall and Brooke both agreed that the Western Allies should husband their resources and prepare to resume the offensive on their own at the earliest possible moment in 1945. For the moment, however, all would remain quiet on the Western Front.

The Reality

Of course, as everyone knows, Bastogne held. In large measure this was due to the stalwart defense of the GIs of the First Army. Although the Germans were able to burst through the positions of the 28th and 106th Divisions, all along the line, isolated groups of Americans held out. After its two sister regiments were surrounded on the Schnee Eifel, the 106th's third regiment held the line at St Vith. In the south, the 28th Division's 110th Infantry Regiment conducted an epic defense that so delayed the Germans that they were never able to recover the time lost.

Other than slightly altering the timetable of the German advance, however, the two main historical incidents that have been changed involved Fritz Bayerlein and his arrival at Marnach and the arrival of the 101st Division at Bastogne. When Bayerlein finally arrived at Marnach on the evening of the 18th he did, in fact, receive information from a local civilian who told him that a force of 40 or more American tanks had passed through the town earlier in the direction of Longvilly. Bayerlein believed this intelligence and, rather than move into Bastogne on the 18th, when he would have encountered little opposition, he delayed his advance and instead moved east where he became involved in a nasty fight against remaining elements of Team Cherry.

The more important twist to history involved the 101st. When McAuliffe left Mourmelon, he believed that his destination was Werbomont. However, as he moved north, he decided to take the detour to Bastogne, where he met with Middleton and was informed of the change in plans. He then placed MPs at the crossroads at Sprimont and elsewhere that were able to direct the trucks of the 101st directly to Bastogne. Traveling through the night, the division was able to reach Bastogne in time to take up positions alongside the three CCB teams on the outskirts of the town and repulse the German attacks. The 101st won the race to Bastogne just in time. Although the Germans would eventually surround Bastogne, with the 101st well-entrenched around it the Germans could never hope to regain the initiative and travel on to the Meuse.

Bibliography

Ambrose, Stephen E., *The Supreme Commander, The War Years of Dwight D. Eisenhower*, University Press of Mississippi, Oxford, 1999.

Cole, Hugh, *The Ardennes: The Battle of the Bulge*, United States Army Center of Military History, Washington, D.C., 1994.

Crookenden, Napier, *Battle of the Bulge*, Ian Allan, Shepperton, England, 1980.

Gavin, James M., *On To Berlin: Battles of an Airborne Commander, 1939–1946*. Viking Press, New York, 1978.

Kershaw, Ian, *Hitler: 1936–1945, Nemesis*, W.W. Norton, New York, 2000.

Koskimaki, George, *The Battered Bastards of Bastogne: A Chronicle of the Defense of Bastogne, December 19, 1944 – January 17, 1945*, Casemate Publishing, Haverstown, PA, 2003.

MacDonald, Charles, *A Time For Trumpets*, Bantam Books, New York, 1985.

MacKenzie, Fred, *The Men of Bastogne*, David McKay, New York, 1968.

Rappaport, Leonard, & Norwood, Arthur, *Rendezvous With Destiny*, 101st Airborne Division, Washington, D.C., 1948.

Ryan, Cornelius, *A Bridge Too Far*, Simon and Schuster, New York, 1974.

Toland, John, *Battle: The Story of the Bulge*, University of Nebraska Press, Lincoln, 1999.

Tolhurst, Michael, *Bastogne: Battle of the Bulge*, Leo Cooper Books, Barnsley, South Yorkshire, 1998.

Notes

1. At this time, McAuliffe was the commander of the divisional artillery.
2. Rappaport & Norwood, *Rendezvous With Destiny*, p. 430.
3. Ryan, *A Bridge Too Far*, p. 31.
4. Ambrose, *The Supreme Commander*, p. 510.
5. Ryan, *A Bridge Too Far*.
6. Crookenden, *Battle of the Bulge*, p. 6.
*7. Josef Goebbels, *The Triumph of Faith*, Der Angriff, Berlin, 1947, p. 146.
8. The prospect of a German–Soviet truce is discussed in Ian Kershaw's, *Hitler: Nemesis*, p. 728.
*9. Goebbels, *The Triumph of Faith*, p. 165.
10. Crookenden, *Battle of the Bulge*, p. 9.
11. Crookenden, *Battle of the Bulge*, pp. 45–7.
12. MacDonald, *A Time For Trumpets*, p. 87.
13. MacDonald, *A Time For Trumpets*, p. 90.
14. *Landser* was the name given to the German infantryman, much like GI for the Americans.
15. Crookenden, *Battle of the Bulge*, p. 55.
*16. Hasso von Manteuffel, *From Egypt to England*, Panzer Publishing, Heidelberg, 1954, p. 325.
17. MacDonald, *A Time For Trumpets*, p. 290.
*18. Manteuffel, *From Egypt to England*, p. 424.
19. Koskimaki, *The Battered Bastards of Bastogne*, p. 22.
20. Koskimaki, *The Battered Bastards of Bastogne*, p. 23.
21. Koskimaki, *The Battered Bastards of Bastogne*, p. 34.
*22. Manteuffel, *From Egypt to England*, p. 589.
*23. Gerd von Rundstedt, *All For the Führer*, Der Angriff, Berlin, 1948, p. 609.
*24. Oswald Mosley, *The End of the Western Alliance*, Blackshirt Books, London, 1954, p. 92.
25. Toland, *Battle: The Story of the Bulge*, p. 123.
*26. Mosley, *The End of the Western Alliance*, p. 101.
27. MacDonald, *A Time For Trumpets*, p. 605.
*28. Goebbels, *The Triumph of Faith*, p. 327.

6
BLUNTING THE BULGE
From the Maas to the Meuse with First Canadian Army

Sean M. Maloney

Operation Wacht am Rhine and a Very Special Operation

At 5:30 a.m., 16 December 1944, the massed tanks of two whole German Panzer armies started to roll lit by artificial moonlight produced by playing searchlights on the low cloud cover. Mark IVs, Panthers, Tigers, all supported by half-track-mounted infantry and self-propelled artillery, poured across a 60-mile front into the Ardennes forest catching Eisenhower's Supreme Headquarters Allied Expeditionary Force and the forward units of the American 106th Infantry and 28th Infantry Divisions unawares. It was the biggest German offensive in the West, ever, and it appeared unstoppable. To the north, there was *Sixth SS Panzer Army*, with its *2d SS Panzer*, *9th SS Panzer*, *1st SS Panzer* and *3d Panzergrenadier Divisions*, plus three other infantry divisions. In the center was *Fifth Panzer Army*, which boasted the *Panzer Lehr*, *116th Panzer*, and *2d Panzer Divisions* and four infantry divisions, while the southern flank of the penetration was covered by the four motorized infantry divisions of the *Seventh Army*. The units of the First U.S. Army, which consisted of tired or relatively inexperienced infantry stiffened by an armored division, staggered under the weight and ferocity of the German assault, code-named *Wacht am Rhine*. Three other armies, First Canadian Army, Ninth U.S. Army, and Second British Army were bypassed by the *Army Group B* forces as they swept into the Ardennes. To the south, below the German penetration, was the Third U.S. Army, staring at the formations of *Army Group G* across the Saar River.

There were plans to keep Third U.S. Army out of the fight. The scarred visage of Otto Skorzeny moved into the light and ground out his cigarette on the burnt table.

"Have the orders for Operation *Greif* been sent?"

"Yes sir," the signals officer replied. "The first teams have deployed and infiltrated the American lines. Radio interceptions already indicate that they

148

are having the desired effect: the disruption of movement of reserve forces in critical areas."

"Send the orders for the supplementary plan. It has been approved at the highest level."

Outside a small town in France, a team of nine men cocked their Thompson submachine guns and waited. They were mounted in an M8 scout car and in a jeep, both equipped with .50-caliber heavy machine guns; the M8 had its 37mm gun, but there was no ammo for it. One man wiped the dirt off his shoulder so that the insignia could be clearly seen.

"Now."

The vehicles rolled out of the barn and into the middle of a convoy of deuce-and-a-half trucks and half-tracks. The jeep pulled ahead of the M8 and vehicles moved out of the way, respectful of the Military Police signs displayed on the hood and the arm brassards of its occupants. Taking a left turn, the jeep pulled up to a checkpoint outside of a château. Silenced pistols disposed of the guards. The M8 continued through and the scene was repeated once again at a second checkpoint.

Colonel Oscar Koch had just finished briefing his G-2 staff when bullets from two .50 caliber machine guns chewed through the intelligence and operations sections in the west wing. Four of the fake MPs raced into the confusion and bloodied bodies,

"G-3 is that way. I'll finish off the G-2 staff. You: cover us."

Automatic fire, and more automatic fire. In short time, most of the Third Army's critical staff officers were dead, including the irreplaceable Oscar Koch. The infiltration team was caught in the open as it tried to withdraw and fought to the death.

General George S. Patton Jr. was away that morning, visiting the front in his Dodge command car. It was cold, but Patton refused to accept creature comforts while he was in contact with his men. The Dodge was moving quickly down the dyke-like road when a P-47 Thunderbolt flew along the road, banked twice and came back. It had no markings. In seconds, the Dodge was a shredded mess and Patton was dead. The KG 200 pilot, a specialist in flying captured American aircraft, returned to German lines and his forward base without incident. Third Army's notoriously poor radio security had cost it its commander.[1]

The Third U.S. Army's divisional and corps staffs put together a back-up army headquarters, but that took several days. Shock at the loss of so many experienced staff officers, men who had worked as a team for the better part of the war, as well as the loss of their charismatic leader, resonated throughout Third Army. A critical meeting between Montgomery, Eisenhower, and Bradley was scheduled for 19 December. The Third Army representative, unfamiliar with the current set of contingency plans, was unable to offer anything other than a series of limited holding operations along the southern flank of the German advance. Cut out of the higher command loop in part due to a personal feud with another officer higher up the food chain in Third

Army, the commander of 4th U.S. Armored Division, Major General John Wood, was disgusted at the indecisiveness. He gathered all the units he could to augment his division, the sum conglomeration making up a mini-corps, and struck out in an attempt to disrupt the inexorable German move on Bastogne.[2]

Wintering on the Maas with the First Canadian Army

Far, far to the north, along the Maas River in Belgium and the Netherlands, sat the units and formations of the First Canadian Army, including the men and tanks of the 4th Canadian Armoured Division, now led by the incendiary and profane Major-General Chris Vokes. Corporal Donald Graff occupied the driver's position on a Sherman Firefly. Equipped with a 17-pounder gun, the Firefly was one of the few vehicles in Allied service that could take on the more heavily-armored German Panther and Tiger tanks. The troop had been sitting in a laager area, cleaning up the rust and mud, making sure that this was time well spent. Who knew what the next move would be?

Graff tilted the hip flask down his throat.

"Graff! You drinking again?" Sergeant Ivan Malikowski yelled from the commander's hatch.

"No, Sergeant."

"Well, give me some too."

The Firefly, named *Brazen*, and its crew had had their share of scrapes since Normandy. The troop had adopted the German method of recording "kills" by painting rings on the barrel. *Brazen* had 15 so far—no thanks to continual re-organization. Fireflys together in a troop, then one Firefly and three regular Shermans. Now together again as a troop. Or was it the other way around? Would it ever end? What was the best way to kill Tigers?

The First Canadian Army, working the lonely and long left flank of the Allied advance, got all the dirty jobs. The fortified channel ports like Dieppe, Bolougne and Calais; nasty little fights all, and then the polders of the Scheldt, the deadly Walcheren operation, where Lancaster bombers were used to breach the dykes and flood out the Germans followed by an amphibious assault. Without cleared flanks, Antwerp was useless and with no Antwerp, there were increased logistics problems for everybody. Now, the Canadians, three divisions of them, plus an attached Polish armored division, the Dutch Princess Irene Brigade, a Czech armored unit, and British and Belgian SAS troops[3] were wallowing in the mud, having replaced British units in the Nijmegen salient and then waited for the next move, Operation Veritable. Montgomery was moving his resources, mostly from Second British Army, into a front which extended from the Nijmegen salient south to Venlo and Geilenkirchen. In some places the front line was only ten miles from Germany. This operation would open up the Germans' northern flank like a chainsaw and, hopefully, act as a turning movement to get the 21st Army Group past Essen and on the road to Berlin, while the American army groups further south pounded into the Germans and pushed them back to the Rhine. As usual, the Canadians would handle the dirty job of cleaning out German resistance in the sodden Netherlands as the British and Americans raced for the prize.

First Canadian Army was normally commanded by Lieutenant-General Harry Crerar; he was ill and supposed to return to duty on 7 November, but his medical recovery was delayed; this put Lieutenant-General Guy Simonds in command, with Major-General Charles Foulkes in Simonds' place as II (Canadian) Corps commander. The right flank of the First Canadian Army abutted the Second British Army, which held the area between Nijmegen and Geilenkirchen, where the Ninth U.S. Army took up its positions. Another corps, I (Canadian) Corps, was supposed to re-deploy from Italy, but none of its units had arrived. I (British) Corps would have to do until then, but Monty wanted it as part of Second British Army reserve for Veritable. A fight for control was brewing, but Simonds was Monty's protégé...

Outside Antwerp, where Simonds had his headquarters, a Canadian Y signals troop, specialized intelligence gathering unit, was carefully listening in on the Germans across the Maas.

"Okay: we have what so far?" asked Major Steve Hutchings.

"The *346th Division*, or what was left of it after we mauled it, still holds a dispersed line on the coast south of Rotterdam; part of it is bottled up on Schouwen and Overflakke islands along with what is left of the *7th Paratroop Division*; neither is going anywhere. There are three other divisions holding the line: the *711th Infantry*, the *712th Infantry*, and the *6th Paratroop Division* up at Arnhem. All three are standard infantry divisions, still in fairly good shape, but lack any significant armor reserves. We are, however, getting indicators that something is up and that it relates to the situation in the Ardennes."

"Like what?"

"Well, we have intercepts indicating that several airfields northeast of Arnhem have been improved by engineer units; that numerous Ju-52 transport aircraft, in squadron strength, have been moving in and out of them. It is possible that the Germans intend to mount some form of airborne operation, but we can't see them pulling out *6th Paratroop* since they have nothing to fill the hole with."

"What else?"

"Another intercepted message says that General Hans Reinhardt has been replaced by Lieutenant General Felix Schwabe as commander, *LXXXVIII Corps*, by the commander of *Army Group H* which holds the Netherlands. Schwabe is a more capable and aggressive leader than Reinhardt. Another message complains that the 150 tanks that were promised to *LXXXVIII Corps* have not yet arrived."

"I'll pass it on."

The Canadian operations staff in Antwerp were assessing what all this meant.

"In addition to the Y information, there are other indicators that between two and four parachute divisions are being made available to *First Paratroop Army* for landing operations, not in a static role or relief role on the front. We don't think they have the lift, but then SHAEF didn't think the Germans had the tanks to conduct the Ardennes offensive either," Major Jim Robertson noted. "Note also that achieving any form of coordination between *First Paratroop Army* operations and what is happening down south may be problematic; *First Paratroop Army* belongs to *Army Group H*, the bulk of which are *Luftwaffe* troops, not *Heer*. As you know, cooperation is not the best between the two services."

Simonds leaned back and looked at Charles Foulkes with upraised eyebrows. "Charles?"

Foulkes brushed his moustache and contemplated the map.

"Put the pieces together. He doesn't have the tanks he wants, therefore, his ground offensive will be shaky. Would you commit airborne forces without a strong ground component? I think not. I think it's a diversion. We should start considering alternatives," he said in his characteristically low voice.

Simonds was no fool, egotistical, but no fool.

"What if Monty becomes pinned down holding the shoulder of the Ninth U.S./Second British Army inter-army boundary? This Ardennes thing could cut him off if it reaches the Meuse and beyond. 1940 all over again." He looked at Foulkes. "Do it."

The Fall of Bastogne

The key was Bastogne, the German staffs knew. Bastogne, Bastogne, Bastogne. It was the key to all road movement in the region; it was a hub. And the Americans were fighting for it tooth and nail. The underequipped 101st Airborne Division and its valiant commander General McAuliffe turned back a German surrender demand with "Nuts!" but defiance was not enough to make a successful defense. With the complete loss of the American 106th Infantry Division in days, and the inability of Third U.S. Army to break through, the Screaming Eagles were fighting a desperate battle. Massive amounts of firepower, *Nebelwerfers*, 150mm artillery, King Tiger tanks, all were thrown at Bastogne. Lightly-equipped infantry and a few tanks were ultimately unable to cope with the onslaught and there were not enough combat engineers to construct adequate field fortifications. Another critical battle, this one fought by Combat Command B of the 7th Armored Division near St Vith, tried to draw off German strength, but its communications were interfered with by the unexpected drop of a *Fallshirmjäger* battle group led by Colonel Baron von der Heydte into the American rear area. In the end Bastogne collapsed as the weight of the German attack shifted to the other axis. The Screaming Eagles fought nearly to the last man and, when the "mini-Stalingrad" gave way, the roads were open to the Panzers. The race for the Meuse was on again.

The Y service was active, but the Canadian Intelligence Corps was also working closely with the Dutch resistance. Normally, relations with that organization's cells was circumspect since it was known that the *Abwehr* had penetrated many of them with Operation North Pole. However, as the Allied armies moved into Belgium and the Netherlands, members of the Free Netherlands Army made contact with family members still in the occupied portion of the Netherlands. Georg Van Houten was one of these.

"Try them again," Captain Reg Walker urged.

"Okay, I've got them. What do you want to know?"

"How many three-engined planes are there?"

A burble of Dutch.

"About 25."

"What about the other airfield?"

"Approximately the same number."

"Are there ground crew? How does he know they aren't wooden dummies interspersed with real planes?"

More conversation.

"They have several hundred ground crew and mechanics."

The phone was replaced. Incredibly, the phone system worked across the lines in some places. In this case, a patrol of the Cameron Highlanders of Ottawa had crossed into German territory, secured a house, and their Dutch liaison started calling until the right people answered.

"Okay sir, correlating with other special information, we have 50 or so Junkers 52s. At 30 paratroops per aircraft, that's enough lift for nearly two battalions at a time," the briefing officer told Foulkes and Simonds. "They have fuel stockpiled and the rigging equipment is there at Deelen airfield."

Simonds considered the situation. "We can suppose that this airborne drop will be triggered by the German advance in the Ardennes reaching a given phase line. What will two battalions of airborne infantry accomplish? Any more word on tanks?"

"They are still complaining that all 150 have not yet arrived. Less than 50 percent, mostly Mark IVs and self-propelled guns with guns of 75mm or better."

"Location?"

"Looks like a rail head near Arnhem. But we can't confirm because of this lousy weather; no air recce."

"So this may be more than a pin-prick raid. Those German infiltration units down south are causing havoc. The level of disruption that the parachutists might cause could be catastrophic if combined with even a limited offensive operation against us. If Second British Army has to withdraw, it will complicate that move. I suspect Monty is trying to preserve his forces for the projected Operation Veritable. He may be gambling that the Ardennes crisis will pass. Then there is the advance on to the Meuse. Gentlemen, it is time to use some initiative before Monty thins out along the Nijmegen–Venlo salient."[4]

Captain Eric Levy checked the map once again. Right on target. The Royal Canadian Engineers were already there with a pontoon bridge section; an infantry platoon crossed to secure the bank and the ferry was ready. No light, no noise. A diversion had been arranged elsewhere on the Maas. Using back roads, the Belgian SAS squadron had been incredibly lucky. So many British jeeps had been captured and pressed into service after the fall of Arnhem that the Germans were mistaking the SAS for their own patrols. After a listening halt, Levy and Chapandrau, his gunner, could hear engine run up tests. Who Dares Wins...

It was over in a couple of hours, but most of the SAS had to escape and evade under cover of darkness. Not all made it back, but the smoldering hulks of Ju-52s littered Deelen and one of its two satellite airfields.[5]

Even Foulkes was impressed. Canadian commanders usually did not have much use for Stirling's people, but in the end Simonds went for the raid. "Better than can be expected," the staff officer finished the briefing.

"The tanks: that will be a risk we'll have to take."

But Montgomery was furious with his Canadian "protégé." Acerbic message traffic and phone calls to Simonds were flowing. Simonds deftly swept them aside and continued with his planning. "*I* am preparing to save the day in the south! *You* will support *me!*" Monty declared time and again. But he was spending too much of his valuable time lobbying Eisenhower to take control of First and Ninth U.S. Armies. While the volume level of that argument increased between Bradley, Monty, and Eisenhower, Simonds had other ambitions. Simonds had a private conversation with Foulkes.

"He wants to know about the disposition of the divisions," Foulkes confided.

"Tell him it's an issue relating to national command. We're Canadians, we report to Ottawa through our headquarters in London. If he has a specific complaint, he can go through channels. It will, of course, take some time... "

"He might take away resources, like 51st Division."

"Let him. Meanwhile, we'll assemble what we need from what we have. There isn't much time anyway and we'll be ready to execute before he knows what's going on."[6]

Operation Gebirgs: A New German Offensive on the Maas

The Ninth U.S. Army's position on the northern flank of the German advance was starting to erode. Montgomery was forced to prop it up with the 51st (Highland) Division which was part of First Canadian Army. Remnants of Combat Command B, and tanks from 3d U.S. Armored Division with the survivors from Bastogne were able to delay the advance on the Meuse yet again, suffering grievous casualties in the process. By this time the 4th U.S. Armored Division was making itself felt on the Germans' southern flank, but it was not enough. Word that the Germans were shooting prisoners was starting to filter through which stiffened the American defensive spirit further, but time was running out and the weather was still bad.

West of Arnhem, Hauptfeldwebel Herbert Trossin helped guide the StuG IIIG assault gun off the railroad car and then spat out some *ersatz* coffee. In a matter of hours, his troop was in a muddy hide opposite Canadian positions. Infantry screened out front, an artillery observer mounted in a Sd Kfz half-track was with them. Operation *Gebirgs* had been put off again, but no one knew why, exactly.

Chris Vokes swore and swore some more. It was too slow. Foulkes had instructed Vokes to pull 4th Canadian Armoured Division off the line discreetly. Nothing Vokes ever did was discreet, but this time it had to be. If the Germans from the opposing two divisions, the *711th* and *712th*, got wind of what he was doing, they might try to pin him down. 4th Canadian Armoured Division was being brought into reserve, along with the 1st Polish Armoured Division, and portions of the Czech armored brigade. It was a risky move; it seemed that every anti-tank gun in First Canadian Army, 6-pounders and 17-pounders from 5th, 6th, and 7th Anti-Tank Regiments, all equipped with the new tungsten-cored APDS round, was being moved in to cover every approach route along the front. Massive stocks of ammo were positioned in depth so that the anti-tank guns could withdraw if necessary and continue to fight. Simonds cajoled the maintainers and every mobile and functional M10 tank destroyer, some of them equipped with 17-pounders, was grouped with 4th Canadian Armoured Division. Every Canadian infantryman who could walk, including some who had up to that afternoon been recuperating in hospitals, augmented select infantry units withdrawn from the line. Canadian Ram Kangaroo armored personnel carriers from the 1st APC Regiment linked up with the infantrymen from three regiments and laagered with the 4th Canadian Armoured Division. Vokes pressed his staff for quicker marshaling and better traffic management on the slippery Belgian roads.[7]

The Allied brigades, Dutch and Belgian, bolstered the Canadian recce units back along the Maas line. During the night, Simonds, ever the gunner, instructed his corps and army-level artillery resources to start pounding suspected and identified German assembly areas. The 5.5-inch guns fired and fired and fired, throwing the Germans of the *712th Division* off balance.

A clean break was made with the two armored divisions, whose tanks moved to assembly areas south of Tilburg. The long-suffering Corporal Graff and the rest of the *Brazen* crew made it into a grove and camouflaged the tank as best they could. No more booze, for the time being.

A dangerous situation was getting worse. German reconnaissance half-tracks were on the outskirts of Liège after a nasty fight for Spa with Seventh U.S. Army units. The defenders were now supported with British artillery which delayed the advance on the Meuse, but not by much. Elements of *Sixth SS Panzer Army*, reconnaissance mostly, were pushing for Maastricht, trying to identify the British formations and pin them down. Further south, Panthers from the *Panzer Lehr Division* were approaching Dinant, the scene of a past German triumph from the 1940 campaign. Some of the Panther crews had manned Mark II tanks with the by now comparatively puny 20mm guns during the Dinant bridgehead operation four years before. This was an improvement. Triumph again was in their grasp. Then on to Brussels, with Antwerp not far away.

Back on the Maas front, Trossin's StuG III assault gun survived the incoming artillery; the forward observer's Sd Kfz did not since it had an open top. The word came over the radio: "Advance!" The three StuG IIIs moved off, with some Mark IVs on their right flank. Immediately, extremely accurate anti-tank fire from Canadian positions brewed up the turreted Mark IVs. Trossin looked for his accompanying infantry. Expecting half-tracks, he was shocked to see truck-mounted infantry. Then there was an explosion as the assault gun hit an anti-tank mine, de-tracking it. Without the ability to pivot the vehicle, the 75mm gun was next to useless. Dazed, Trossin climbed down the back deck just before a 17-pounder APDS round penetrated the right-hand skirt and ricocheted inside, killing his crew and starting a catastrophic fire. Without adequate armor and direct-fire artillery support, the attack bogged down. With no half-tracked or tracked carriers, the infantry's trucks made little headway in the mud and became easy targets. In hours, *LXXXVIII Corps* called off Operation *Gebirgs*.

On the Ardennes front, Cromwell tanks from armored regiments attached to XXX (British) Corps advanced south of Maastricht, on the eastern bank of the Meuse. Montgomery ordered Horrocks to deploy armored recce units to secure bridges over the Meuse. Horrocks' staff decided that securing the bridges between Liège and Maastrich was best done from both banks at once. Catching German reconnaissance units from *Sixth SS Panzer Army* off guard, the Irish Guards maintained the pressure, passing the flaming hulks of half-tracks and eight-wheeled armored cars until they started running into fixed positions equipped with 88mm anti-tank guns. After the eighth Crowell brewed up, it was time to retire, at least until American artillery could catch up. Other XXX Corps units made it into Liège, to be absorbed by the vastness of the city and its ancient defenses. There would be no rapid exploitation south to Namur yet.

Preparations for Operation Lynx

The improvized Canadian-Polish armored corps, code-named "Lynx Force" by Simonds to disguise the size of the formation from Monty and to deceive German signals into believing that it was merely a temporary reserve battle group,[8] was taking shape. Elements of the 16th Polish Armoured Brigade, part of the planned Polish corps, were arriving but only an additional regiment was available to augment 1st Polish Armoured Division; there had been some delays in November since tank crews had to transition from Crusaders to Shermans.[9] Sexton and Priest self-propelled artillery units were grouped; the less mobile towed artillery stayed put on the Maas. Aggressive night patrolling, a hallmark of the Canadian way of war, coupled with selective artillery shoots kept the staff at *LXXXVIII Corps* guessing after their assault failed. By Christmas, Canadian armored recce units were deploying in a line south of Hasselt to Brussels. The 1st Polish Armoured Division and 4th Canadian Armoured Division were now commanded by an *ad hoc* corps headquarters based on men Simonds trusted from First Canadian Army headquarters. A much stripped down II (Canadian) Corps headquarters, under Charles Foulkes, would continue to hold the Maas River line against further encroachment by the Germans.

The German logistics system was in crisis. The weather which worked for them, covering preparations for the initial assault on 16 December, now worked against them. Trucks were jammed up on the icy roads from the dumps at Prüm to Spa and Rochefort. Without fuel, the Panzer spearheads were going to have to slow down. Dinant was in German hands, with Charleroi not far away; there was bitter fighting in Liège and any Allied approach from Maastricht was screened off. This left Namur. A German reconnaissance company had made it into the outskirts and even crossed one of the bridges, but no main force units had arrived to hold the city. Reconnaissance forces, lightly equipped, were merely tourists in Namur. On the American side to the north of the penetration, the unnecessary losses in the Hürtgen Forest taken by First U.S. Army since September had stripped units of experienced combat leaders; the level of initiative was low. The 82d Airborne Division was the exception and, with tanks of the 7th Armored, was the steel core holding the shoulder together.

The Panthers and Mark IV Panzers from *2d Panzer Division* were refueling when orders were given to break off and move out. The *Panzer Lehr Division* at Dinant was refitting, while *116th Panzer* was already headed for Namur. The decision had been made, despite the protests of Sepp Dietrich over in *Sixth SS Panzer Army*; success would be reinforced. The drive would be made on Brussels. Only then would *Sixth SS Panzer Army* break the back of the Allied forces as they tried to withdraw from the Nijmegen–Venlo salient. If the supply lines remained open. If American forces were unable to re-take Bastogne. If Monty kept arguing over who commanded what and where.

The 29th Reconnaissance Regiment from the 4th Canadian Armoured Division, better known as the South Albertas, moved into the western outskirts of Namur. The regiment's Shermans, leapfrogging by bounds, turned a corner and in no time there were rounds down range. Two German halftracks with *116th Panzer* markings on them erupted in flames. Their escaping crews were machine-gunned to a man. The battle for Namur was on. Whoever controlled Namur controlled the south-easternmost routes to Brussels and then Antwerp.

After the yelling had died down, Montgomery agreed that his forces, based on Horrocks' XXX (British) Corps, would take Liège away from the SS and hold it. Plans were made to extract Ninth U.S. Army to positions west of Aachen. Simonds' staff continually checked the dispositions of the *Panzer Lehr Division*. Was it at Charleroi yet? That would alter the plan. Not used to a mobile battle like this one since Simonds preferred to fight set-piece actions, the staff were getting a lot of on the job training. For Simonds, it was a risk.

It was uncharacteristic of him, but this was an opportunity at many levels and he had seized it. Could the student outstrip the teacher?

The Battle of Namur

The fully-tracked Ram Kangaroos of the 1st Armoured Personnel Carrier Regiment swept into Namur, followed by trucks towing 17-pounder anti-tank guns from at least two different regiments, soon to be reinforced by two more. Deployed in an arc south of the river, covered by the machine guns of the Lincoln and Welland Regiment ("the Lincs"), this hedgehog provided Simonds with options. He had the bridges at Namur and could defend them against German assaults which meant that a secured crossing threatened the German *116th* and *2d Panzer* with a head-on encounter battle south of the city. If the German Panzer flow went south to bridges between Namur and Charleroi to avoid it, Simonds had a protected left flank. What would the enemy do?

Hauptmann Winter was having problems. Thus far, the two bridges he had reconnoitered west of Namur were incapable of supporting the weight of his regiment's Panthers. They might get one or two across, but the flimsy structures would collapse with the abuse. It they could not use Charleroi, bridging equipment would have to brought forward.

That equipment, however, was not a priority for movement through the shaky supply corridors—fuel and ammo were. So Hauptmann Winter was not getting his bridging any time soon. By this time, *116th Panzer* had bumped the Namur hedgehog and got a bloody nose. The Mark IVs were no match in the built-up areas especially when 17-pounders could be brought to bear. The *116th*'s infantry regiment was already suffering from attrition taken on the race to the Meuse and a major assault stalled at the wrong time. As the camouflaged Panzergrenadiers moved up in an open area to flank the Lincs, a horrible screaming sound shocked the battle-hardened troops. Rockets started to explode amongst the platoons, which suffered grievous losses.

"*Mein Gott!*" a prisoner noted during interrogation, "We thought we were the only ones with rocket artillery. This was worse than Russian Katyushas." This was duly passed on to the CO of the 1st Rocket Battery, Major Jim Greengrass, who led the new Land Mattress rocket projector unit.[10]

The staff of the *Fifth Panzer Army* now had to decide its next move. Reconnaissance companies had crossed the two bridges west of Namur and reported that no enemy forces were present, but that there was a blocking force just to the west of the city. There appeared to be little opposition within five miles north of the Charleroi–Namur road. With no prisoners taken at Namur, it was unclear who *Fifth Panzer Army* was facing. Sherman tanks, anti-tank guns, and rocket artillery. No unit markings, no flags. There was almost no radio traffic, and what there was was mostly American and then from Ninth U.S. Army units. Intelligence analysts assumed that the force holding Namur was some advanced guard from XXX (British) Corps that had moved down from Liège. Brussels or Namur? Clearing a river from both sides at once

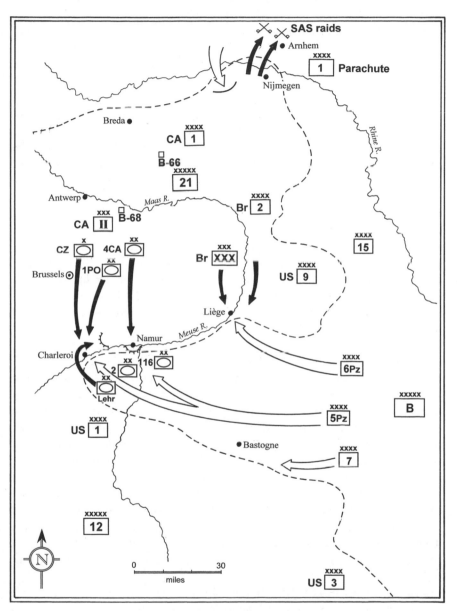

Battle of the Meuse Crossings

had an appeal and that would clear the way if *Sixth SS Panzer* hoped to swing south and avoid Liège.

The weary remnants of *116th Panzer* picqueted Namur for the time being. *Panzer Lehr* was instructed to cross at Charleroi and proceed east to clear the north bank. *2d Panzer Division* was in reserve and would exploit whichever opportunity presented itself. With a strong flank guard in place, *Panzer Lehr*'s Panthers and Mark IVs approached the western parts of Namur. Reconnaissance companies were taking severe damage to the front from the Canadian resistance, this time provided by the Algonquin Regiment and M10 tank destroyers. The bulk of *Panzer Lehr* was strung out on the road network between Charleroi and Namur, reconnaissance units trying to find a way to flank the city and get around the hedgehog. Missing, however, were the numbers of tracked and half-tracked quad 20mm self-propelled anti-aircraft guns necessary to protect ground formations from Allied airpower. And the weather was improving…

Before the *Panzer Lehr* tank regiment's commander could react, his command post was inundated with reports of multiple incursions by tanks supported by large numbers of ground support aircraft. The sheer numbers overwhelmed the hard-pressed and strung-out German reconnaissance units. In effect, the combat elements of *Panzer Lehr* were broken up into three segments, each fighting its own battle, all with their backs to the Meuse. It was a fierce fight; there was nowhere to run. The droop-snouted Royal Canadian Air Force Typhoon fighter-bombers from 126 and 127 Fighter Wings located at the forward airfield code-named B-68, poured rocket after rocket into the massed *Panzer Lehr* columns, preying on the tanks. R.C.A.F. Spitfires raked the logistics lines snaking to Charleroi. Only minutes from B-68, the sortie rate for the Canadian fighter squadrons was so high that the airfield was running out of rockets; these had to be shipped in from the B-66 site which covered the Maas sector. There was one unfortunate loss to an Me-262 which, taking advantage of the improved weather, wandered into the zone and bagged an R.C.A.F. Spitfire recce bird that was looking for *2d Panzer* units south of Namur.[11]

A Jagdpanzer IV tank destroyer platoon was quickly wiped out when caught on its left flank by a group of Shermans exploiting the effects of the air strikes. The shocked survivors were rounded up and placed against a wall. Their captors were not speaking English; indeed, some spoke German with a market accent.

"Are you SS? Identify yourselves."

"No, no we are not SS," pleaded one officer.

"How many of you served in Poland?"

There were no replies. Machine guns were turned on the tank destroyer crews.[12]

The *Fifth Panzer Army* staff was on the verge of panic. Communications with *Panzer Lehr* were intermittent and there was a significant amount of jamming from unknown sources. The air strikes caught the planners completely off guard. It was difficult, if not impossible to ascertain the fate of the division. Couriers were employed, crossing the Meuse in rubber boats. Few returned, but one who did informed commanders that a reduced *Kampfgruppe* still held out, but it had no fuel. Attempts were made to move fuel across the river, but accurate artillery fire from Canadian Sexton self-propelled guns supporting the Poles and the Czechs put an end to that activity. One group of Panthers broke out of the trap and made it to Charleroi, before running out of fuel and the few quad 20mm anti-aircraft guns that *Panzer Lehr* possessed tried to drive off Canadian Typhoons as they made runs on the retreating German vehicles. Several 1st Polish Armoured Division tanks and some Czech Shermans were left smoldering in their wake, but to no avail. The bulk of *Panzer Lehr* was destroyed. *Fifth Panzer Army* ordered *2d Panzer* to prepare to move to Charleroi and along the river to support *Panzer Lehr*. Canadian counter-battery fire was just too accurate for effective artillery support to be provided.

The 1st Polish Armoured Division re-grouped and mopped up *Panzer Lehr* remnants. Led by Chris Vokes, the 4th Armoured Brigade, augmented with two other Sherman-equipped armored recce regiments, ploughed through the remnants of the *116th Panzer* south of Namur. Instead of consolidating on that objective, the units of the 4th Canadian Armoured Division then slammed into the outer cordon of *2d Panzer Division* units north of Dinant.

Brazen was racking up the kills. Corporal Don Graff jockeyed the Firefly back and forth on the ridge line. They had caught the advance elements of the Panther battalion and were engaged in a real gun-fight. More rings would be added to the 17-pounder barrel. Enemy armored vehicles were cooking off, but the Canadian force, particularly the non-Firefly Shermans, was taking hits. Fortunately, Graff thought, it was not as bad as Normandy; emplaced 88mm anti-tank guns had wiped out entire regiments during the battle of Bourguébus Ridge south of Caen in July. Another Mark IV Panzer exploded when the fire set by a previous penetrating round reached the ammo storage compartments. A Sherman was lost to a Panzergrenadier wielding a *Panzerschreck*, but there was not much left of him when several .50-caliber machine guns fired in his direction. Maultier half-tracks and trucks were blown apart, along with their valuable loads of ammunition and fuel.

Then the withdrawal order came. Back to Namur. It was no mean feat, taking an armored brigade plus, turning it on a dime and heading back, but that was the plan. The fight had been sharp, but short, as it was intended to be. Contact was broken cleanly in most sectors, though the Governor General's Foot Guards took a few too many tank hits which rendered an entire squadron unserviceable. The force retreated behind the Namur hedgehog.

Simonds was pleased. More and more towed artillery was arriving which only increased the amount of Canadian firepower that could be brought to bear. Every time the Germans went after Namur, they were confronted with fighting in a built-up area where fire dominance was out of their hands. They simply did not have enough infantry to take the city. The uncommitted remnants of *Panzer Lehr* held Charleroi, but to what end? The division's ability to project power to the north or east was minimal. Between *2d Panzer* and *116th Panzer*, there were barely enough serviceable tanks left to constitute one quarter of a normal division's complement.

The tip of the spear held at the Allies' throats had been snapped off. The Bulge had been blunted. Over the next week, the 4th U.S. Armored Division operating with the 11th American Armored Division broke through to Bastogne, which disrupted the logistics net supplying *Fifth Panzer Army*. Under pressure, the remnants of the three Panzer divisions withdrew to positions around Rochefort and then back to a cluster of villages north of Bastogne to rationalize the newly-stabilized lines. The Ardennes Crisis was over. American forces, now strongly reinforced, ensured that the Ardennes salient remained contained. Montgomery could focus on Operation Veritable, the drive into northern Germany. There would be no Anglo-American race for the Rhine. The disorganized leadership of Third U.S. Army fell into a period of bitter personal in-fighting which damaged the effectiveness of the formation and limited its ability to act as the shock force that it once was. With no decisive rout of German forces in the Ardennes, Veritable and its subsequent operations threatened to encircle the *Wacht am Rhine* forces, forcing them to withdraw to the Rhine. As usual, First Canadian Army got the dirty work of the war, clearing out the unglamorous long left flank…

The Reality

A decapitation strike against Third U.S. Army obviously didn't take place, but the capability was there and in Skorzeny, there was a mind that could have thought it up. Operation *Greif* was real and caused serious disruption in the Allied rear area, including rumors of a plot to assassinate Eisenhower.[13] The attack on Patton's convoy by an unmarked American fighter aircraft did take place on Christmas Day 1944; whether it was from KG 200 is unknown,[14] but KG 200 was a real unit and portions of it specialized in flying captured Allied aircraft and even engaging in combat with them.[15] The loss of Colonel Oscar Koch, perhaps the only G-2 man convinced of the seriousness of German moves, this early in the battle would have caused serious problems, as would the loss of the experienced staff team assembled by Patton.[16]

The Canadian command personalities for First Canadian Army were shifted one up for this alternate scenario, with the exception of Major-General Chris Vokes, who swapped command of 4th Canadian Armoured Division with Major-General Harry Foster, who went to command a Canadian division in Italy. Lieutenant-General Harry Crerar, a more plodding politically-minded officer then Lieutenant-General Guy Simonds was in command at this time, having just come back from sick leave.[17] The German airborne option against the Canadians did exist, as did the command change for *LXXXVIII Corps*, the improvement of the airfields, the allocation of additional airborne resource, and the problem of getting the 150 tanks to *LXXXVIII Corps*. None of the 150 tanks made it, so no ground option was implemented. The air assault was postponed due to lack of aircraft and poor weather, though the von der

Heydte drop did take place. It just was not as effective as portrayed here.[18] There was some debate as to whether the German moves on the Maas were deliberately designed to pin down First Canadian Army to prevent the maneuver depicted in the piece; evidence is fragmentary, but the possibility exists.[19] Canadian signals intelligence capabilities were pretty good by this time, as was radio discipline (at least compared to the Third Army).[20]

The British-Canadian command relationship problems were real, despite the laudatory front put up by official historians. Simonds was just ambitious and egotistical enough to have attempted to beat Monty to the punch, if the opportunity presented itself. Indeed, Monty was suspected of husbanding resources for Veritable by the Canadians[21] for the first phases of the Ardennes Crisis (as it is known in Canadian military history, as opposed to the Battle of the Bulge) despite the seriousness of the situation, and Monty did maneuver deliberately to humiliate Omar Bradley over commanding the two nearly cut-off U.S. armies to the north of the German penetration.[22] All of the First Canadian Army units in the piece were real, (though the three independent brigades were not attached at the time of the Ardennes Crisis) as were the equipments that are portrayed: Land Mattress, Firefly Shermans, Ram Kangaroo APCs. First Canadian Army commanders were circumspect about the use of what we today call special operations forces, but later on in the campaign to liberate the Netherlands, their capabilities were increasingly respected and employed during Operation Amherst.[23] I have merely moved this up a bit in time to coincide with the changes in command personalities. As for Canadian close air support, the system had improved to the point where it had become this effective in the war. The serendipitous location of the B-68 airfield not only assisted the forces effectively for this scenario, it was critical in efforts to blunt the Bulge during the actual campaign; once the weather improved, of course.[24]

Bibliography

D'Este, Carlo, *Patton: A Genius for War*, Harper Books, New York, 1995.

Graham, Dominick, *The Price of Command: A Biography of General Guy Simonds*, Stoddart, Toronto, 1993.

Greenhous, Brereton, *et al.*, *The Official History of the Royal Canadian Air Force*, Volume III: *The Crucible of War 1939–1945*, University of Toronto Press, Toronto, 1994.

Hamilton, Nigel, *Monty: The Field Marshal 1944–1976*, Sceptre, London, 1987.

Lucas, James, *Kommando: German Special Forces of World War Two*, Castle Books, Edison, 2003.

Stacey, C.P., *The Official History of the Canadian Army in the Second World War*, Volume III: *The Victory Campaign: Operations in North-west Europe 1944–45*, Queen's Printer, Ottawa, 1960.

Stahl, P.W., *Geheim-Geschwader KG 200*, Motorbuch Verlag, Stuttgart, 2002.

Whitaker, W. Denis & Shelagh, *Rhineland: The Battle to End the War*, Stoddart Books, Toronto, 1989.

Zebrowski, Marian W., *Polski Broń Pancerna: Zarys Historii, 1918–1947*, London, 1971.

Appendix
Order of Battle, First Canadian Army December 1944[25]

Army Units

     1st Army Group, Royal Canadian Artillery (4 regiments)

     2nd Army Group, Royal Canadian Artillery (4 regiments)

     1st Rocket Battery, 1st Radar Battery

     1st Armoured Personnel Carrier Regiment[a]

I Canadian Corps[b]

     1st Canadian Infantry Division

     5th Canadian Armoured Division

     1st Armoured Brigade

     2nd Armoured Brigade

II Canadian Corps

     2nd Canadian Infantry Division

     3rd Canadian Infantry Division

     4th Canadian Armoured Division

     1st Polish Armoured Division

I British Corps

     49th (West Riding) Infantry Division

     51st (Highland) Infantry Division

     52nd (Lowland) Infantry Division

Attached Formations

     1st Belgian Infantry Brigade

     Royal Netherlands Brigade (Princess Irene's)

     1st Czechoslovak Independent Armoured Brigade Group

     Belgian and French elements of the Special Air Service Brigade

a. Normally under 79th British Armoured Division.

b. All re-deploying to Northwest Europe from Italy and unavailable for operations.

c. Command of the armoured formations shifted as necessary from corps to corps.

Notes

*1. Paul Krausemann, *The Patton Assassination: Death of a Myth*, Munich: reVision Verlag, 2008, p. 67.

*2. U.S. Army Historical Office, Stuttgart. (unpublished) "Report on the Aftermath of 3rd Army Headquarters Raid, 16 December 1944: Classified Annex."

 3. See appendix for order of battle.

*4. National Archives of Canada, RG 24 Acc 2004/167 file TS997–UOU, "Intercepted Messages: Ardennes Crisis, December 1944."

*5. Hugh Ernest Rextion, *The Dead Die Harder: The SAS in Northwest Europe 1944–45*, Virgin Exploitative Books, London, 2004, pp. 45–7.

*6. Guy Simonds, *War as I Saw It: An Autobiography of Canada's Greatest Soldier Ever*, S & M Publishing, Toronto, 1972, p. 948.

*7. Peter Seagrave, *From the Profane to the Ridiculous: a Biography of General Chris Vokes in War and Peace*, Ottawa Valley Books, Perth, 2005, p. 541.

 8. A battle group would be the equivalent of an infantry battalion plus a tank squadron, or a tank regiment with an infantry company attached.

*9. John Grodzinski, *To Warsaw and Back: The Polish Corps at War 1941–45*, Brassey's Poland, Gdansk, 2005, pp. 234–50.

*10. National Archives of Canada, RG 24 Acc 2004/167 file TS2100–9XR, "CIC German Interrogation Reports December 1944."

*11. Scott Robertson, *The Storm Birds: Canadian Typhoon Squadrons in the Second World War*, Canwarav Books, Kingston, 2006, pp. 252–5.

*12. Jan Haglunden, *Great Allied War Atrocities: Another View*, Neu Stasi Verlag, Leipzig, 2007, chapter 5.

 13. Lucas, *Kommando*, pp. 127–35.

 14. D'Este *Patton: A Genius for War*, p. 691.

 15. For details see Stahl, *Geheim-Geschwader KG 200*.

 16. For more on Koch, see D'Este's *Patton*, p. 676.

 17. Stacey, *The Victory Campaign*, pp. 426–7.

 18. Lucas, *Kommando*, pp. 127–35

 19. Stacey, *The Victory Campaign*, pp. 440–50.

 20. Carlo D'Este notes the poor radio discipline issue several times in *Patton: A Genius for War.* See particularly chapter 43.

 21. See Whitaker and Whitaker, *Rhineland*.

 22. Hamilton, *Monty: The Field Marshal*, pp. 238–50.

 23. Stacey, *The Victory Campaign*, pp. 552–6.

 24. Greenhous *et al.*, *The Crucible of War*, pp. 323–53.

 25. At least for the purposes of this scenario. The three Free Belgian Dutch and Czech brigades were attached to, and detached from, First Canadian Army on numerous occasions from July 1944 to May 1945.

7
GO HOME, THIS IS OUR GODDAM SHOW![1]
Monty pulls it off

Charles Vasey

"War without allies is bad enough—with allies it is hell"[2]
Of all the disciplines of war there can be none more trying than command of a coalition. The whole concept of a modern army is of a hierarchical organisation with responsibility and power cascading down from the highest to the lowest. Yet in a coalition force an extra-military factor arises—some commanders will not blindly follow the orders of their superior without reference to their own governments. Military jurisprudence does not, of course, expect absolute obedience to a superior but it does not typically encompass command by consent. It requires considerable skill on the part of commander and commanded to manage a relationship where dissent is to be accommodated. Where different armies, with different styles, different languages and different political agendas supplied by their political masters are to be successfully commanded then the art of the general is not one just of command but also of persuasion. A commander moves from being a leader of men to a herder of cats.

The Allies in Northwestern Europe were fortunate to have in Dwight Eisenhower just such a commander. Despite derogatory opinions as to his military ability and sniping from his own compatriots—"the best general the British had"[3]—he managed to keep his coalition armies moving. This was so even if that movement tended to be more of a random walk than a Prussian General Staff solution. Eisenhower had rediscovered the art of leadership from pre-industrial times where the *amour-propre* of each general needed careful consideration. Bonnie Prince Charlie at Culloden Moor beset by clan claims on the position of honour would have recognized the issues that faced Ike.

Eisenhower's problems were not merely a number of political masters, but a collection of *prima donnas* in his army and army group commanders. Not since Agamemnon enraged Achilles over Briseis has a commander suffered from as much sulking. The abilities of Bradley, Montgomery and Patton will be subject to debate for a long time to come, but their egos seem indefeasibly large even by present celebrity standards. The animus between Bradley and Patton (though *both* agreed Monty was a shit) commenced in Sicily. The career of George Patton slowed but Omar Bradley was there to keep the home fires burning with Monty. The body language in many of the group photographs is very interesting. In some photographs Monty struts in front of Eisenhower. In other photographs Bradley stands off to one side as if faintly embarrassed to be with these people. One feels for Eisenhower even if, at times, his supply decisions were more a Judgement of Solomon than a Napoleonic analysis.

The British and Canadian forces (with their other European allies—Poles, Belgians, Dutch and others) were reducing in relative size as fresh American divisions landed and French divisions were formed. In modern warfare quantity has a quality all of its own and this disparity did matter in terms of coalition politics. This advantage at least gave Eisenhower an opportunity to read the Riot Act to Montgomery even if he had, at other times, to assuage wounded feelings. However, the expansion of the U.S. Army brought with it other non-coalition problems. Generals (like Patton) who were pleased with their performance in other campaigns found themselves commanding armies beneath others (like Bradley) who had formerly been less celebrated. The opportunities from U.S. Army expansion whet their appetites for personal advancement as much as the decline in importance thinned the skins of their Commonwealth colleagues.

"I am envious only of glory; for if it be a sin to covet glory, I am the most offending soul alive"[4]

The commander of the First U.S. Army Courtney Hodges was just as careful in guarding his honor and prerogatives as the more imposing George Patton. He had understudied and then replaced Omar Bradley at First Army. As such he had seen the furore between Bradley and "Bimbo" Dempsey (commanding Second British Army) in the drive to the Seine.[5] Hodges was not a media player like so many American generals. He was courtly rather than self-promoting, brave (his calm bearing during the Bulge on hearing the news that Peiper was driving on his HQ drove his staff officers to distraction—a common destination for staff officers) but undemonstrative (by American standards). What was more he had failed at West Point and had enlisted as a private—this was no typical officer. This in no way made him any different from his more excitable compatriots in the key matter of substance. Hodges was raised on the American doctrine of constant attack, if Queen Mary's heart had "Calais" engraved upon it, then an American general had "attack" on his heart and on his forehead.

How galling therefore to Hodges to find his army under attack in the Ardennes in December 1944. Troy Middleton's VIII Corps (HQ at Bastogne) was faced by major attacks from three German armies (two of them Panzer armies). Hodges' attention (and that of his army group commander) had been quite rightly to the north of the Ardennes and he was as surprised as anyone by the attack. Unfortunately he had to deal with the surprise while everyone else simply looked on. He had no armchair from which to be a general. On 19 December 1944 at the Verdun Conference Patton's Third Army was tasked with driving into the German mass from the south. Hodges was not in a position yet to dispose of reserves capable of succouring his own corps. He was already on the back foot.

Yet in all honesty Hodges could look with pride at his force's conduct. V Corps under Gerow formed the northern shoulder of First Army and was not only concentrated but giving the Germans a bloody nose. Attacks on the Elsenborn Ridge were driven off, the breakthrough by Peiper was sealed off by 30th Division's recapture of Stavelot, the 82d Airborne was deploying at Werbomont, and St Vith was held (although this was not yet known). Faced with an attack by powerful German formations, and the confusion concomitant with such attacks the U.S. forces had moved quickly and had moved *forward*. This was an army that believed in its own qualities and in hustle. Jochen Peiper's breakthrough, which should have rolled back the "terror-stricken doughboys," was almost rudely disregarded. There was, it is true, a very large hole to the south of St Vith down to the forming Bastogne block, but north of St Vith the Germans were faced with a forming and solidifying line. Hodges' First Army was surprised, and his formations were outnumbered, but they were reacting with aggression. He had reason for some quiet confidence. It was annoying that George Patton would be bustling up to "rescue" him, but there was an opportunity here for victory for Hodges and for First Army.

It might reasonably be objected that this "forward policy" flew in the face of good sense when facing a major attack, but (it might also be argued) wars are not won by falling back in the face of a bold attack—they are won by advancing. In any case Bradley was still under the impression that this was a spoiling attack until the third day of the battle. Hodges was still in the dark about much of what was happening, but he was well aware of Peiper's breathrough, and had echeloned the newly forming airborne corps at Werbomont. He saw no reason to retire. And who would have disagreed with this, knowing only what was then known?

"Gardez Bien"[6]

At this stage, so Hodges might be forgiven for thinking, his own side heaped further pains on him. At his chief of staff, Bedell Smith's, suggestion Eisenhower had decided to hand the northern sector of Bradley's command to Montgomery, leaving Bradley to oversee the southern half of the Ardennes. Unusually the defenders were choosing to provide the attackers with an army group boundary right in front of their attack. Montgomery could provide a strategic reserve—XXX Corps—and could form the heavy anvil to block and cover the Meuse until the hammer of Patton could smash the Germans asunder. The roles offered played to the strengths of Montgomery and Patton, but neither Hodges nor Bradley might be expected to view matters in so analytical a way. This was their army, not just a pawn in a game of chess.

Montgomery arrived at Hodges' HQ with all the fervor (it is said) of Christ come to cleanse the Temple. Given his notoriously high-handed manner one might expect serious difficulties but Monty was a (relatively) humbled man since the fall. Monty's demands to be commander of land forces had almost caused Eisenhower to sack him then (only the diplomacy of Monty's chief of staff, Francis "Freddie" de Guingand, had saved his master). Yet even a diplomatic Monty was not going to be any easier for Hodges to accept. That Montgomery was a careful man whose skills were matched to the task of holding the Meuse was clear, that he had a great interest in success—his army group would be cut off if the Germans reached Antwerp—was obvious, but he remained a man who had raised condescension to an art form. It was truly said of him that he was unbeatable in adversity and unbearable in victory.

Montgomery had already sent his assistants to discover on the spot how the U.S. forces were performing. His view was that the Germans had very powerful forces but that the Allies should not allow the U.S. forces to be smashed in halting them. Instead, Monty wanted the American line to pivot under German pressure and fall back towards the Meuse. As First Army's lines shortened, a reserve would form under Collins to allow the riposte. As the Americans fell back to cover the east end of the Meuse (Liège to Namur) British divisions were moving up to cover the west. They would jointly form their line on the Meuse with key reserves ready to meet a *German Army* that would then be well forward of its supply lines. In the manner of a martial artist Montgomery proposed to pivot away from the German blow on his right and then, having overstretched his opponent, give him a strong shot to the head with his left. It was undeniably a clever plan, but it was an un-American plan. American blood had been spent getting this far; it seemed foolish to set that for naught by falling back under an attack that was being ably dealt with by American forces. It sounded like just the sort of plan that had caused Monty to take so long to capture Caen. No American general wished to contemplate that analogy.

Montgomery's suggestion (for he had to avoid his imperious prescriptive ways with the task-orientated Americans and suggest rather than command) was to "refuse" the line back from Stavelot towards Marche. German forces would drive into the gap (glissading off the forming American line). They would move westward it was true but *south*-westward and not north-westward towards the Meuse and Monty's own line of communications. Advancing west merely bagged more Germans and depleted their fuel.

Hodges preferred a more forward policy. He felt there was presently no need to retreat. He had finally received news that Hasbrouck had held St Vith; this extended First Army's forming line even further south than had previously been imagined. Rather than abandoning this post (so gallantly and unexpectedly held) he wanted to push forward the troops at Werbomont to form that link. Hodges proposed no feinting pivot, like a boxer he wanted to move up close to his opponent to slug it out. Here was a moment where the American perception of Montgomery in Normandy—as a "sticky" general who had no plunge and liked artillery plan solutions—must have had an impact. The German attack was a great surprise to all, but in the north of the salient the Americans were limiting its impact. Why yield territory that would have to be repurchased with American blood?

The news of St Vith and Hodges' arguments persuaded (at least openly) Montgomery not to order the withdrawal from St Vith at that time. 20 December passed with First Army still pushing forward to link up with St Vith and to complete the discomfiture of Peiper's units. But it takes two to tango and the Germans fancied a quickstep instead.

"In view of past experience, it can be assumed that the enemy will not quickly recover from his unexpected reverse"[7]

The Germans planned a major secondary offensive for 21 December; 12 divisions (seven of which were armored) were ready to break into the Allied positions. This was to occur in four main attacks:

The most northerly attack on Malmedy-Butgenbach-Monschau was intended to pin the six U.S. divisions in that area.

The second was to force the St Vith position and free the St Vith–Houffalize–St Hubert roads.

In the third attack *2d* and *9th SS Panzer* were to push on the Vielsalm salient and drive back the 82d Airborne.

Finally attack four was the push towards Marche, deep in the west towards Dinant.

This plan was not to be put fully into effect, however. At some point late on the 20th German commanders conferring together decided to encourage the forward American position. St Vith must fall it was true for without it vital road networks were not available. But to the north of there German formations were to engage and hold in a less overtly offensive manner. Pinning not assaulting was the order of the day. This allowed a southward drift of German units to get round the American right flank. Against a pinned target the Panzer formations were to hook through St Vith and behind the U.S. forces at Vielsalm as the Americans moved forward. The new target was not to press on to Marche and to Dinant but to try a shorter maneuver, cutting behind the new American line at Vielsalm and drive towards the crossings closer to Liège than Dinant. This was to be a short rather than long hook. That there were traffic problem aplenty for the Germans was certain, that American forces had proved able to stand with a breakthrough behind them was also the case, but the shorter hook, if it worked, might bag more Americans for less fuel. In short, had the Germans sat at Tongres with First Army command, they would have agreed with Monty's analysis. They had no intention of driving miles into southern Belgium towards France yet away from Antwerp.

Who devised this plan is now subject to debate as many of the German field commanders died later in the campaign. Sepp Dietrich as commander of *Sixth SS Panzer Army* was certainly involved, but it was *German Army* generals whose

Panzers were closest to breakthrough. The commanders of *2d Panzer* and *Panzer Lehr* (both pulled away from Bastogne) were the men on the ground. Post-war scholarship has clearly seen a political aversion to awarding any part of this clever plan to Dietrich (a former butcher and Nazi heavy) rather than to the more chivalric commanders of the two forward units—Fritz Bayerlein of *Panzer Lehr* having been "elected" the champion of the Army. It might more correctly be argued that the solution was the last gasp of the German General Staff from the days of Imperial Germany.[8] It has also been argued that (in the northern part of the front at least) it was not a plan but an appreciation of the weakened abilities of the German Volksgrenadiers. We cannot at this remove be certain.

The first attack was designed to engage the U.S. divisions but also to limit German casualties and allow formations to extend southwards. The St Vith attack was to proceed with all speed, but the Vielsalm salient was only to be engaged and pinned, one Panzer unit moving to support the left hook. The drive on Marche was shelved, though reconnaissance units were allowed to press westwards looking for fuel dumps and spreading alarm and dismay.

In St Vith Brigadier General Robert Hasbrouck was all too ready to withdraw once he had obliged the Germans to give battle. He skilfully pulled back towards Vielsalm. The U.S. line continued forming more solidly but was not pinned back on the Meuse (which Hodges wished to avoid). The German forces now had their road to the west, a road that, near Houffalize, would allow them to drive north. Elsewhere the battles of the 21st put 82d Airborne under considerable pressure but did not indicate a major problem, German forces seemed content to engage and then use mortar and sniper fire to limit any forward U.S. movement. By this date XXX Corps (a British formation) was arriving on the Meuse on the line Namur–Dinant–Givet, holding the bottom of the funnel down which Monty intended the Germans to go. The Germans were not to know it but the Meuse to the west was therefore blocked. However, from Namur to Liège there was a gap on the Meuse. This was a gap into which the German short hook might yet drive. Both sides awaited the morrow with the usual mixture of warfare—great hope and profound ignorance.

The Germans used 22 December to push southwestwards towards Houffalize and to begin to drive north on the road to Liège. Their left wing was pushing into an open gap but moved carefully, unaware of what, if any, American formations were in that area. They would have been cheered by news from the U.S. lines (but were not to discover this until later). Matthew Ridgway, commanding the newly formed XVIII Corps, instructed Hasbrouck with his St Vith forces (7th Armored and various infantry units) to press forward to test the German flank. Hasbrouck refused. Believing the Germans to be in strength to the south, he saw no reason to imitate General Custer. He was relieved of command. The ensuing attack by 7th Armored, delivered late following command confusion, met significant German resistance but few counterattacks. Ridgway felt vindicated to that degree. There were, of course,

Germans in the Amblève valley and to the west but these were taken to be the remnants of Peiper's breakthrough. Indeed Peiper was to order his own breakout on the next day, unaware of his compatriots' changed plans—much to the dismay of armchair generals everywhere.

At this stage Hodges had committed himself to a policy of steady forward movement—in the north (his left) he was of course fully engaged—but there were no breakthroughs and morale was growing. The news of Hasbrouck's removal was accepted as a command difference—U.S. generals lived in an environment of ruthless (if not fatal) pruning. Montgomery had left First Army HQ that morning to meet some of his liaison officers who had been scouting U.S. formations to the south. This untypical tactfulness was an attempt to lighten pressure on Hodges. Freddy de Guingand, wishing to avoid any unpleasantness, had recommended a policy of some distance. Unfortunately physical distance from the First Army HQ meant that, if the situation changed, Montgomery would not be there. Hodges was concerned in case he was commanded to retreat but at present he had no such orders and intended to make hay (if one may use an unseasonal comparison) while the sun shone.

23 December dawned with significant German forces building to the right of the American line. At this stage the Montgomery Plan of wheeling back towards the Meuse (or to Werbomont at the very least) would have effectively defeated the German hook. Such foresight was denied to both sides at the time.

Montgomery's influence was in any case not to be felt. He was moving towards Werbomont to meet Hasbrouck and a young British liaison officer briefed by Hasbrouck. His escort ran into a force from Peiper's command which had decided to break out to the southwest rather than the southeast at about 12:00 p.m. The ensuing firefight destroyed most of Montgomery's vehicles and his travelling caravan. His escort units engaged forward and drove back the German troops. There is no evidence that the SS troopers were aware of who or what it was that they engaged that day, although after the war a number of soldiers who may have been present wrote an exciting account of how they laid an ambush for Monty.[9] This book created something of a storm in the German and British press, involving one distinguished British historian who had to make a retraction from his authentication of their accounts. Whatever the truth was as to motive, the results were undeniable— for most of the afternoon of 23 December Montgomery was awaiting the solution of his immediate security needs and the arrival of fresh transport. This arrived (rather unexpectedly) from the south with a small convoy of jeeps bearing the rusticated General Hasbrouck and Montgomery's staff officer. The staff officer explained to "the Master" that, in his view, Hasbrouck had been correct in his appreciation of the situation. Had Montgomery been at HQ the officer had intended to request that Hasbrouck be reinstated. Montgomery chose his aides with care, he already trusted Hasbrouck.

Hasbrouck's briefing convinced Montgomery (or perhaps confirmed his own conviction) that the U.S. line was still too far east and that there was a risk of being caught by a hook from the south. His communications officers could not achieve a link with First Army, however (and Montgomery decided a face-to-face meeting with Hodges was in any case politic) but contact was achieved with British 21st Army Group and Montgomery ordered his staff there to move armored forces towards Liège in case the U.S. line needed an armored reserve. It was already dark when a convoy of jeeps started out for First Army HQ. Neither Montgomery nor Hodges had any idea of what was heading north towards them.

24 December dawned with Montgomery in conference with Hodges. Hasbrouck explained his concerns before withdrawing from the meeting. Hodges pointed out that he was committed and holding everywhere. Montgomery countered that Hodges was without a significant reserve. To this end Montgomery had put his own favourite veteran division—51st (Highland) Division—under First Army command. There may also have been another attempt to mollify Hodges' here.

Montgomery insisted that the line must shorten in order to give Collins the spare divisions to form his new corps which was to counterattack. Hodges was backed by Ridgway who joined the conference late from his attacks in the south. Montgomery was used to the habit of command but recognized that he must be careful. (There is evidence from Churchill's doctor that instructions had been sent by the Prime Minister to Montgomery to act with extreme courtesy.) Montgomery insisted that withdrawal from the Vielsalm salient was as necessary as withdrawal from St Vith had been—yet opened no new roads for the Germans. In a short break in the conference de Guingard took the two American generals aside and stressed that this might go to Eisenhower if they did not accede—Montgomery *would* force his views through. Ridgway was disgusted but Hodges gave in; he had fought the good fight. Ridgway departed to organize the withdrawal. Two hours later a message arrived at First Army headquarters. A small *ad hoc* U.S. force at Baraque de Fraiture had been overrun by units of three Panzer divisions (a pardonable exaggeration) barrelling north. The signal was followed by another stating that the Germans were past the Grandmenil junction heading towards Werbomont. Ridgway's movement was to be too late. The First Army was facing major German formations within 20 miles of Liège!

"Nothing is to be feared but fear"[10]

The Christmas Day staff conference at First Army HQ was not the cheeriest there could have been. For it transpired the German indirect strategy and the lost day had effectively left Ridgway's XVIII Corps out of the line; it (and the accompanying units of 7th Armored Division) had a difficult task to get back towards what would be the likely line on which the First Army aimed to stop the Germans. The question now was where would that line form? Montgomery had favoured Werbomont with its ridge position, but the

Germans were very close to it by this point and there were German forces engaging all the way along the American line. If some delay could be mounted at Werbomont the line could begin to form at Aywaille where the Liège road crossed the valley of the Amblève river. This would guard the flank of the Stavelot position, although leaving it dependent on the line back through Aywaille. What might be disastrous would be if the first stop line could only be formed at Aywaille.

Hodges and Montgomery concentrated on the task in hand. Faced now, as they were, with defeat they found a commonality of purpose. The northern forces were ordered to strip out two divisions and despatch them to Collins at Romsee near Liège. Complaints were met with a frosty response. The 30th Division at Stavelot despatched a regiment to hold Trois Ponts as Ridgway's men retreated north, while the rest of 30th Division fell back to Malmedy to ensure the route north to Spa was protected. There would be a gap in the line between Stavelot and Malmedy but there was no major road through that gap.

Ridgway, realising his position, had responded with ferocious speed. One regiment of the 82d was told off to hold Vielsalm and the rest plus armored units drove north to Trois Ponts and the welcoming arms of the 30th Division. A retreat under attack is a most difficult procedure. It might be argued that such a retreat had shattered less elite American divisions during the early stages of the Bulge battle. The 82d, however, was made of stern stuff. The manoeuvre tested the 82d but *9th SS Panzer* was slow to recognize the retreat, and though it followed up late in the day, by nightfall the 82d's rearguard was approaching Trois Ponts, and some 7th Armored tanks were at Aywaille. This process once completed was intended to leave the First Army south of the Meuse protecting its supply line, but it still left the Meuse uncovered between Liège and Namur. If German forces took Werbomont they could drive northwest to Huy and be across the river. The question then was what could be done at Werbomont?

There is a wreckage of small units that follows an army and two units of this kind were to be found at Werbomont. Monty's liaison officers accompanied by General Hasbrouck arrived at Werbomont early on Christmas Day. The 99th Battalion (Separate) was an untypical unit formed out of Americans of Norwegian stock for a planned operation in Norway. The battalion had suffered a backlash not of its own making in the Bulge. Ottto Skorzeny's Trojan Horse units had infiltrated the U.S. rear areas creating a miasma of fear and suspicion. The result had been to put all Americans very much on their guard against foreign-sounding GIs. In an army where many Americans were of German stock this was a dangerous occurrence. The arrival of large numbers of blond highly-accented troops in a funny unit had excited the attention of sentries and military police whose ancestors hailed from Ireland and Italy. The battalion had been despatched to the comparative quiet of Werbomont early in the battle and had been joined there by a battalion of Belgian Fusiliers. This rather unlikely force dubbed the League of Nations by

Hasbrouck (and Fred Karno's Army[11] by the accompanying British staff officers) was tasked with holding Werbomont while the line formed elsewhere. Hasbrouck, though, was game for anything and the arrival of an engineer unit led to some imaginative mining of the roads as the two battalions settled down to hold the ridge. Hasbrouck would have liked some of his armor (now driving to Aywaille) with him but could not make contact with Ridgway in time.

The fall of Werbomont was a practical certainty so First Army also needed to block the road towards Huy in case the Germans merely masked Aywaille and drove northwest. Until Collins could extricate his new divisions and prepare for the counterattack First Army had (for practical purposes) no reserves. Hodges had to look to Montgomery's forces and here Fortune favoured the Allies. The original plans for British XXX Corps troops was for them to hold the section of the Meuse south from Namur, long stops in cricket parlance. To reach there many had first to move through Brussels which was closer to the now-exposed section of the Meuse than their destination areas. Montgomery's orders to 21st Army Group HQ had been passed to "Pip" Roberts at 11th Armoured Division and his units were now heading towards Huy after collecting their old Sherman tanks from Brussels (the units were hoping to receive new Comet tanks).

11th Armoured was at first blush the poor relation of the British armored divisions, with less social cachet than Guards Armoured (though rather more tank experience) and less military fame than 7th Armoured. 11th Armoured instead had pursued its course for military excellence, learning from each of its campaigns especially in the flexible treatment of infantry–tank co-operation. It was a meritocratic organisation by this stage. It had also (in Normandy) fought alongside U.S. formations. It was ordered to Huy rather than Givet, with 3d Royal Tank Regiment and 8th Rifle Brigade leading the way for 29th Tank Brigade. Other formations were following. The New Model Army quality of 11th Armoured was admirably suited to a battle where planning was judged in hours not days. Its men reacted promptly and professionally, Roberts in briefing his brigadiers noted that he wanted "no stopping for tea"—a reference to Guards Armoured on the road to Arnhem. (If recrimination between the Allied generals was bad, the cap badge rivalries of the British Army were worse.) He wanted tank support for the Americans soon, and he knew the conditions in the Ardennes from a motoring holiday in the thirties.

Montgomery's original plan foresaw the mass of German tanks pushed westward toward the British XXX Corps' blocking positions. Now that the Germans had committed *northwards* Montgomery felt no qualms about weakening that long-stop screen. If the Panzers were halted on or before the Meuse between Huy and Liège both Montgomery and Hodges agreed they would be hard pressed to attempt yet a further hook westward short, as they would be, on time and fuel. Montgomery therefore instructed Roberts to secure Huy and push on to Werbomont and sent a signal to XXX Corps to push forward from the Meuse.

Hodges took Collins aside and mentioned to him that the British were "riding to the rescue." It seemed so unfair he mused that some might think this would be a British victory. Collins took the hint and ordered the forming 3d Armored Division to expedite its movement to Aywaille and beyond. The hopes of German commanders—that panic would grip the Allied command—proved barren. Instead both British and American armored formations had a race, not since Messina had there been a steeplechase like this. The sporting rivalries of the Allied officers overcame the concern about defeat. They had two opponents: the Germans and their own allies. Defeating both was their target.

But this rosy picture of cheery Allied rivalry is painted with hindsight. If Werbomont had not held would the Americans have broken? One cannot say, but, the nearer to the Liège bridges the Germans got, the more likely that practical restrictions on supply would have had an impact on U.S. formations. The Bulge campaign was a madcap attack as it was, but judging when an army will crack is a difficult and uncertain matter.

"What God abandoned, these defended"[12]

At this stage, while the Allies marshalled their forces, the Germans, who had guessed correctly so far, experienced a moment in which the fog of war seeped into their command posts. With their Panzers committed northward *en masse*, their westward-ranging reconnaissance units near Marche were in contact with armored cars of an unknown enemy unit. After a brief clash near Rochefort these were identified as belonging to 53d British Division. This formation was not on the list the German intelligence officers had prepared as likely to be met. Clearly the British were in the west; it was to be hoped they were not in the north too. The news arriving on Christmas morning prompted a radio staff conference; were the British flanking the Germans? It was concluded that there was no immediate threat though one brigade was committed westward.

The disquiet grew when the forward forces moved on Werbomont and were met with a hail of fire. Hasbrouck had put everything in the shop window and even commandeered some artillery units to make the maximum noise. However, he lacked any form of armor apart from two tank destroyers, also commandeered, both of which were destroyed in the first half hour of combat. He was aware that forward units of British armor were approaching Huy, so the best hope of the Allies was (he felt) to make the Germans think twice about continuing their headlong advance. If he could but encourage the Germans to halt, and deploy into attack formation he might yet gain time.

Hasbrouck was unaware of the brief German scare in the west but was pleased to see the German commanders had halted, called up infantry and artillery, and ordered the refuelling of their tanks. The attack started just after 1:00 p.m. and was engaged with all strength by the "Americans." The two

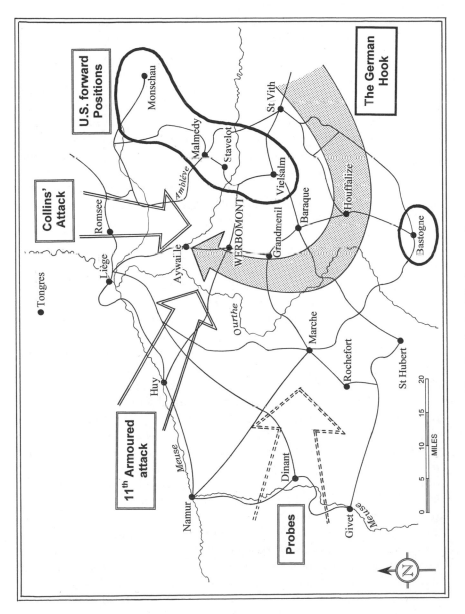

The Battle for Werbomont

infantry battalions held on as long as possible but German attacks were pressed hard. By 3:00 p.m. Hasbrouck could see the end was near. He had contact with Collins and knew American armor had arrived in the next village but he also knew that it could not save him.

Hasbrouck pulled the few remaining troops back in a steady retreat but by now the experienced German Panzergrenadiers had "smelled a rat." The level of fire support and the thinness of the line indicated this was window-dressing. The mines in part cleared, tanks were sent forward and by about 3:15 p.m. Werbomont was in German hands and its few defenders (American and Belgian) were retreating north, marshalled by Hasbrouck. If victory was to be illusory for the Germans, defeat was bitter for the Belgians and Norwegian-Americans. With little ammunition and few supplies they struggled into the woods trying to keep warm and to keep the walking wounded alive. Both formations were trained for cold-weather combat but both had left behind their seriously wounded comrades. These were fortunate indeed that no *SS* units had faced them. It was by now abundantly clear to the Germans that they had been fighting a very small force and had taken half a day to clear it. It was a bitter moment.

Already 3d Armored was at Aywaille. Aided by the British liaison officer Hasbrouck's HQ staffscanned British frequencies and were delighted at 4:00 p.m. to contact the tanks of 3d Royal Tank Regiment about ten miles to the west. At 4:15 operating off map co-ordinates radioed by the liaison officer the accompanying guns of the Royal Artillery were contacted and a shoot arranged. Darkness had already fallen as the German forces were struck by artillery fire from British 25-pounders. Uncertain as to the provenance of this fire the formations targeted had no choice—they had to press in two directions. The Germans were loath to travel at night in woods but needs must where the Devil drives. The Germans pushed forward *Kampfgruppen* on Aywaille and towards Huy. Both were met during the early evening by Allied armored formations. In the poor light both sides feared infantry attacks with bazooka or *Panzerfaust*. The disadvantages of warfare in December were made all too obvious. Both sides halted and spent a cold night facing each other without any real knowledge of the situation. By now, however, German HQ was aware it no longer faced a screen, there were British and Americans, artillery, infantry and armor.

During the night of the 25th both British tanks and infantry flowed in to support the drive towards Werbomont and from the north came Collins, taking practical control of the battle and bringing a combat command of 3d Armored. The mixed force that now pressed on the ridge was far too strong for a major German attack. Allied signals traffic was already indicating to German intelligence officers that the Meuse was blocked in this direction. At a hurriedly assembled radio conference Dietrich agreed that further forward movement would be difficult, and reported that 82d Airborne and 30th Division had both managed to disengage successfully. The Americans had, once again, refused to panic. German eyes were turning back toward Marche and the west or toward Bastogne where the 101st Airborne was holding von Manteuffel's forces at bay. Liège was safe, though it would take hard fighting to drive back the Germans. Two young German officers claimed next morning that they could see Liège from the German positions. Doubtless this was just imagination but it made the halting of the break-in all the more bitter.

"The Führer's Final Gamble"[13]

Rising to the challenge of the feared breakthrough the U.S. forces had shortened the line exactly as Montgomery had wished (though not as he had intended). While Ridgway and the 30th Division sorted out their battle lines Collins began to push the Germans facing him. 11th Armoured, now up in full strength, was sent westward to attack down the roads towards Marche. The Norwegians and Belgians took the opportunity to recuperate from their Christmas Day battle while Collins' infantry pushed into the German lines to allow the engineers to clear the defensive mine fields.

During the 26th and 27th further German attacks on the Werbomont ridge met with vigorous artillery and tank responses. The Germans had by this stage concluded that the north sector of the Bulge was no longer possible to break through and were acting to tie down an Allied break-in. The weather was changing and both American and British fighter-bombers were patrolling the skies.

The First Army had not been trapped south of the Meuse in such a way that it could be cut off and overwhelmed. Some of its formations had been mauled but in general it remained in strength in defensible positions. How close the Germans had come to success was then, and has remained, a matter of considerable argument. So has the whole concept of how much the German commanders had operational control of the battle.[14] Although Ridgway's divisions had been trapped too far forward, they had not broken. Having an elite formation as rearguard had been useful to that extent, but the 82d was too shattered to be used in combat as a division for the rest of the war. There was fortunately no argument between Collins or Roberts since neither had "rescued" the Werbomont force whose fortuitous existence took the laurels. The Germans were then and remain to this day (if one believes the memoirs) surprised at the resilience of the Americans. They had twice been turned (by Peiper and by the hook) but in neither case had major retreats ensued.

But the U.S. Army was a jealous god demanding sacrifice from its votaries. Since Hasbrouck had been right (as it transpired) and Ridgway had been wrong (as it transpired), Ridgway was relieved of command and Hasbrouck reassigned to command. In typical fashion Ridgway attracted a number of supporters (including his British and Polish parachute counterparts) who felt he had been hard done by, but Eisenhower had already suggested him for a command in Operation Olympic—the attack on the Japanese Islands—a fate from which *Enola Gay* was to rescue him.

But other than this an almost eerie calm descended on both Hodges and Montgomery who issued a joint statement whose rolling tones and language suggested a provenance closer to Downing Street than Tongres. So unusual was this silence that George Patton (who had raised the siege of Bastogne) was given to claiming it was "a damned fix." After the Prime Minister's death Winston Churchill's doctor revealed to Chester Wilmot that Churchill had indeed flown to Brussels and had debriefed Montgomery personally. The result was an uncharacteristic silence at the press conference where de Guingand stood in for Montgomery. Hodges was retained in command but his army reduced in size. The Allies still had plenty of fighting ahead of them (both internally and externally). But now the Germans had spent their best troops, little remained to defend the *Volksdeutsch* of the east, and Model's assessment of American troops had proved wrong. As Model said to Hitler, echoing Friedrich II but referring to the *Amis*—"these are not the same Austrians." Neither side paused to consider that it was a polyglot force of Belgians and Norwegian-Americans who cost the Germans vital hours on Christmas Day at Werbomont.

The Reality

Montgomery never ran into an SS ambush during the campaign, unlike the one O'Connor had suffered during the Desert Campaign. Montgomery believed very much that it was a commander's duty to command, not lead from the front. One wonders what might have happened if the Germans had assassinated Eisenhower as Ike's security men feared once Skorzeny's poison had entered the body of SHAEF. Without that steady hand on the tiller what then might have happened?

In fact the replacement of Hasbrouck was countermanded and the Allied forces pulled back in an ordered fashion. The Germans continued to press southwestward looking for a break in the line and met none. Bastogne absorbed a considerable quantity of German resources and occupied them until Patton broke through. The reserve Montgomery had fought so hard to build was never really applied as he wanted. Lightning Joe Collins started to move forward as soon as he could mass his troops. But they moved forward into victory from an ordered defense line. One could blunt the American offensive spirit but not change it. The Germans and Americans fought a number of actions on the crossroads that might have permitted a northern hook until eventually the Germans collided with British formations in the west. The inspiration for the Werbomont fight was the defense of the Baraque de Fraiture.

In bad terrain, with shortened days and fuel difficulties the Germans only hope for success was a collapse of American morale but this simply did not happen in strength in the north. The pocketing of Peiper early in the campaign summarizes how unrealistic German hopes had been. Had a mere breakthrough been enough to undo the Americans then Peiper might have expected victory. As it was he suffered the embarrassment of being himself cut off and having to retreat, abandoning his equipment. Bradley and Hodges have been criticized for taking the view that the Ardennes was an unlikely place for a breakthrough, but one must in all honesty admit that they had good reason to doubt its qualities. In the end the Ardennes was sound and fury signifying nothing.

And yet, when in 1940 the French generals proclaimed that the Germans would not cross the Meuse, they were so very nearly right. War is like entering a darkened room, one does not know what it is like until one switches on a light—so it is with campaigns. Surprise and élan have sometimes won great victories.

I regret to say that Montgomery did not adopt a retiring mien after the battle, instead issuing some statements that led the Americans to believe that he was insulting their army. Bradley claimed that Montgomery had portrayed himself, "as having single-handedly rescued our shattered American armies." With Montgomery's gift for putting his foot in his mouth and Bradley's thin skin the issue turned toxic very quickly.

Montgomery never did learn the real lesson of coalition warfare, but then neither did Patton nor Bradley. Whatever quality of general he was, Eisenhower had abilities as a *commander* that far outweighed those of his subordinates. It cannot have been a great surprise that he was eventually to become American President and therefore commander-in-chief. One wonders if he preferred politicians to his warring generals.

Hodges died in 1966. After the Bulge he had led his men over the Rhine and been sent to the Far East. Ridgway died a highly decorated officer in 1993 avoiding the unfair fate I have sketched out for him. Montgomery died in 1976 and had continued to argue about his record until his health collapsed. Patton died in 1945 in a car accident—speed was his trademark and once again he arrived before Monty. Eisenhower died in 1969.

Bibliography

The major shape of this article is that of Chester Wilmot's *The Struggle for Europe*. Published in 1952, this is a masterful summary of the ETO by a war correspondent who was embedded before we knew what embedding meant. I cannot recommend it too highly.

Cavanagh, William, *A Tour Of The Bulge Battlefield*, Leo Cooper, Barnsley, 2001.
Delaforce, Patrick, *Monty's Highlanders*, Tom Donovan Publishing, London, 1997.
Delaforce, Patrick, *Taming the Panzers*, Sutton Publishing, Stroud, 1993.
Delaforce, Patrick, *The Black Bull*, Sutton Publishing, Stroud, 1993.
D'Este, Carlo, *Decision in Normandy*, Collins, London, 1993.
MacDonald, Charles, *The Battle of the Bulge*, Weidenfeld & Nicolson, London, 1984.
Slessor, John, *Strategy for the West*, Cassell, London, 1954.
Toland, John, *The Battle of the Bulge*, Frederick Muller, London, 1959.
Wilmot, Chester, *The Struggle for Europe*, Collins, London, 1952.

Notes

1. Said to Trooper Les Slater of 3d Royal Tank Regiment by an American tanker – before offering Slater some fuel. Delaforce, *Taming the Panzers*.
2. Slessor *Strategy for the West*.
3. Patton's witty but cruel view.
4. Horatio Nelson, letter to Lady Hamilton.
5. Carlo D'Este is very useful in explaining the legacy of ill feeling between the allies in his *Decision in Normandy*.
6. The family motto of the Montgomeries – "Watch (or guard) Well."
7. Intelligence appreciation sent to Field Marshal Walther Model see Wilmot.
*8. Paul Carrell, *Decision at Werbomont*, Cologne, 1987.
*9. See *Die Bild* 3 December 1953 (trans.) "The Plot To Assassinate Montgomery."
10. Francis Bacon "Essays".
11. Fred Karno was a notable star of stage amongst whose troupe was to be found a young Charles Chaplin.
12. Lines on the BEF in 1914 by A.E. Housman *Epitaph for an Army of Mercenaries*.
13. The title of Chester Wilmot's chapter on the Bulge in *The Struggle For Europe*.
*14. See Michael Siggins, *Saved by the Cavalry*, London, 1995; Stephen Kosakowski *Betrayed By Montgomery*, Colorado, 2001; and John Foppington, *Chaos: the American Way Of War*, London, 2001.

8

OPERATION *HERBSTNEBEL*
Smoke Over The Ardennes

John Prados

Most observers agree that the Battle of the Ardennes was born in Adolf Hitler's mind in the heat of the 20 July Plot. Certainly 1944 had been a tough year for the German dictator, the hardest yet. Military reverses had ejected his armies from Russia, the Anglo-American Allies had landed on the continent, then broken out of Normandy and were overrunning France. The bomb plot against Hitler himself only confirmed that without some victories the situation would worsen, not only at the front but in German politics. The National Socialist loyalty campaigns Hitler ordered could go just so far in shoring up his support, but if Hitler could turn the tables, win battles and do damage, his political flank would be secured, the *Wehrmacht* would be on the move once again, and he might be able to gain enough time to employ his newest secret weapons effectively.

Though Hitler survived the bomb set off at his headquarters by conspirators he was injured and spent some time bedridden, during which he could ponder the war situation. Not even Hitler was blind to the growing disparity between Nazi Germany and the Allies—speaking to *Wehrmacht* operations staff chief General Alfred Jodl on 31 July Hitler remarked, "an operation in France... is totally impossible in a so-called open field of battle under today's circumstances." He went on, "We can move with some of our troops, but only in a limited manner. With the other ones we can't move, not because we don't possess air superiority, but because we can't move the troops themselves: the units are not suited for mobile battle."[1] As the *Führer*'s thinking evolved, the realization that the *Heer*'s (*German Army's*) capability for mobile warfare was diminished remained with him. Later he understood better the *Luftwaffe*'s incapacity as well. In the context of winning victories, these factors set his boundaries; he had to mount an attack, but it had to be an offensive in which troops with limited mobility could achieve decisive results, while Allied air superiority dictated an attack under poor weather conditions. In addition, assembling the forces to go on the offensive required husbanding new production and gathering reserves, in effect, starving the front, and therefore accepting further territorial losses while preparations were made.

Where to try an offensive also loomed as a key question. In Italy troops that were not mobile could fight easily, but there were no decisive objectives and the most likely outcome was more positional warfare. On the Eastern Front the Russian enemy was so powerful that a force the size Hitler could muster would achieve little but attrite an inexhaustible adversary. That left the West. Attacking in the West had some other attractions for Hitler. The Nazi leader believed that the British and American alliance was unstable and he might drive them apart if he could achieve large enough results. The Allied military command, integrating American and British leaders at every level, might be less flexible than the Russians in responding to a rapidly evolving situation. And, unlike the Russians, the Western Allies did not have a bottomless supply of manpower to replace their losses. Anglo-American logistics capabilities also remained limited due to the continued resistance of German garrisons in a number of the Atlantic coast and English Channel ports which had been bypassed in the breakout and pursuit. The West would be the theater for action.

Orchestrating the Offensive

Talking to Colonel-General Jodl and others on 19 August, Hitler issued orders to begin preparations for an offensive. He specifically envisioned an attack in November, "when the enemy air force cannot fly," using a force of about 25 divisions. The *Armed Forces High Command* staff (*Wehrmachtführungstab*) put out the first directives for an "offensive rebound" the next day.[2] On the 21st German Foreign Minister Joachim von Ribbentrop told the Japanese ambassador not to expect any large-scale German offensive for at least two months, but that after that the creation of new divisions would begin to make one possible. Ribbentrop's off-hand estimate was close to Hitler's actual idea. He also noted that territory taken by the Allies before the attack would not matter because Germany would regain all the ground lost. On 23 August the commander of the *Home Army*, the organization responsible for troop training, similarly informed the *Kriegsmarine* that an offensive was in prospect for November or December. On 2 September Hitler instructed *OKW* to assemble a strategic reserve in the West of 25 divisions. Also at the beginning of September, the *Führer* summoned Field Marshal Gerd von Rundstedt, whom he had previously relieved of command in the West for defeatism, and asked von Rundstedt to resume his post as Commander-in-Chief West (*Oberbefehlshaber West* or *OB West*). Von Rundstedt had earlier gone out with a blast at Hitler—advising the *Führer* to make peace—but now permitted himself to be convinced to return to command, resuming his *OB West* post on 5 September.

Preparations were barely begun when Field Marshal Montgomery's 21st Army Group broke into Belgium and captured Antwerp on 3 September, the same time as the *OKW* concocted its initial plan, which was for an offensive against General George Patton's Third Army in eastern France. When Jodl met Hitler again on 6 September the *Führer* was all for concentrating on the

Vosges mountains, even further to the south. The *Fifth Panzer Army* on that sector continued to attempt offensive operations with whatever forces it could scratch together in service of Hitler's orders. Reinforcements of two somewhat worn-out divisions, *3d* and *15th Panzergrenadier*, were brought up from Italy. They were not especially powerful formations at the time but were at least more troops. Patton's soldiers, who were encountering a rapidly increasing scale of German resistance, were seeing the business end of Hitler's strategic plan.

The *Home Army* proceeded systematically to muster forces in support of the concept. The key would be a new series of divisions, the Volksgrenadiers. These would be units with reduced establishments, less firepower, and personnel from new drafts or combing out of the *Luftwaffe* and *Kriegsmarine*, about 10,000 men per Volksgrenadier division but there were a lot of them. Organization of the units was underway before the end of August. *Home Army* was also creating a series of new, small Panzer brigades, and some horse-drawn artillery corps. On 2 September Hitler ordered that all new production of artillery and assault guns be earmarked for the West and reaffirmed earlier instructions that the bulk of new tanks also be sent there.

Some forces slated for the offensive, such as the *9th* and *10th SS Panzer Divisions*, taken out of the line for rest and replacements just before Montgomery struck with his operation Market-Garden, were inevitably drawn in to the fight for Arnhem in late September. They gave Hitler a defensive victory but at the cost of delaying their refit program. Throughout the period of preparations a constant tension existed between building up reserves and using the gathering forces to intervene in local engagements where important terrain was threatened.

Strategic reconcentration of forces centered on the newly formed *Sixth Panzer Army*, an all-*SS* entity commanded by trusted Nazi General Josef "Sepp" Dietrich, which Hitler ordered on 11 September. Before the end of the month the *OKW* had ordered *9th SS Panzer* out of the line, along with the *1st SS Panzer Division "Leibstandarte Adolf Hitler"*, *2d SS Panzer Division "Das Reich"*, and *12th SS Panzer Division "Hitlerjugend"*, all to be refitted east of the Rhine and subordinated to Dietrich. The battle for Aachen obliged *OKW* to recommit *I SS Panzer Corps* (*1st* and *12th SS*) temporarily in October, but presently they were back in reserve. The *II SS Panzer Corps* (*2d* and *9th SS*) was ordered to be in reserve by 22 October. The Panzer army retrained in Westphalia. *Heer* armored units would also be refitted. The *Panzer Lehr Division* had been ordered into reserve along with the SS but its relief from the front line was delayed by combat. The *11th Panzer Division*'s relief was similarly delayed, and further complicated by lack of railroad rolling stock. At the higher command level, headquarters of the *Fifth Panzer Army* and the *XLVII* and *LVIII Panzer Corps* were similarly withdrawn from the front. The army command went to General Hasso von Manteuffel, an experienced leader of armored troops. Also relieved from front-line duty as quickly as possible once the Arnhem fighting died down were several *Luftwaffe* paratroop divisions.

There remained the question of what to do with the forces *OKW* was accumulating, and how to accomplish anything in the face of Allied air superiority, overall predominance on the ground, and (unknown to the Germans) intelligence advantages from codebreaking. Hitler had at first been inclined to aim his attack at western France and Patton, but that was rather far from the *Sixth Panzer Army* concentration area on the right bank of the Rhine. An offensive build-up would be difficult to accomplish, while the sector was devoid of real strategic objectives, and attack here would not directly effect the split between Americans and British that Hitler hoped to create. In the Low Countries Montgomery's 21st Army Group had just established itself and an offensive might regain the critical port of Antwerp, lost during the period of planning (Antwerp had been captured on 4 September, but its port would not be open until early November, when the Scheldt entrances were captured, and the need for minesweeping delayed an initial convoy up until 28 November), and the British could possibly be dislodged.

Antwerp especially seemed a decisive objective. Its capture would physically divide the 21st Army Group from the American forces in France, much as the Germans had done to the British and French in 1940 at Dunkirk. The separation would instantly bring into play the Anglo-American differences Hitler wanted to use as a wedge to complicate the Western Alliance. In 1940 Germany had attacked through the Ardennes, close to *OKW*'s new concentration areas and where the Allies would not expect an offensive precisely because of the poor terrain. The distance from German positions in the *Westwall* to Antwerp was just over 110 miles, over which the *Wehrmacht*'s less mobile formations could hope to be effective, and which the mobile forces could cover with the least expenditure of Germany's limited fuel resources. At a planning conference on 16 September Hitler tapped a map of the Western Front at this point and declared, "I shall go over to the offensive, that is to say, here, out of the Ardennes, with the objective, Antwerp!"[3]

The idea of an Ardennes offensive was bold—too bold in 1944 even for Germans—and only Hitler's will made it happen. Instructed on 25 September to draft operational plans, the *OKW* operations staff came back with a series of options, none of them Hitler's Ardennes–Antwerp concept. The Antwerp attack option in this scheme would have been launched from Venlo, Holland, north of the Roer, where the front had stabilized. The Ardennes was involved in one option, but it was a more limited one, with attacks out of Luxembourg and from north of Aachen to capture Liège on the Meuse River. A different Luxembourg option involved an attack into northeast France to clear the Saar of Patton's troops, and another attack against Patton from Lorraine formed the fourth possibility. Finally there was an option for an offensive in Alsace. For any of the plans to work Germany had to have a period of 10–14 days of bad weather predicted, a necessary minimum of fuel reserves, and a force of 29–30 divisions. *Army Group B* and the *OKW* reserve would have 2,168 tanks and assault guns plus 1,900 artillery pieces. Jodl counted on rapid destruction of Allied forces along the attacked front to compensate for the fact that *OKW* did not anticipate much ability to supply the attack force from the zone of the interior once the offensive had begun. General Jodl briefed the various plans on 11 October, recommending either the Venlo or Liège options. Hitler accepted the concept for the offensive but bypassed the *OKW* options in favor of his Ardennes– Antwerp attack. Even then opposition did not die away— both Field Marshal von Rundstedt and the frontal commander, Field Marshal Walther Model of *Army Group B*—came back with different proposals. The so-called "Small-Solutions" (*OB West* and *Army Group B* each submitted a variant) envisioned attacks without quite the scope of Hitler's offensive. The *Führer* rejected them all. On 27 October he received the plans and pronounced them "incapable of producing decisive results."[4]

The Ghost Front

The German military leaders may not have been in agreement with Hitler's strategic concept but they proceeded faithfully to execute it. The most important factor in favor of the German offensive would be success in assembling the attacking armies while still achieving surprise. That proved possible due to a very clever deception plan combined with Allied overconfidence and intelligence failures. A second key advantage would be that the Germans were able to assault a lightly defended Allied front. The second advantage would obtain precisely due to German success on the intelligence and deception front.

American forces held the Ardennes and had done so since elements of the 5th U.S. Armored Division had bumped up against the *Westwall* on 11 September. Lieutenant General Courtney H. Hodges' First Army was responsible for the front. Hodges had 14 divisions to cover a sector of 150 miles, within which his forces were concentrated in groupings on his left flank to contribute to the battle for Aachen and fight for the Roer River dams. The only way to cover the ground and also maintain the offensives in progress was to skimp somewhere, and that place became the Ardennes. In a calculated risk there, a frontage of about 65 miles was held by Major General Troy Middleton's VIII Corps, with four divisions on the front and the equivalent of an armored division in reserve. Hodges could have stood down his offensives to reinforce, or reinforcements could be sent by Lieutenant General Omar Bradley of the 12th Army Group, or by General Dwight D. Eisenhower, the commander-in-chief at Supreme Headquarters Allied Expeditionary Forces (SHAEF). Consequently what the Allies knew about German dispositions became more important than ever.

Thanks to sophisticated intelligence the Allies knew a great deal. Codebreakers reading Japanese diplomatic codes reported the earliest conversations between Japanese ambassador Oshima and the German leaders, meaning that the Allies received strategic warning three full months before the offensive. The Dutch resistance reported on the relief from the front of the

Luftwaffe paratroop divisions. Codebreakers working the German codes intercepted and decrypted numerous messages on the formation of *Sixth Panzer Army* and regrouping of its units, even down to the scale of their equipment, as well as scattered messages pertaining to refitting of other Panzer formations. By 11 November the Allies knew that five *Heer* Panzer divisions were being rebuilt in addition to those of the *SS*. Also intercepted, and reinforced by combat intelligence, were instructions to comb out English-speaking troopers and captured equipment for the creation of a special Panzer brigade that could masquerade as an American unit. There were also orders to the *Luftwaffe* to transfer vehicles from its rear services to the parachute divisions, and to furnish dawn fighter cover for unloading at rail yards close to the Ardennes front. Most significant, the *OKW* had planned a rapid concentration of German air units to support the ground attack and the Allies decrypted numerous *Luftwaffe* messages pertaining to preparations for this aspect of the operation, including advance stocking of airfields, anticipation of converting interceptor aircraft to fighter-bomber mode, units involved, concentration of known ground-attack units, and so on, beginning as early as 27 October. Quite revealing *Luftwaffe* messages in late November were also decrypted containing orders for photo reconnaissance of the Meuse River bridges from Namur to Liège and other key portions of the Ardennes.

Hitler's offensive would be made possible by a clever effort to fool the Allies. Realizing that their extensive preparations could not be carried out without the Allies learning *something* about them, the *OKW* concocted a cover plan designed to give the Allies something different to believe in. The plan, *Wacht am Rhein*, made it seem the German efforts were to assemble forces for a spoiling attack that could break up an Allied offensive across the North German Plain. The deception plan proved highly successful. Allied intelligence analyses were full of discussions of the probable German spoiling attack, speculations as to its timing or locale or the events that might trigger it. Passage of time was also a factor—as more days passed with no sign of the German attack it began to seem remote. Continued Allied military success filled staffs with overconfidence as well. Predicting how soon the Allies might reach Berlin seemed more useful than estimating the German spoiling attack than never seemed to materialize. The closest to divining German intentions were the G-2 intelligence staff of First U.S. Army, which on 10 December predicted a German attack, albeit north of the Ardennes. Even that staff did not follow through, however, and its subsequent analyses stepped back on 15 December to speak of "a limited scale offensive... for the purpose of achieving a Christmas morale 'victory.'"[5]

Adolf Hitler kept his finger on both the *Wacht am Rhein* deception and on the attack preparations. He was in on every decision, down to tactical arrangements such as the length of pre-assault artillery bombardment, whether there should be night attacks, or whether Panzers should be committed to stiffen the infantry in certain sectors. Some 20,000 tons of fuel were allocated for the offensive: 8,000 tons to carry the armies to the Meuse, an equal amount to reach Antwerp, and 4,000 tons for a fuel reserve. A hundred trains a day were headed for the West. On 6 November the *Sixth Panzer Army* began deploying to assembly areas closer to the Ardennes. In a typical exchange with Colonel-General Jodl on the same day, Hitler got the operations staff chief to point out the attack sector.

"No changes on the whole front," Jodl explained. "It is still just the American V Corps, with thin occupation; there are about four divisions in the whole corps sector."

After further discussion, Hitler came back to the subject and spoke wonderingly, "Twenty kilometers per division!" Then: "One can only imagine, if we consider our own proportions: the attack against Verdun at that time took place with 7 divisions on a front of — km. Here there are — divisions on 11 km."[6]

Actually the V U.S. Corps, on the immediate left flank of Middleton's VIII, began an offensive of its own against the Roer River dams on 16 November.

But there was so much to do that the Germans could not meet the planned date of 25 November for the offensive. On the 23d Hitler met with von Rundstedt and Model, the army commanders, Sepp Dietrich of the *Sixth Panzer Army*, Hasso von Manteuffel of the *Fifth Panzer Army*, and Erich Brandenberger of the *Seventh Army*, and their chiefs of staff and agreed to postpone the operation until 10 December. The group made final plans for deployment to the attack sector. Movement at night, Panzers to be kept back from the front, and a move to the line of departure only just before the assault were all laid on. Model issued a directive for the attack by *Army Group B* on 25 November. The code-name for the offensive would be *Herbstnebel* (Autumn Mist). A further conference with Hitler took place on 2 December when Model made a last plea for the "small solution" but the *Führer* would have none of it. That same day *Sixth Panzer Army* commanders held a wargame exercise to rehearse their plans. At the last moment Hitler pushed *Herbstnebel* back to 15 December, when weather was predicted to turn worse for a longer period, and in the end he would authorize one more postponement of 24 hours. The offensive armies assumed responsibility for logistics in the Ardennes sector on 8 December, and tactical command of the front on the 11th.

The *Führer* justified himself to senior officers, the higher commanders and division leaders in a secret speech at Ziegenberg given on 12 December, the day after headquarters moved there in preparation for the big show. After lengthy historical explanations for why Germany had to prevail, and exhortations to the generals ("It is important to rob the enemy of his certainty of victory from time to time, and to show him through offensive strikes that his plans are doomed"), Hitler argued that "wars are finally decided by the recognition on one side or the other that the war can't be won any more," that official reports had shown that the Americans alone had lost 240,000 men ("These numbers are just gigantic") since the invasion, "far higher than we thought they would lose," and that the Allied coalition consisted of "heterogeneous elements with... extremely different and conflicting goals."

"Now gentlemen," Hitler continued, "I have accepted sacrifices on other fronts—which weren't necessary—to create the necessary conditions that will allow us to move forward offensively." The *Führer* discounted the differences between 1940 and 1944, and minimized Germany's difficulties: "For the upcoming offensive we don't have only first-class units available. But on the enemy side they are not all first-class units either." Victory or death was what the crisis demanded.[7]

Breakout and Pursuit

Herbstnebel went into execution at 0530 of X-Day, 16 December, with a half-hour artillery preparation. The troops then began to edge forward. American commanders were shocked, Germans were ecstatic. On the *Sixth Panzer Army* sector infantry and engineers composed the first wave. The surprise proved such that U.S. artillery needed two hours to organize defensive fires. Dietrich had four Panzer divisions plus a parachute and four infantry divisions on a front of less than 20 miles. Manteuffel of *Fifth Panzer Army* included armor in his leading waves to hasten the break-in of the American front. His army had three Panzer and four infantry divisions with a front of roughly 25 miles. The U.S. 28th Infantry Division on this sector managed some local counterattacks. A third German formation, General Erich Brandenberger's *Seventh Army*, with a parachute and three infantry divisions to cover a front of about 20 miles, moved forward to protect the left flank of the mobile forces. Elements of the 28th and 4th U.S. Infantry Divisions defended their strongpoints fiercely in this sector, but were still hampered by the surprise of the German attack.

American positions in the Ardennes had certain advantages, but also some disadvantages. From north to south the front was characterized by distinct terrain features. On the north side the U.S. left flank was anchored on the Elsenborn Ridge, where both the 2d and 99th Infantry Divisions were present due to unit relief and American concentration for the Roer attacks. Here the Americans benefited from both high ground and a series of villages to aid the defense. To the south of this position was the Losheim Gap held by the 14th Armored Cavalry Group, a sector that opened to good tank country and represented a weak point. South of here was the 106th Infantry Division, a brand new formation with two of its three regiments occupying part of the *Westwall* the Americans had captured in the Schnee Eifel. Its third regiment connected with the 28th Division. This sector rested on the Our River, whose strong current and high banks made it a good defensive position. The 4th Infantry and a combat command of the 9th U.S. Armored Division completed the defenses, also holding the Our and Sauer River lines. Behind the front the Ardennes as a whole were characterized by a limited network of narrow roads, water barriers as difficult as the Our, heavy forest, and hill and valley terrain gradually sloping down to the Meuse River, whose crossings were dominated by the cities of Liège and Namur and the smaller towns of Huy, Dinant and

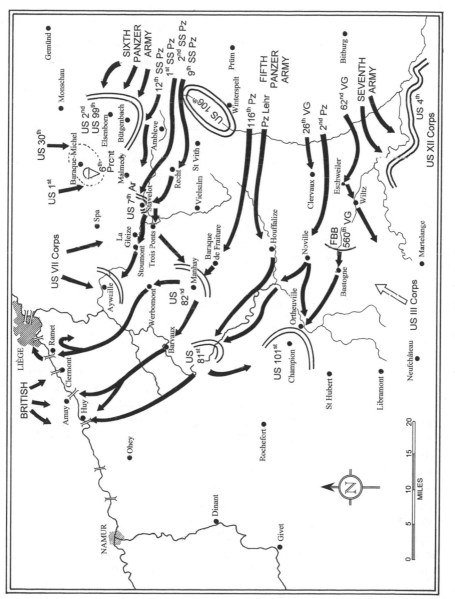

Operation Herbstnebel

Givet. The Meuse had formed a barrier to Germany in 1914 and 1940 and it would do so again. Beyond that river the terrain opened up toward Antwerp, though numerous rivers and canals broke up the going for motorized forces.

The attack began with great expectations. Lieutenant General Hermann Preiss' *I SS Panzer Corps*, with two Volksgrenadier divisions plus *3d Paratroop* on the line and *1st* and *12th SS Panzer* echeloned behind them, went in against the Elsenborn Ridge and Losheim Gap. Within an hour and a half Preiss was reporting that everything was progressing well but he was wrong. The *277th Volksgrenadier* attack on Elsenborn bogged down, and its assault company was late arriving, giving the Americans time to recover. Elements of the *12th Volksgrenadiers* came in on the flank to extend the attack but the Americans held the line, establishing the northern shoulder of what would eventually become a huge bulge in the front. Even the commitment of *Kampfgruppe* (Battlegroup) *Müller* of *12th SS* Panzer, was not able to lever out the Americans from their defenses.

The remainder of *12th SS* Panzer would be inserted into the line to the right of the infantry, striking into the American rear. This depended on opening the Losheim Gap, a task assigned to *3d Paratroop Division*, fighting with the 14th U.S. Armored Cavalry. A road overpass near Losheim collapsed under artillery fire and *1st SS Panzer* engineers had to reconstruct it. The advance was also slowed by an old German minefield the planners had not noticed. Nevertheless, the path was opened for *Kampfgruppe Peiper* (Lieutenant Colonel Jochen Peiper) to break through into the rear. Peiper thought the roads more suitable for bicycles than tanks, but his unit would play a key role in the offensive.

How the Americans reacted to the attacks figured critically in the potential for Hitler's offensive. Only limited reserves were available to General Hodges and First Army. The surprise attack prevented Hodges immediately realizing how serious the situation was, but he took prudent countermeasures. A regiment of the 1st U.S. Infantry Division was ordered down from the north, and it could have successfully blocked *Kampfgruppe Peiper* had it arrived in time. The Germans had taken precautions, however, laying on a special operation, code-named *Stösser*, in which 870 paratroops of the *6th Paratroop Regiment* (Colonel Freiherr von der Heydte) were landed on a drop zone near Baraque Michel on the night of 15 December.

The air drop turned out to be virtually the last act before the weather closed in and made flying impossible. In fact, the major *Luftwaffe* fighter strike prepared so carefully for months had to be postponed on the actual day of the attack. The Germans gladly exchanged that support for a sky clear of Allied aircraft, however, a trade decidedly to their advantage. Bad weather would cripple Allied air operations until Christmas Day.

In any case, the 26th Infantry of the U.S. 1st Division, speeding south into the breakthrough zone, ran into von der Heydte's paratroops. Instead of creating a barrier to further German advance, the American infantry were pulled into a firefight with the German airborne troops. A special unit, the

506th Panzer Battalion with eight monster Tiger II tanks, came to the support of von der Heydte and enabled the German paratroops to hold back the Americans on the northern flank for a critical 48 hours.

Meanwhile on the *Fifth Panzer Army* front the *18th Volksgrenadier Division*, reinforced by an assault gun brigade, had also attacked into the Losheim Gap. It broke into the rear of the American 106th Division, two regiments of which were trapped in their *Westwall* positions when the *26th Volksgrenadiers* also broke through to the south of them. Assault across the Our River was critically slowed, however. At first only infantry weapons, then some motorcycles and Volkswagens could be ferried across one by one. Only by mid-afternoon were the engineers, hampered by the strong current, able to complete a bridge. Then the *2d Panzer Division* began to cross in force. Elements of the 110th Infantry Regiment of the 28th U.S. Division, and Combat Command R of the 9th Armored, were able to mount a counterattack outside Clervaux, the first significant American reaction of the campaign. Major fighting developed around the villages of Marnach and Kacherey as the Americans committed more forces. Spurred by the emergency, *2d Panzer Division* accelerated its arrival on the battlefield, broke up the U.S. attack, and captured Clervaux in the evening. Behind it the *116th Panzer Division* had also begun crossing the Our and positioning itself to attack. On *2d Panzer*'s right the *Panzer Lehr Division* was coming into play as well. By the end of the day the Americans had sustained heavy casualties and their 9th Division armor had essentially been played out.

On the *Seventh Army* front *5th Paratroop* and *352d Volksgrenadier Divisions* spearheaded the attack against the 109th Infantry of the 28th U.S. Division. The paratroopers had to ferry across the Our, and Brandenberger's army was deficient in bridging equipment. Even so the Germans quickly overran Weiler and bypassed other American strongpoints. A key objective was Diekirch, but here the Americans quickly concentrated Combat Command A of the 9th Armored Division and the Germans slowed down. A southern shoulder for the bulge began to form here.

Although German forces were on the move throughout the Ardennes, spotty reporting, confusion, and outdated assumptions about the strategic situation hindered the Allied command in understanding the extent of the German offensive. Only on the second day did General Middleton at VIII Corps realize he had come up against a major frontal offensive. Middleton had already ordered in his last reserve, Combat Command B of the 9th Armored Division, to restore contact with the two regiments of the 106th Division that were being cut off in the *Westwall*. Appeals to First Army for reinforcements brought dispatch of the 1st Infantry Division and the 7th Armored Division but the 1st Division was critically slowed by the German airborne drop, and the 7th Armored, ordered to St Vith, a critical road junction behind the front, would encounter troubles of its own. Combat Command R of the 7th was speeding south and approaching the village of Malmedy, setting the stage for a key battle.

The Germans thought they had enough fuel to reach Antwerp but there could be no doubt fuel was a problem, and there was little assurance that fuel stored in rear areas would reach the front. The Americans had fuel depots in the villages of Büllingen and Stavelot in the *Sixth Panzer Army* sector. Dietrich wanted that gasoline, *1st SS Panzer Division* was ordered to get it. *Kampfgruppe Peiper* got to Büllingen successfully, then moved through Faymonville and Waimes toward Stavelot, but on approaching the objective Peiper encountered Combat Command R of the 7th Armored Division, which was on its way toward St Vith. That left the task to *Kampfgruppe Hansen* (Colonel Max Hansen) of *1st SS*. Hansen's battlegroup had driven through Amblève and Recht, where he brushed aside CCB of 9th Armored, then turned north toward Stavelot, where he ran into the remainder of 7th Armored Division. The biggest tank battle in the initial phase of the campaign would take place here on 18 December.

At noon on the 17th General Dietrich issued movement orders to *II SS Panzer Corps* (Lieutenant General Wilhelm Bittrich) with *2d* and *9th SS Panzer Divisions*. Bittrich was to activate Brigadier General Sylvester Stadler's *9th SS Panzer*, which slipped in to the right of the *Leibstandarte*. Moving through Amblève, Stadler's reconnaissance troops found elements of Combat Command B of the 9th Armored, which Troy Middleton had now ordered to secure the junction at St Vith. Stadler instantly turned his division toward the junction and, in the evening of the 17th, Stadler's 40 Mark IV and 48 Panther tanks smashed Combat Command B. He then turned north, coming up on the flank of the Americans engaged with *1st SS Panzer*. As 18 December dawned, the 7th Armored already had its hands full with the battlegroups of *1st SS* when, three hours into the battle, *9th SS* barreled into its left flank. The American tankers were forced to retreat north of Stavelot and assume defensive positions. In the midst of battle part of the American fuel dump was destroyed but the rest fell into German hands.[8]

Major American reinforcements arrived that day in the shape of the 30th Infantry Division, which was inserted into the line to link the 7th Armored with the 1st Infantry, extending American defenses along the northern face of the bulge and preventing a German eruption into the First and Ninth U.S. Army rear areas behind Aachen. Local counterattacks around Malmedy were the most the Americans could manage.

Along the *Fifth Panzer Army* front 18 December would be the day the Germans really broke into the open. Manteuffel had steadily increased his pressure on the U.S. VIII Corps defenses through 17 December, grinding forward and bringing more forces to bear. The *116th Panzer*, *26th* and *62d Volksgrenadier Divisions* brought their weight to bear, capturing the towns of Wiltz and Eschweiler. The army's left pincer, based on *Panzer Lehr*, had its way smoothed by the fall of St Vith to Dietrich's Panzers. Not having to mount an attack for that key road junction, *Panzer Lehr* covered half the distance to Houffalize. Manteuffel left headquarters to visit the command post of Colonel Günther Hoffman-Schonborn's *18th Volksgrenadiers*, now his left flank unit.

The *560th Volksgrenadier Division* and *Führer Begleit Brigade* (*Begleit* = Escort) had been kept in army reserve for a St Vith attack, and Manteuffel now released them to speed the advance.

On the American side, Troy Middleton's VIII Corps had been largely destroyed. Combat engineers and military police, plus a few remnants of the 28th Division were all he had left to defend the key junction of Bastogne, where his headquarters was located. As a precaution he moved HQ to Neufchâteau. On 18 December Middleton received a key reinforcement, the 10th Armored Division (Major General William H. Morris, Jr.) sent from Patton's Third Army. Middleton ordered Morris to defend Bastogne.

The arrival of 10th Armored represented the beginning of the SHAEF strategic response to the *Herbstnebel* offensive. General Eisenhower had now ordered a major redeployment, with offensive operations on other sectors discontinued, Ninth Army to take over part of the First Army area of operations north of the bulge, and First Army to pull back its VII Corps and send it into the Ardennes from the north. Patton was to send up his XII Corps from the south, 10th Armored was the first wave of that movement. Eisenhower also released XVIII Airborne Corps from SHAEF reserve and ordered it to the battle front.

Much depended on whether the momentum of the German attacks could be slowed, and 10th Armored was critical here. But Morris had no time to organize a defense of Bastogne. Manteuffel's *XLVII* and *LVIII Panzer Corps* were arriving on the scene as quickly as he did. Combat Command B of the 10th, the lead element, split into several groups of battalion size to cover different road approaches to Bastogne, with a couple of engineer battalions stiffening the defenses. Reconnaissance troops of *2d Panzer Division* discovered the Americans when they neared Noville, sent back word, and the division then hit with most of its 120 tanks and assault guns. The fresh *Führer Begleit Brigade* (Colonel Otto Remer) attacked down the Longvilly road with armor almost as strong as a division—43 tanks and assault guns plus a further 28 assault guns with an attached unit. The *26th Volksgrenadier Division* came through in the intervals. The Germans simply had too much strength. Through a long day they leaked past the American posts, and *2d Panzer* broke through from Noville at 3:00 p.m. Morris ordered Combat Command B to withdraw down the road to Neufchâteau. The following elements of his division halted and assumed position on the southern face of the bulge.

The American fight for Bastogne had the important consequence that it gained most of a day. During that time the 101st Airborne Division (Brigadier General Anthony McAuliffe in acting command), which had also been ordered to Bastogne, got most of the way there. Remer's brigade, exploiting to the west, ran into elements of the 101st near Ortheuville as darkness fell. McAuliffe deployed his troops for a desperate defense that night. Colonel Meinert von Lauchert reoriented his *2d Panzer Division* and struck out cross-country toward Bertogne. Meanwhile Major General Fritz Bayerlein's *Panzer Lehr Division* had a clear run west through Houffalize, reaching La Roche by that night. In the *LVIII Panzer Corps* area, *116th Panzer* moved west through Vielsalm to reach Baraque Fraiture.

Eisenhower's other strategic reinforcement, the 82d Airborne Division (Major General James M. Gavin), had been ordered to St Vith but that town fell long before the division could reach the battle area. It began to deploy on the night of the 18th around Manhay and sent one regiment to Hotton. Manteuffel would face serious resistance the next day. On 19 December the *Führer Begleit Brigade* attempted to cross the Ourthe River and move through Ortheuville but was stopped cold by 101st Airborne. The *Panzer Lehr* reached Hotton but encountered more American airborne troops and had to halt, while *116th Panzer* was stopped outside Manhay by the rest of the 82d Airborne. The *2d Panzer* moved up the valley of the Ourthe, nearing Hotton that night. By this point Manteuffel's Panzers had far outrun his infantry and new arrangements had become necessary.

Along the *Seventh Army* front, General Brandenberger had a hard time keeping up with the thrusting Panzer spearheads. American resistance was stiffening perceptibly as Major General Manton S. Eddy's XII Corps began arriving from Patton's army. Though not fully on line until 21 December, Eddy's three divisions gave the Americans a coherent defense along the southern face of the bulge. Brandenberger simply ran out of forces. Manteuffel's *18th* and *62d Volksgrenadier Divisions* had to be committed on this flank to extend the German line out to Bastogne.

Meanwhile there was Dietrich's *Sixth Panzer Army* in the north. On 19 December the *3d Paratroop Division* relieved *12th SS* Panzer at the heel of the bulge so that mobile unit could get back in play. The key here, however, was the grouping of mobile formations around Stavelot. The *3d Panzergrenadier Division* was committed here to free the armor, and *9th SS* Panzer began moving to cross the Salm River at Trois Ponts. The Germans' good fortune was limited, though. At Trois Ponts stood Company C of the 51st Engineer Combat Battalion, which had wired two of the three bridges for demolition. The Germans had another element to bring into play, Operation *Greif*, a set of special assault commando teams drawn from the English-speakers of the *150th Panzer Brigade*, who were supposed to function in exactly these sorts of situations. Fanning out behind American lines with the initial breakthroughs, the teams were to ensure that important bridges were not destroyed before the exploitation forces crossed them. One of these teams reached Trois Ponts but the Americans caught the *Greif* men trying to cut cables on one of the bridges and shot them. When General Stadler's *9th SS* spearhead appeared, the Americans duly blew the bridges and the German advance halted.

Dietrich's bridging equipment had fallen behind during the advance and was now interspersed among the marching columns of the *12th SS*. Just getting it forward would take another day. Only then could a new bridge be erected.

The very limited road network of the Ardennes cost the German offensive dearly. The other element of Bittrich's corps, *2d SS Panzer Division* (Major

General Heinz Lammerding) had not so far been able to get into action at all. On 19 December it finally came up, but only by moving through Vielsalm and taking off cross-country on the west bank of the Salm. Both *Sixth* and *Fifth Panzer Armies* had had to enter each other's command areas in order to find their ways forward.

Meanwhile the *1st SS Panzer Division*, reconcentrated at Stavelot, took off up the Amblève River valley toward La Gleize. By now the units of U.S. VII Corps (Major General J. Lawton Collins) had begun to appear from the north. Elements of the 3d Armored Division (Major General Maurice Rose) and 30th Infantry Division (Major General Leland S. Hobbs) were closing into the La Gleize area as the *1st SS* arrived there, led by *Kampfgruppe Peiper*. On 19 December Peiper was repulsed with heavy losses. The German Panzers drew off to lick their wounds and prepare for the next day.

A Day of Battle

The battle of La Gleize headlined Sepp Dietrich's efforts on 20 December. Peiper led off at dawn with a fresh assault but strengthened American troops stopped him cold. At mid-morning *Kampfgruppe Hansen* joined in for a combined assault. Battle raged for hours. In the late afternoon Colonel Hugo Kraas' *12th SS* Panzer began arriving and went into the attack off the march. Peiper tried a flank attack through the villages of Bergoumont and Monthouet, taking the brunt of counterattacks from two task forces of the 3d Armored Division. Peiper had to be reinforced by troops from *12th SS*, while others fought hand-to-hand in La Gleize. By midnight the Americans were in retreat toward Stoumont. Peiper's battlegroup, once the pride of *1st SS*, had been reduced to less than half its original strength.

At Trois Ponts the *9th SS* got infantry across the Salm and drove the U.S. engineers out of the town. In the afternoon German pioneers arrived with their bridging equipment and began work both on a pontoon bridge and on restoring the span the Americans had blown up. Stadler's Panzers began rolling once again just before noon of 21 December.

Manteuffel, faced with concentrated resistance at Manhay and with no forces at hand to stiffen his *116th Panzer Division*, had gone to *Army Group B* and asked Field Marshal Model to direct *Sixth Panzer Army* to support him. Model did so, with the result that Lammerding's *2d SS Panzer Division* combined with *116th*, attacking from the northeast as *116th* assaulted from the southeast. The American airborne troops resisted fiercely. The battle of Manhay raged throughout the day and night.

In Manteuffel's center the *Panzer Lehr Division* made a concentrated assault on Hotton. Here the Aisne River valley was extremely narrow, and Fritz Bayerlein could not deploy his formations effectively. Americans of the 508th Parachute Infantry Regiment slowly pulled back in the face of Bayerlein's assault—though *Panzer Lehr* could not deploy, Bayerlein's attack still benefited from tank support and the airborne troops had only limited heavy weapons. By late afternoon Bayerlein was coming into more open country to the north and west of Hotton, threatening an encirclement of the U.S. position. Colonel Reuben H. Tucker, the U.S. commander, reluctantly decided to retreat. To preserve his potential to cooperate with the remainder of the 82d Division, he moved north toward Barvaux. This opened the road to the Meuse to the Germans.

Meanwhile the *Führer Begleit Brigade* made no progress against the "Screaming Eagles" of McAuliffe's 101st Airborne Division. In the afternoon of the 20th the first troops of Colonel Heinz Kokott's *26th Volksgrenadier Division* came up in support and toward nightfall the infantry succeeded in crossing the Ourthe River on McAuliffe's left flank. Leapfrogging forward, the grenadiers began to outflank the Americans while Remer's Panzers kept the pressure up on their front. At 10:00 p.m. General McAuliffe was forced to order a retreat to Champion, leaving a battalion of the 502d Parachute Infantry as a rearguard. The American paratroopers held on to Ortheuville until dawn, when they made an orderly retreat behind McAuliffe's new defense line. Remer's armor pursued cautiously.

Manteuffel's real problem was now his left flank. When Eisenhower had ordered George Patton to send a corps from Third Army up in support of the bulge defenders, the dynamic Patton had rejected half-measures and argued instead that he pivot two entire corps to the north. The SHAEF commander-in-chief accepted the idea. Patton's XII Corps had shored up the defenses, but his III Corps (Major General John Millikin) provided a real offensive mass with the 4th and 6th Armored Divisions and the 26th and 35th Infantry Divisions. On 20 December the 4th Armored and 26th Infantry arrived to begin hitting the southern face of the bulge on *Fifth Panzer Army*'s sector. Here the *62d Volksgrenadier Division* was hard-pressed to hold back these energetic counterattacks.

This day of fighting had witnessed great losses on both sides and had major implications for the campaign. On Dietrich's front the *I SS Panzer Corps* had taken La Gleize but was now able only to slog forward toward Stoumont against Lawton Collins' VII U.S. Corps. Beyond Stoumont were more high hills and narrow valleys, but the terrain opened up past Aywaille, less than ten miles ahead. After that would be Liège. Bittrich was in somewhat better shape with his *II SS Panzer Corps*, whose *9th SS Panzer Division* was at Trois Ponts and poised to advance the following day. Its road through Chevron and Werbomont was open, though a crossing of the Ourthe River still lay ahead. Bittrich's other division, *2d SS Panzer*, together with *Fifth Panzer Army*'s *116th Panzer*, was locked in battle at Manhay. Manteuffel led the Manhay battle. West of there, *Panzer Lehr Division* had opened a road to exploit to the Meuse. Manteuffel needed to broaden that opening but the Americans defending Champion prevented this. The slow pace of the infantry was holding back the potential of Manteuffel's Panzers. At the same time a major American threat had now materialized from the south with the appearance on Patton's III Corps. The previous day *OKW* had released the *Führer Grenadier Brigade* from high command reserve, and *Army Group B* had directed *Fifteenth Army* at

Aachen to send its *246th Volksgrenadier Division* to the attack front. Both these formations would be committed against Patton. The major units left in *OKW* reserve were now the *10th SS* and *11th Panzer Divisions*. Field Marshal Model would release the *79th Volksgrenadier Division* from *Army Group B* reserve on 21 December. This unit would be deployed to extend the northern face of the bulge.

General Eisenhower and his subordinates faced an equally complex and very threatening situation. The Germans could not be permitted to reach the Meuse but blocking them seemed almost impossible. Ike had faced up to realities and on 20 December reorganized the commands to give all forces north of the bulge to British Field Marshal Bernard L. Montgomery, keeping those to the south under command of Bradley's 12th Army Group. Montgomery began ordering troops from British XXX Corps to the Meuse line. Meanwhile Collins' VII Corps had another division coming up, and that was ordered to the Aywaille area. The 82d Airborne received orders to abandon Manhay and disperse its regiments to ensure at least a modicum of blocking forces on several routes the Germans might use. This resulted in a defense line of sorts along the Ourthe, with the U.S. paratroopers stiffened by small units of tank destroyers, field artillery, and engineers that had come up over the past couple of days. The hope was to hold off the Germans long enough to deploy the British forces, and buy time for Patton's counter-offensive to become effective. The Battle of the Bulge was approaching its climax.

On to the Meuse

As *Fifth Panzer Army* stood poised to forge ahead to the Meuse, its spearheads were subject to a very real threat from the rear. The stand of McAuliffe's 101st Airborne Division around Champion effectively left open a road into the heart of the German position. While the Americans scrambled to build a front this did not matter, but with George Patton coming up from the south it became important. Manteuffel could have organized his own defense of the Ourthe River line, along the axis Hotton–Houffalize, but he lacked the forward-deployed infantry to do that. The easier solution would be to capture Champion and seal off this avenue of advance. General Heinrich von Lüttwitz of *XLVII Panzer Corps* was put in charge of this operation on 21 December. To effect it, Lüttwitz would commit *560th Volksgrenadier Division* to reinforce the *26th Volksgrenadiers* and Remer's *Führer Begleit Brigade* driving on Champion from the east. Lüttwitz also ordered Fritz Bayerlein to detach a battle group from *Panzer Lehr* and take the Champion position from the rear. The strategy was impeccable.

German pressure against the "Screaming Eagles" built rapidly. McAuliffe shuffled troops to meet a succession of attacks and was doing well when bad news arrived. A dispatch rider coming from Paris with documents from SHAEF had been riding through Marche-en-Famenne, about ten miles in the division's rear, on the morning of 21 December, when he saw German troops approaching that town from the direction of Hotton. Assuming these Germans would turn toward Champion, McAuliffe's 101st Airborne Division suddenly needed an almost all-around defense. He ordered some combat engineers, a tank destroyer unit, and two battalions of the 501st Parachute Infantry to prepare positions along the hill line west of the town. It was about 2:00 p.m. when Lieutenant Colonel Joachim Ritter von Poschinger's battle group made contact. *Kampfgruppe Poschinger* was built around the *902d Panzergrenadier Regiment* plus two tank companies and other elements. Von Poschinger went straight into attack mode and gained some ground against the American paratroopers.

Meanwhile, Colonel Remer launched an attack of his own, combining with the fresh *560th Panzergrenadiers*, which pressed the Americans sorely. By noon McAuliffe had expended the American reserves. By 4:00 p.m., attacked from two sides, the "Screaming Eagles" were under intense pressure. The Germans thought they could bag another formation, as they had with the 106th Division in the *Westwall* so Remer sent officers under a flag of truce to offer the Americans surrender terms. McAuliffe kept the German plenipotentiaries in the cold outside his headquarters. After about a quarter of an hour he emerged and rasped a simple reply to their demand, "Nuts!"

The Germans, blindfolded, were sent back to their lines.

By then it was after 5:00 p.m. and dusk was approaching. Remer resumed attacking. Word of McAuliffe's response spread like wildfire among the American positions and the paratroopers fought like wild men. *Führer Begleit Brigade* made no progress at all, while *Kampfgruppe Poschinger* was driven back with a loss of four Panther tanks.

That night Colonel von Poschinger tried a novel maneuver, dismounting one of his rifle battalions and sending it tramping through the wooded hills to block the Champion–St Hubert road, McAuliffe's last route to the outside. At dawn a passing U.S. supply convoy spotted the Germans descending toward the road. McAuliffe scraped up a battalion of the 327th Glider Infantry Regiment to secure the road and a sharp firefight erupted to the south of Champion.

German troops now attacked all along the perimeter and McAuliffe had nothing left to throw in. Reluctantly he determined to make a fighting withdrawal to St Hubert. The 101st Airborne Division abandoned Champion at 1:30 p.m. on 22 December.

The defense of Champion gained the Americans vital time, however. By now Patton had an additional division on line, with plentiful supplies and artillery support. McAuliffe withdrew towards these reinforcements and was able to turn around immediately and join in a steady push against the German bulge. The forces that had overwhelmed Champion were obliged almost straight away to switch over to defending a new defensive line Ourtheville–Champion–Hargimont.

The remaining units of *Panzer Lehr* had been prepared to exploit out of Hotton on 21 December. Bayerlein did so, only to encounter the new U.S.

defense of the Ourthe at Grandhan that morning. There was only a battalion of paratroopers defending the town, but they fought hard and *Panzer Lehr*, short of ammunition, was unable to use its artillery to full effect. *Panzer Lehr* managed to cross the Ourthe River only the next day. The *116th Panzer Division* moved through Manhay on the 21st, finding the U.S. 82d Airborne had disappeared overnight, but found the Americans again on the Ourthe at Bomal. Again the division had to deploy for an attack.

The *2d SS Panzer Division* also left Manhay, north toward Werbomont, where it encountered a full regiment of the 82d primed for defense. This time the Germans did better. The *9th SS*, the other division of *II SS Panzer Corps*, had left Trois Ponts and came up on Werbomont from the east. The combined might of Bittrich's Panzers ejected the Americans from the town. The 82d fell back behind the Ourthe, which *II SS Panzer Corps* reached on 22 December. Meanwhile, *I SS Panzer Corps* fought for Stoumont on the northernmost axis of the German advance. Its grinding battle against VII Corps continued. On 22 December the corps broke into the open, with *1st SS Panzer* heading for Aywaille, and *12th SS* for Harze. When *1st SS* reached Aywaille it found Brigadier General Robert C. Macon's 84th Infantry Division already in position. *Kampfgruppe Hansen* was unable to break through, and *Kampfgruppe Peiper* now lacked strength to do more than fix the Americans in place. The *1st SS Panzer Division* went over to the defense.

The German high command realized its offensive forces were weakened from losses and acted to reinvigorate the offensive. On 22 December *Army Group B* directed the *Fifteenth Army* to release the *9th Panzer* and *15th Panzergrenadier Divisions*. Moving from a front remote from the bulge, however, it would be some time until these forces could make their weight felt.

Now the campaign approached its climax, with the focus on the center of the bulge. On 23 December, Germans of both Panzer armies launched concentric attacks to overwhelm the Ourthe River line. The 82d Airborne Division had conducted a lengthy fighting retreat, but by now its commander, General Gavin, had his troops stretched thinly and they had suffered tremendous losses. When the Germans attacked in strength the line along the Ourthe simply collapsed. Remnants of the 82d retreated behind the Meuse.

At this point the Germans brought into play their special unit, the *150th Panzer Brigade*. The unit had been following along behind the *II SS Panzer Corps*. Led by commando specialist Colonel Otto Skorzeny, the *150th* was equipped with a mixture of German and captured Allied equipment, and now it was thrown forward to help capture the Meuse River bridge at Ramet. The *150th* approached with its two M4 Sherman tanks in the lead, followed by a number of American half-tracks and trucks. The bridge was defended by elements of the 309th Engineer Combat Battalion, who saw nothing amiss as Skorzeny's troops closed in. Suddenly German fire erupted in all directions against the defenders, driving the engineers away from the bridge. Only an hour behind Skorzeny came the lead elements of Lammerding's *2d SS Panzer*

Division, the freshest of the German armor, which still had 110 of its original 134 tanks and assault guns. By midnight, Christmas Eve, Germany had a bridgehead across the Meuse with most of Lammerding's troops across.

The *9th SS Panzer Division* made directly for Liège but it ran into the British 29th Armoured Brigade in the eastern suburbs and was unable to reach the Meuse bridges. General Bittrich ordered the division to leave a covering force behind, then head for Ramet and cross the Meuse there, afterwards advancing against Liège on the west bank of the Meuse. Hitler's early planning had been that the Panzer forces should avoid fighting for the city, leaving it to infantry and assault engineers, but as the campaign had proceeded Liège had loomed larger and larger, and now there was no infantry unit within reach. Bittrich made a try for Liège on Christmas Day, just as the British 53d Infantry Division and 33d Armoured Brigade arrived on the scene. Hitler would not receive Liège for his Christmas present.[9]

On the *Fifth Panzer Army* front, the *116th Panzer Division* made it to the river and crossed at Amay. The wait for follow-on forces would be a lengthy one. One of the two new mobile divisions had been diverted to face Patton. The other, *9th Panzer* had 75 armored fighting vehicles, a tower of strength compared to *Panzer Lehr*. Bayerlein was now down to just 20 tanks. Arrayed along the Meuse these formations were miles ahead of their support. On Christmas Day also the weather cleared and Allied air forces attacked everywhere, further complicating the movement of fuel and ammunition to the advance forces.

On 24 December *Army Group B* ordered in a corps of two Volksgrenadier divisions. One was going to have to fill the gap between the *I SS Panzer Corps* units around Aywaille, the other could help relieve the *SS* Panzers in the Ramet bridgehead, but the German mobile forces simply lacked the strength to make it all the way to Antwerp. In addition, the campaign in the Ardennes had consumed far more fuel than anticipated, even with the supplies captured from the Americans. While the weakened armor might have been able to make Antwerp with the remaining fuel, they would have little ability to maneuver and might not be able to return if they attained the Antwerp position.

At a difficult map conference on Christmas Day at his western headquarters in Ziegenberg, Adolf Hitler made the reluctant decision to suspend the *Herbstnebel* offensive. He sweetened the bitter pill by returning to the idea of an attack in Lorraine. Orders to the *Fifth* and *Sixth Panzer Armies* to go over to the defensive were increasingly necessary. By 26 December the scale of forces opposite the Germans on the Meuse had built up to three British divisions and the equivalent of three U.S. ones. On the 28th the Germans withdrew their bridgeheads to the right bank to benefit from the river for their defense.

Summing Up

The *Herbstnebel* offensive would be the greatest attack ever mounted by Hitler in the Northwest Europe campaign of 1944–45. In the face of Allied forces that had every advantage of strength, matériel, mobility and air support, a *German Army* deficient in all these categories was able to launch an immense effort. It proved unable to win the victory Hitler wanted, and the offensive did not break up the Western alliance—though it did cause discomfort among SHAEF and the respective U.S. and British higher commanders. On the other hand, *Herbstnebel* was a palpable German victory. It put the Allies on notice that Germany was not to be trifled with. When, between 29 December and 10 January, the Germans executed an orderly withdrawal before Patton's Third Army could pinch off their salient, they ended their action with some real tactical advantages.

American losses totaled some 96,000 men, including 12,000 killed in action and twice that many prisoners. Almost 900 tanks and other armored vehicles were destroyed. That put the Americans at the very limit of their replacement capacity, and several months would be required to make good the equipment losses. British losses were only some 15,000, but the British had already exhausted their replacements and had to break up two armored brigades and an infantry division to bring other units back to strength. But Germany also could not afford losses, and *Herbstnebel* had added another 70,000 to its toll, among them 10,000 dead and 20,000 prisoners permanently lost to the Reich. The 350 tanks and assault guns destroyed could hardly be replaced from new production, which was now allocated to the Eastern Front.

German morale went up a notch, and that helped with the Lorraine offensive launched in January 1945. But the mobile reserve, *Sixth Panzer Army*, had to be diverted to the Eastern Front also, critically weakening the West. On balance the *Herbstnebel* campaign gained Hitler perhaps three of four extra months for his Thousand Year Reich to live. These results were far from what he had anticipated.

The Reality

The German offensive in the Battle of the Bulge is very interesting from the standpoint of casting an alternate reality. First of all, not very much needs to change for the outcome to be different. The German preparations, while not flawless, were close to optimum for generating a surprise attack with overwhelming force. I have stuck precisely to the real history in delineating this part of the story. Second, much of what stopped the German attack was friction caused by the isolated, defiant, and lucky actions of small American units. Just a few of these were changed to make the progress of the German offensive look very different.

I have attempted to generate this alternate history while controlling for various factors. Historical weather, historical air capabilities, historical unit strengths were all applied. Reinforcement rates were kept identical except for the initial 48 hours of the campaign, where I assumed a greater degree of German surprise and therefore a slower Allied response. The greater surprise also permits a less successful first-day defense by the Americans, and that single fact sets up early German captures of critical road centers at St Vith and Bastogne. In the actual campaign the defense of St Vith through 20 December, and the absolute ability of Bastogne to hold out through German attack and siege, set up what ultimately became a German defeat. Hitler's unwillingness to execute a timely withdrawal further magnified the adverse consequences of the campaign. Here it is assumed the withdrawal is an early one.

Given these factors, though other observers may assess other consequences, I conclude that the overall result could not have been hugely different. Here the Germans make the line of the Meuse where in actuality they fell short about 20–25 miles. I assess there was no possibility of making Antwerp. Allied casualties are evaluated at about 20 percent greater than the historical and German ones at 12 percent less than the actual. The three extra months gained in this alternate history would not have been sufficient to reverse the tide of World War II.

Bibliography

Cole, Hugh M., *United States Army in World War II: European Theater of Operations: The Ardennes, Battle of the Bulge*, Office of the Chief of Military History, Washington, D.C., 1965.

Eisenhower, John S.D., *The Bitter Woods*, G.P. Putnam's Sons, New York, 1969.

Elstob, Peter, *Hitler's Last Offensive*, Secker & Warburg, London, 1971.

Gavin, James M., *On to Berlin: Battles of an Airborne Commander, 1943–1946*, Viking Books, New York, 1978.

Heiber, Helmut, and Glantz, David M., eds. *Hitler and His Generals: Military Confrences, 1942–1945*, Enigma Books, New York, 2003.

Hinsley, F.H., *et al.*, *British Intelligence in the Second World War, Its Influence on Strategy and Operations,* Volume [V.] 3, Part II, Cambridge University Press, New York, 1988.

MacDonald, Charles B., *A Time for Trumpets: The Untold Story of the Battle of the Bulge*, William Morrow, New York, 1985.

Megaree, Geoffrey P., *Inside Hitler's High Command*, University Press of Kansas, Lawrence, 2000.

Merriam, Robert E., *The Battle of the Bulge*, Ballantine Books, New York, 1966.

Messenger, Charles, *Hitler's Gladiator*, Brassey's, Washington, D.C., 1988.

Nobecourt, Jacques, *Hitler's Last Gamble: The Battle of the Bulge*, Schocken Books, New York, 1967

Parker, Danny S., *Battle of the Bulge: Hitler's Ardennes, Offensive*. Combined Books, Conshohocken, PA, 1991.

Parker, Danny S., ed., *Hitler's Ardennes Offensive: The German View of the Battle of the Bulge*, Greenhill Books, London, 1997.

Parker, Danny S., ed., *The Battle of the Bulge: Perspectives from Hitler's High Command*, Greenhill Books, London, 1999.

Quarrie, Bruce, *The Ardennes Offensive: VI Panzer Armee*, Osprey, Oxford, UK, 1999.

Quarrie, Bruce, *The Ardennes Offensive: V Panzer Armee*, Osprey, Oxford, UK, 2000.

Quarrie, Bruce, *The Ardennes Offensive: I Armee & VII Armee*, Osprey, Oxford, UK, 2001.

Reynolds, Michael, *Men of Steel: I SS Panzer Corps: The Ardennes and Eastern Front, 1944–45*, Sarpedon, New York, 1999.

Reynolds, Michael, *Sons of the Reich: II SS Panzer Corps: Normandy, Arnhem, Ardennes, Eastern Front*, Casemate, Havertown, PA, 2002.

Shulman, Milton, *Defeat in the West*, Masquerade, London, 1995.

Strawson, John, *The Battle for the Ardennes*, B.T. Batsford, London, 1972.

Strong, Kenneth, *Intelligence at the Top*, Cassell, London, 1968.

Toland, John, *Battle: The Story of the Bulge*, Random House, New York, 1959.

Warlimont, Walter, (trans. R.H. Barry), *Inside Hitler's Headquarters*, Praeger, New York, 1964

Wilmot, Chester, *The Struggle for Europe*, Harper & Brothers, New York, 1952.

Notes

1. Heiber and Glantz, *Hitler and His Generals*, p. 445.
2. Warlimont, *Inside Hitler's Headquarters*, quote p. 475.
3. MacDonald, *A Time for Trumpets*, quote p. 11.
4. Parker, *Battle of the Bulge*, quote p. 22. It should be noted that the *OKW* war diarist, Percy Schramm, in his detailed presentation of German planning for the Ardennes, writes that *OB West* and *Army Group B* were purposely kept ignorant of the Ardennes plans until October 28, when the chiefs of staff of both organizations were first briefed by Hitler himself. (Percy Schramm, "The Preparations for the German Offensive in the Ardennes," in Parker, ed., *The Battle of the Bulge: The German View*, p. 61.
5. Merriam, *The Battle of the Bulge*, quote p. 68.
6. Heiber and Glantz, *Hitler and His Generals*, p. 527. The omissions shown in the text are also missing in the original.
7. *Ibid.*, pp. 539–41.
*8. Lawrence Bascher, *Disaster at Stavelot: A Tank Battle in the Snow*. New York, Harper Brothers, 1958, *passim*.
*9. Wilhelm Bittrich, *The Road to the Meuse*, Mann Verlag, Stuttgart, 1974, pp. 158–279.

9
HOLDING PATTON
Seventh Panzer Army and the Battle of Luxembourg

Kim H. Campbell

A Change in Plans

General der Panzertruppen Erich Brandenberger stared at the situation map. He was tired and yet this was only the beginning. He had been working day and night on the preparation for the offensive since that day in early November when Field Marshals Walther Model and Gerd von Rundstedt had called him to headquarters and unveiled the *Führer*'s grand offensive into the Ardennes, code-named *Wacht am Rhein* (Watch on the Rhine). Model, commanding *Army Group B*, was Brandenberger's immediate superior. Model, in turn, reported to von Rundstedt, who commanded all the German forces in the West (*OB West*). Brandenberger's mission in this offensive would be to protect the southern flank of the main thrust conducted by *Sixth* and *Fifth Panzer Armies* towards Brussels and Antwerp. The two field marshals explained how they had tried to reason with Hitler to reduce the scale of the attack to one that would have a greater chance of success but to no avail.

There was one exception to their pleadings; Hitler had allowed a proposed offensive in Lorraine to be postponed. But Lieutenant General George Patton's Third U.S. Army's continual advances convinced Hitler that something must be done to keep this army from turning north and attacking into the southern flank of the Ardennes Offensive. He knew Brandenberger's *Seventh Army* with only four infantry divisions was too weak to stop Patton by itself. It was the consensus of senior officers in the west as well as Hitler that Patton was the most dangerous general the Allies had. The field marshals had suggested that the best way to occupy Patton was by strengthening and expanding the role of Brandenberger's army. No longer would it just be defending the left flank of *Wacht am Rhein*. Instead, *Seventh Army* would have a much greater offensive role with the primary mission being to tie down Patton. Brandenberger had to keep Patton from interfering with the timetable of the offensive.

Even with the additional forces promised, von Rundstedt confided his skepticism about the whole affair. Primary among the reasons for this was the fact that the *Führer* had really taken hold of this additional attack and insisted that the objective be the capture of Metz. Hitler claimed that this would force the Americans to evacuate all the way back behind the Moselle River, allowing for the retaking of Strasbourg and relieving the pressure on Colmar.[1] "May as well make Paris the objective" was von Rundstedt's feeling. Reaching Metz was well beyond the capability of the forces made available to Brandenberger. And yet he was thrilled to have such powerful forces under his command. Brandenberger wiped his hand across his face. The heat from the stove wasn't helping him stay awake and he no longer got a rush of adrenaline from combat operations. He had been a fighter for too many years now for that.

The operational plan drawn up by his staff was simple enough for the troops of 1940 or even 1943. But now, with these boys, old men, and half trained *Luftwaffe* and *Kriegsmarine* personnel, he was not so sure. The bulk of his army consisted of the *212th*, *276th*, and *352d Volksgrenadier Divisions*, and the *5th Fallschirmjäger (Paratroop) Division*. True, he had been provided with several additional good units, at least in name, he thought to himself. "They now have their chance to show their mettle," he said half out loud. He looked over at his order of battle board. Topping the list of his additional units was the *6th SS Gebirgs Division "Nord"*. This SS mountain division had been secretly shipped from Norway where it had been in *OKW* reserve. The *6th SS Gebirgs Division* was one of a kind. With over 18,000 men it had 80 percent more manpower than most Volksgrenadier divisions. The division had two exceptionally large infantry regiments, each having three battalions. Additionally, *Nord* had Panzergrenadier, reconnaissance, engineer, and flak battalions.

It had taken every favor, numerous threats and every ounce of strength he could muster, to get the German railroads to move the division to its deployment area in time for the attack. Brandenberger hoped this, the largest infantry division on the Western Front, would provide the breakthrough needed for his little offensive.

Next on the board was the *11th Panzer Division*.[2] Getting the *11th* pulled out of the line and refitted in time had been another of Brandenberger's many headaches. Nevertheless, it was ready, with over 130 tanks and assault guns, including 60 Panthers. Then there was the *15th Panzergrenadier Division*, the *Führer Grenadier Brigade*, and the *Führer Begleit Brigade*. Altogether they could pack quite a punch. It had been tough convincing Model, and even more Hitler, that these units could better protect the left flank of *Fifth Panzer Army* by taking part in *Seventh Army*'s attack.

Then there was also the carrot. If the attack was going well, von Rundstedt had held out the possibility of committing the *10th SS Panzer Division "Frundsberg"*, if it could be refitted in time. A similar proposal had initially been made about the 21st *Panzer Division* and the *17th SS Panzergrenadier Division*. Brandenberger had made a convincing argument that once Patton's

Third Army began shifting troops north, *Army Group G* would no longer need them and they could then be transfered to his *Seventh Army*. It was agreed that as soon as the Third U.S. Army began moving north, the *21st Panzer* and *17th SS Panzergrenadier Divisions* would follow. Brandenberger had often found himself daydreaming about what he could do with nearly 500 tanks and assault guns. He would demonstrate, both to the *Führer* and to the *Amis* (Americans), what a *General der Panzertruppen* was still capable of doing.

Already replacement equipment and troops for the 21st *Panzer Division* and *17th SS Panzergrenadier Division* had been prepositioned so that both units could refit on the march. There would be no time for training the replacements; they would have to learn their trade in the crucible of battle. There had only been one catch, Sepp Dietrich, commanding the *Sixth Panzer Army*, had insisted that if the *10th SS Panzer Division* and *17th SS Panzergrenadier Division* were both assigned to *Seventh Army*, they should be placed in the same corps. It was obvious to all that Dietrich was hoping to eventually have both SS units placed under his *Sixth Panzer Army*.[3] Brandenberger, eager for the troops, agreed that if the situation allowed he would use the two SS divisions as a corps entity.

The Dance Begins, 16 December 1944

The first day of the offensive was not yet over and already Brandenberger had asked for the release of the 21st *Panzer Division* and *17th SS Panzergrenadier Division*. There had been no clear signs that Third U.S. Army was moving troops north, but its offensive operations had noticeably decreased. That was good enough for General Brandenberger. He knew it would take several days to get the two divisions redeployed and refitted even with all his preparations. "If," he thought, and then, to himself said, "No, not if, but when Patton turns north, I will need those two divisions and I will need them to be already at hand and ready to fight."

The *Seventh Army's* plan of attack called for an initial attack by its *212th*, *276th*, and *352d Volksgrenadier Division*s (from left to right), with the *5th Fallschirmjäger Division* on the far right tying in with the *Fifth Panzer Army* to the north. All they needed to do at this point was to draw the 4th U.S. Infantry Division's reserves north, away from his main attack. In fact, Brandenberger hoped that the weight and scope of the attack of *Sixth* and *Fifth Panzer Armies*, as well as the attack of his northern (right) wing, would force the Americans to commit not only their divisional reserves but, he hoped, most of their corps level reserves as well.

As a result of the difficulty in getting the *6th SS Nord* deployed in time for the offensive, Brandenberger had requested a two-day delay to the start of the battle. Hitler exploded at the suggestion and was adamant that there would be no more delays and that the attack would go forward on 16 December, as planned. After Hitler calmed down and it was made clear that it was impossible to have the *6th SS Nord* ready on 16 December, he relented. Hitler stated that every effort must be made to attack on 16 December. If it could not be done, then he would allow a one day delay for the *Seventh Army's* left wing forces to attack on 17 December, but no later. All other attacks must take place on 16 December as per the operations order.[4]

Gradually it dawned on Brandenberger to turn the necessity of the delay into an attribute. If his right wing attack on 16 December could draw in upon itself U.S. divisional and corps reserves, it would facilitate the success of the main attack by his left wing on 17 December. As the initial reports came in during this first day, Brandenberger was satisfied that his four committed divisions had all made some penetration of the American positions. Not as much progress as called for in the plan, but not bad considering the lack of armor support, the caliber of the troops and the terrain where the attacks had been launched. Now, with the first day fighting drawing to a close, he was confident that the enemy's reserves were moving toward his right wing and thus preparing the way for a major breakthrough by his left wing the next morning.

The main attack by his left wing would be launched by the newly created *LXXXI Corps* with the *6th SS Nord* and the *11th Panzer Division* against the weakened remainder of the 4th U.S. Infantry Division's front. After smashing through the 4th, the German left wing forces would turn southwest and race for Luxembourg City using the Moselle River to protect their exposed left flank. The *Seventh Army's* frontage would widen during the advance allowing additional units to be fed into the line. While the *Führer* still talked of the attack proceeding all the way to Metz, Brandenberger knew his real mission was to delay as long as possible, and do as much damage as possible to Patton's Third Army when it responded to the Ardennes offensive.

With that overall mission in mind, Brandenberger's offensive was only to advance to areas that would give him defensive advantages for his coming engagement with Patton. Accordingly, he determined to use the Moselle from Wasserbillig down to Wormeldange to protect the left flank of his main defense line once he obtained it. The main defense line would run from Wormeldange on the Moselle west through Luxembourg City and then northwest to Arlon. He would anchor his defense on the Moselle on one end, Luxembourg City in the center, and Arlon in the west. The key was to reach these positions and prepare to defend them before the Third Army could arrive.

There were other potential benefits if *Seventh Army's* offensive was successful. The left wing attack would outflank the 4th and 28th U.S. Infantry Divisions. Brandenberger hoped this would unhinge the defenses of both American divisions and force them to fall back, allowing the four divisions of his right wing to advance west to defensive positions tied in with his left wing at Arlon and proceeding northwest to Neufchâteau. This would protect *Fifth Panzer Army's* southern flank, at least for a while. If things went fairly well, they might cut off portions of several American divisions.

Finally, Brandenberger knew he could capture the Radio Luxembourg transmitters at Junglinster. These transmitters were some of the most powerful in Europe and their capture would be a real coup. If the offensive moved quickly enough it might even capture the commander of 12th Army Group, Lieutenant General Omar Bradley, whose headquarters was in Luxembourg City. Now that would be a triumph.

Bradley was so concerned with the declining rifle strength of his infantry divisions that he was personally escorting his personnel officer on the first part of his trip to the Pentagon. They were supposed to fly to Versailles on the morning of 16 December but heavy fog had grounded their aircraft. Instead, Bradley elected to make the four-hour journey by car over the icy roads. It was not until late in the afternoon, nearly 12 hours after the Ardennes offensive had begun, that the initial, sketchy reports of an attack in the U.S. VIII Corps sector finally reached Eisenhower's headquarters and Bradley found out that his army group was under attack. The initial reports only indicated that it was probably nothing more than a spoiling attack involving perhaps four or six divisions. A short time later word arrived that at least eight divisions, previously unidentified, were involved. Eisenhower immediately gave Bradley two armored divisions, the 7th Armored Division from Lieutenant General Simpson's Ninth U.S. Army to the north, and the 10th Armored Division from Patton's Third Army to the south. Bradley further told Simpson and Patton to put any division they had out of the line on alert for movement to the Ardennes. Once they became aware of the German attack, the U.S. higher commands reacted quickly and forcefully, even though they were not fully aware of the magnitude of the offensive.

Commander of the First U.S. Army, Lieutenant General Courtney Hodges, whose army was bearing the brunt of the attack, reacted quickly as well. Hodges ordered an armored division's combat command to the sector of the front he perceived, correctly it turned out, to be the most threatened. Furthermore, he placed several divisions on alert for possible movement to the Ardennes. At the corps level, the commanders were uneasy and sensed that things at the front were not "in hand," though this was what their divisional commanders were reporting. There is a natural tendency to down-play problems in your own sector so as to give the impression that you are competent and have things under control.[5]

The 4th Infantry Division's commander, Major General Raymond Barton, knew by late afternoon on 17 December that his 12th Infantry Regiment was hard pressed. Still, he hesitated to call on his other two regiments for help. There was no guarantee that the Germans would not expand their attack against his division the next day. He did, however, take the precaution of ordering the reserve battalion of his 22d Infantry Regiment, his southernmost and farthest from the fighting, to move north on the morning of 17 December. Barton also moved most of the division's artillery north to assist the 12th Infantry. Additionally, he put the division's reconnaissance troop and the 4th Engineer Battalion on one-hour standby for movement to the endangered sector of the front line.[6] Finally, Barton ordered that there would be no pulling back. He did not know for sure yet, but from the look of the

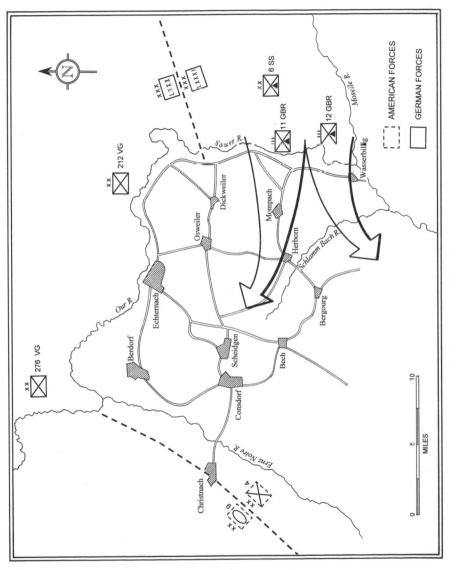

6th SS Mountain Division's Attacks

first attacks, there was a good chance that he might be holding the shoulder of a German attempt to break through.

For George Patton, 16 December was a very frustrating day. First he had to give up the 10th Armored Division to Hodges' First Army. Then, even more disturbing, he had to call off his offensive just as he was on the verge of beginning his final attack to break through Germany's *Westwall* and release his vaunted army into the guts of Germany. All through the fall, at a cost of tens of thousands of casualties, Patton's army had slugged its way through German defensive lines. Now that he was finally in position for the final breakthrough, he had to call off the entire attack. All this because of what should be an easily managed spoiling attack up in First Army's sector. Nevertheless, based on his intelligence officer's suggestion that something big might be brewing, Patton directed his staff to do some preliminary studies on moving elements of Third Army to the north. That precautionary planning now looked rather fortuitous.

Nord Enters the Battle, 17 December 1944

Private First Class Harry Johnson could feel the cold starting to invade his clothes as he stumbled along at the tail end of his squad moving up the forest trail to the forward outpost. They had the 5:00–7:00 a.m. shift. They began to pick up the pace because they knew that, if they were late relieving Sergeant Joe Schmitt and his squad, they would get every lousy detail for the next week. Schmitt had been with the 4th Infantry Division's 8th Infantry Regiment since it landed in France. He had proved to be a fine combat soldier but had also taken a fancy to French wine and his reward was to have been promoted to sergeant three times and busted twice. He had been wearing his stripes for six weeks now, a new record.

Private Johnson missed his warm bed in Cherbourg where only two weeks ago he had been dispatching Red Ball Express supply trucks to the front lines. Then the comb-out came and he found himself on one of those same trucks heading for the front. As his squad approached the outpost, Schmitt came out from behind a couple of trees. Johnson looked up as he heard a strange sound he had never heard before, kind of a screech. Schmitt yelled "screaming meemies" as he dove for cover. Before he hit the ground, the six men were tossed in the air.

The *6th SS Nord Division*'s *11th SS Gebirgs Regiment* crossed the Sauer River at 6:00 a.m. on 17 December. The first assault battalions, in their rubber boats, suffered no casualties during the crossing, thanks in part to a heavy, low-lying fog that blanketed the entire river valley. Brandenberger had taken the extra precaution of having a 15-minute barrage across the entire *Seventh Army* front to help hide the new fires coming from the *6th SS*. However, many of the artillery battalions had not repositioned in time to shoot. Horse-drawn artillery has its disadvantages. Then there was the problem stemming from his orders to the *212th*, *276th*, and *352d Volksgrenadier Division*s to continue attacking through the night to make up for falling behind schedule on the first day. Naturally, this led to many units being either too close to, or too intermingled with, American units for the artillery to risk firing.

Still, the barrage did help conceal the opening fire of the *6th SS Nord*. The *11th Panzer Division*'s artillery had also moved forward to add extra weight to the *6th SS*'s efforts. The barrage concentrated on rear areas where there were known headquarters, artillery, and reserve positions. The German shelling succeeded in knocking out most of the wire communications between battalion headquarters and their subordinate companies.

It was nearly 7:00 a.m. when the lead elements of the *11th SS Gebirgs Regiment* finally began pushing through the outpost line of Company K, 8th Infantry Regiment, 4th Infantry Division. The squad-size outpost positions were quickly overrun or their defenders fell back on their main battle positions. In either case, the attack of the two lead battalions of the *11th SS Gebirgs Regiment* began to pick up momentum. But just as quickly as it had begun, the forward momentum stopped dead in its tracks. Company K regained its balance and held firm in its main defensive positions. The lone artillery battalion Major General Barton had left in supporting distance of his 8th Infantry also began to execute its preplanned fires.

Casualties among the exposed mountain troops began to mount. *Nord's* commander, *Generalmajor der Waffen-SS* Karl Brenner was on the banks of the Sauer River urging his engineers to speed up the construction of bridges at his two crossing sites. Brandenberger had stressed to him that getting armor across the Sauer quickly was the key to victory. So Brenner chose to put the added inspiration of his presence into the bridging effort.[7]

Brenner received word, from up on the ridge above the river valley, that the attack had already stalled. Immediately he set off on foot up the road to the sound of the guns.

He had attacked with both regiments abreast. The regiments were attacking with two battalions on line and their third battalion following behind to reinforce whichever lead battalion's attack looked the most promising. That was the plan once the division was across the Sauer River and had enlarged the bridgehead enough to bring all the battalions over.

For now Brenner only had about a battalion and a half across the river in each regimental sector. As he reached the rear of his lead battalion he began barking orders. Within minutes, a German barrage rained down on the Company K positions. The American mortars were quickly silenced. The U.S. artillery had shifted its fire down to the river but the guns were firing blindly and the shells only occasionally landed near Brenner's bridge building engineers. The bombardment had only a minimal affect on the bridging effort. Under Brenner's personal leadership, the attack began to make progress again. By 9:00 there were signs Company K was starting to give way.

To Company K's right, Company L was holding its own against the *12th SS Gebirgs Regiment*. It was almost as though, without Brenner's guidance, the attack could not make any progress. In reality, the terrain was more difficult in the *12th SS*'s crossing area and Company L had better ground for siting its defenses. For both regiments, the lack of heavy weapons, against the prepared defenses, was making progress very costly.

By 9:30 a.m. most of the machine guns and mortars were finally across the river and being moved into firing positions to help the battalions in contact with the Americans. Once the heavy weapons opened fire the effect was quickly apparent. The already weakening position of Company K started visibly to deteriorate. To make matters worse, Company K's ammunition was beginning to give out. Under the intense German fire it was nearly impossible to resupply most of the positions.

The earlier piecemeal attacks had been straining Company K, but it had held. Now Brenner put together a fully coordinated assault with the two lead battalions of the *11th SS Gebirgs Regiment* supported by artillery from across the Sauer. The newly deployed mortars and machine guns added even more weight to the attack. Within 10 minutes the thin center of Company K's position gave way, making the entire line untenable. The survivors fell back on reinforcements but these arrived too late to save the position and were too weak to attempt to retake it. With no decent defensible terrain, the entire force fell back on the village of Mompach and set up a hasty defense.

The mountain troops followed hot on the Americans' heels, but stopped short of assaulting the village off the march. Brenner now ordered the *11th SS* commander to take Mampach without delay. The assault came with a vengeance. The *11th SS* suffered heavily in the initial rush but the attack continued on and was soon into the outer houses of the village. In close house-to-house fighting numbers quickly began to tell. By 1:00 p.m. it was over except for a handful of isolated hold-outs. The survivors fell back on Herborn. The Americans had lost 27 men in Mompach, 16 of them captured. The Germans had suffered over 35 dead, mostly in the initial attack. For nearly six hours of heavy fighting, Brenner had only gained about two and a half miles. But on the other hand he was closer to piercing the American lines than he realized.[8]

The loss of Mompach was a devastating blow to the 8th Infantry Regiment. To the north, Company M, 3d Battalion, 12th Infantry Regiment was forced to pull back its right flank to the south of Dickweiler which was under increasing pressure from the *212th Volksgrenadier Division*. The area around Osweiler and Dickweiler was starting to develop into a potential pocket for the better part of two battalions, 1st/12th Infantry Regiment and 2d/22d Infantry Regiment, which had been the 22d Infantry Regiment's reserve. Barton took a chance that the German attack would not spread further to the south and moved the 2d/22d up to counterattack the *212th Volksgrenadier Division*.

To the south of the growing gap created by Company K's defeat, Company L found its left flank dangerously exposed. To Company L's front, the pressure from *12th SS Gebirgs Regiment*'s attacks was increasing. To make matters worse, with Company K gone, *6th SS Nord*'s artillery now focused its efforts on

Company L. When a strong German force was detected moving around its left flank, Company L began to pull back.

Back at 4th Infantry Division headquarters, Barton, who had perceived the greatest threat to his division to be on his left flank, was finally getting word of the extent of this new threat. He reacted quickly with the limited reserves he had, though most of his reserves had already been committed to rescue companies cut off during the attacks on 16 December. On the first day, Barton had weathered fairly well the attacks by the *212th Volksgrenadier Division* and parts of the *276th Volksgrenadier Division* against his 12th Infantry Regiment reinforced with his attached armor. Barton had gambled that the German attack would not spread further down his front and had stripped the reserves from the rest of his division to use for counterattacks on 17 December. To his dismay, the dawning of 17 December brought exactly the events he had hoped would not happen. As the attack on his right developed, Barton's reserves were ill positioned to meet the developing crisis. Now he was forced to shift some of those reserve units from the 12th Infantry to the 8th Infantry.

The division's attached armor battalion had been severely depleted during the heavy fighting in the Hürtgen Forest in late November and had only 11 operational tanks when the German offensive had began. With those and a tank company from the 9th Armored Division's Combat Command A, Barton had judiciously parceled out his armored forces in penny packets to the most threatened portions of his line. Often they arrived just in time to keep a position from falling or to prevent a breakthrough. The line had held, but nowhere was there enough strength to defeat the Germans decisively. Now he committed the seven remaining tanks to help Company K retake Mompach. After the two lead tanks were knocked out by *Panzerfausts*, the attack faltered and fell back yet again to Herborn.

The attacks of the German *Fifth* and *Sixth Panzer Armies* to the north were commanding the attention of the higher U.S. chain of command, and General Barton realized he might have to rely on his own assets and abilities for a while. He was able to take comfort in the knowledge that 10th Armored Division's CCA was on the way and would be available on 18 December. Surely he could hold on his own for a day. Like the Dutch boy trying to plug the dike, Barton found himself trying to plug a growing number of holes, with a limited number of fingers.

Along the banks of the Sauer River, the engineers of the *Seventh Army*'s left wing were doing much better than their *Fifth Panzer Army* comrades on the Our River to the north the day before. By mid-afternoon two bridges were fully operational. Assault guns from *11th Panzer Division* were given initial priority for crossing. They quickly moved off to support the *6th SS Nord* which had been lucky in repelling one armored counterattack already.

The remnants of Company K, 8th Infantry, and their supporting tanks were now subordinated to Company K, 12th Infantry. Its mission was to defend Herborn, which lay in a cleared depression and was dominated by the surrounding wooded high ground.

To the Americans, their armored attempt to retake Mompach seemed to have taken the wind out of the German attack. In reality, the delay was the result of the *6th SS Nord* pausing to regroup, resupply, and bring up armor support now that the bridges had been completed. The Germans did not remain passive long. One of the *11th SS Gebirgs Regiment*'s battalions moved through the wooded high ground north of Herborn, cutting the road between Herborn and Osweiler. A second battalion deployed along the road from Mompach. The reserve battalion, finally over the river, deployed through the woods to the high ground south of Herborn. Herborn was for all practical purposes surrounded—though the only the road leading west across the Schlamm Bach was still open it was subject to direct fire from German positions on both sides of the road. The Schlamm Bach is not a big river, but the banks on both sides are swampy and difficult to traverse.

No assault on Herborn came. Brandenberger had urged Brenner to push on and bypass pockets of resistance. So Herborn was screened off by the reserve battalion and pounded by artillery. The other two battalions of the *11th Gebirgs Regiment* pushed northwest toward Scheidgen in the rear of the 12th Infantry. Brandenberger hoped the capture of Scheidgen would bring about a general collapse of the entire American line along the Sauer River. Such a development would allow the *LXXX Corps*, with its two Volksgrenadier divisions, to get moving again. During the night of 17 December, *11th SS Gebirgs Regiment* troops linked up with elements of the *212th Volksgrenadier Division* near Scheidgen effectively cutting off two battalions of the 12th Infantry.

Brandenberger Commits His Panzers, 18 December 1944

On the *6th SS Nord*'s left flank the *12th Gebirgs Regiment* had taken Wasserbillig, where the Sauer empties into the Moselle, and was threatening Lellig. The division was now attacking in two different directions. The *11th SS Gebirgs Regiment* was attacking to the northwest into the rear of the left wing of the 4th Infantry Division. The *12th SS Gebirgs Regiment* was attacking to the southwest pushing the remainder of the 4th Infantry Division back toward Luxembourg City. With the frontage of *6th SS Nord* widening, Brandenberger felt he now had room to commit his armored forces. He also perceived that a breakthrough in the 4th Infantry Division sector could be possible the next day. With daylight fading on 17 December, Brandenberger ordered the remainder of the *11th Panzer Division* forward to take up positions for an assault on Herborn at first light on 18 December. The *11th Panzer Division* was to smash through Herborn and push on all the way to Junglinster and the Radio Luxembourg transmitters. From Herborn to Junglinster was only ten miles as the crow flies.[9]

Once the *11th Panzer Division* had cleared the bridges over the Sauer, one of the bridges would be dedicated to bringing the *Führer Begleit Brigade* over. The *Führer Begleit*, with 23 Mark IVs and nearly 50 assault guns, would move into a forward reserve position.

During the evening of 17 December Barton met with the commander of the 10th Armored Division, General Morris, in Luxembourg City. The two men agreed that the 10th's CCA should attack the *6th SS Nord* through Herborn and drive it back across the Sauer. At the same time, 4th Infantry Division would launch an attack to link up with the two battalions of the 12th Infantry cut off in the Echternach–Dickweiler pocket. The 4th Infantry Division's attack would consist of eight patched-up Sherman tanks, an engineer battalion from corps fighting as infantry, and an infantry company from the 22d Infantry Regiment that had managed to avoid being caught in the pocket.

Herborn awoke to an intense barrage on the morning of 18 December. All night the garrison could hear German armored vehicles moving into positions. The commander was planning on pulling out under the cover of darkness until he received word that an armored counterattack was to take place on that day and that it was vital that the town be held until then. Out of the morning mist came Panzergrenadiers and SS mountain troopers, well-supported Jagdpanzer IV assault guns and Mark IV and Panther tanks. The garrison's remaining Shermans accounted for themselves well, knocking out four German assault guns and three Mark IV tanks, before being destroyed themselves. Bazooka ammo ran out early in the fight, but not before taking out several more armored vehicles. The house-to-house fighting was vicious, but when the garrison no longer had any effective means to combat the German armor, the end result was no longer in question. Houses putting up stiff resistance were blasted to rubble by direct tank fire. Less than an hour after the fight had begun, the remnants of the garrison attempted to run the gauntlet to reach the apparent safety of the far side of the Schlamm Bach. The few who made it found themselves forced off the road and into the woods.

Commander of the *11th Panzer Division*, Major General von Wietersheim, had held the *111th Panzergrenadier Regiment* in reserve, along with most of his 56 Panthers. He committed them to push west even before the fighting in Herborn ended. It took less than half an hour to cover the two miles to Berbourg and seize the town. No sooner had the town been secured than reconnaissance troops reported a large American armored force approaching on the road from Bech. Wietersheim deployed his forces to meet the Americans. He also got the rest of the *11th Panzer Division* back on the road and moving to attack the flank of the approaching enemy force.

Retreating rear service troops warned the 10th's CCA that Herborn and Bergourg had fallen and that there was a lot of German armor at both locations. This was a new development. Only a few assault guns had been reported on 17 December. CCA deployed and moved forward to attack Bergourg. About a half mile north of the town, the advancing Shermans began to receive fire from defensively deployed Panthers. Losses quickly mounted for CCA, and it pulled back out of range to begin probing the German position.

An armored infantry platoon working through the woods to find the right flank of the German position ran headlong into Panzergrenadiers, supported by a couple of Jagdpanzers, moving up from Herborn. Halftracks were quickly burning. Several of the armored infantry troopers managed to escape by retreating deeper into the woods.

The Panzergrenadiers discovered a logging cut capable of handling vehicles and a Panzer company was quickly dispatched to reinforce the attack through the woods.

A series of small actions flared up and died out all through the area as both the *11th Panzer Division* and CCA probed for weaknesses in each other's positions. Finally, the *11th Panzer Division* attacked straight into CCA's defenses. Panthers and Shermans exploded and burned, but for once in such a punching match, the Shermans were killing more than being killed. Just as the Panthers were going to start pulling back, the German force advancing through the woods attacked just behind CCA's left flank. Several American tanks and a number of halftracks were quickly hit. Seeing confusion among the Americans, the main German force renewed its attack. The confusion was more apparent than real, however, and the Americans reacted quickly and knocked out several of the lead German vehicles coming out of the woods. The last one actually blocked the trail, and the remainder of the armor was unable to advance. The Panzergrenadiers continued to attack without armor support.

An uneasy feeling began to settle over CCA. Their exposed flank, the renewed pressure on their front, mounting losses and the deaths of several battalion commanders, combined to convince General Morris to pull CCA back to better defensive terrain. Once the supporting units were safely withdrawn, the speed of the Shermans allowed them to break contact under fire. The withdrawal was conducted in good order. The question now was where to make the next stand.[10]

Patton Moves North, 18 December 1944

On 18 December Patton came to Bradley's headquarters in Luxembourg City (closer to the front than most army and many corps headquarters) and finally learned how bad the situation was. Most troubling to Patton was the surprise appearance of the *6th SS Gebirgs Division* and the *11th Panzer Division*. Bradley asked for help, and Patton promised three divisions, not including the 10th Armored Division already sent. Patton ordered the 4th Armored and 80th Infantry Divisions to prepare to move north into Luxembourg and another infantry division to follow the next day.

By the time Patton got back to his own headquarters, the situation of the First Army had gotten much worse, prompting Bradley to call Patton and order the promised troops north immediately. By midnight on 18/19 December, 4th Armored Division was on the march and by first light the 80th Infantry Division would be on the move as well.

Late on the morning of 19 December, Eisenhower held a conference with his senior commanders at 12th Army Group headquarters in Verdun. Patton was directed to launch an attack to relieve the growing pressure against Bastogne, and then push on to the north and effect a junction with the Ninth Army. Eisenhower asked Patton, "When can you start?" Patton answered, "As soon as you're through with me." Eisenhower wanted a more specific answer to which Patton replied, "The morning of December 21st, with three divisions, if First Army can protect my assembly areas."[11]

Eisenhower ordered General Devers' 6th Army Group to take over the two southernmost corps sectors of Patton's Third Army. This move freed up more troops for Patton, who now envisioned eventually having at least two of his corps headquarters and six divisions for his counterattack. But first he had to get to Bastogne.

From Bad to Worse, 18–20 December 1944

For General Barton, the situation on 18 December went from bad to disaster. First there was the loss of Herborn, then the repulse of CCA, which was quickly followed by the defeat of the relief column trying to break through to the Echternach–Dickweiler pocket. The column was nearly totally destroyed when it ran head-on into the *11th Gebirgs Regiment* which was now well supported by assault guns. Now, with daylight running out, word came that Manternach, in the south, was under heavy pressure. But the biggest blow had been the loss of the key road center of Bech. CCA was again roughly handled by the *11th Panzer Division*, and pushed off to the northwest. Barton had no reserves left to commit and his veteran division was being sliced into three distinct pieces, with one surrounded and running low on ammunition.[12]

Drastic situations call for drastic measures. Fearing the piecemeal destruction of his division, Barton ordered the forces in the pocket to break out that night. He was determined to pull his division back and reunite his regiments in order to exert stronger control. This, he hoped, would allow him to establish a defensive line behind the Ernz Noire River from Christnach in the north down to Junglinster, then southeast through Rodenborg and then east to Grevemacher on the Moselle. It was too much frontage for the division to cover even at full strength, but with CCA and the arrival of CCR and most of 10th Armored Division's divisional assets, Barton thought he would be able to hold long enough for additional forces to arrive.

At *Seventh Army* HQ, Brandenberger had been worried by an armor attack trying to break through to the pocket earlier in the day. It had been beaten back only with great difficulty. He decided to relieve the *11th SS Gebirgs Regiment* with the *Führer Begleit Brigade* after dark. This strengthened his hold on the trapped American troops and also allowed the *6th SS Nord* to be reunited. The *Führer Begleit Brigade* would be committed to attack the forces holding up the *276th Volksgrenadier Division*, while the *212th Volksgrenadier Division* reduced the Echternach–Dickweiler pocket. The *6th SS Nord* would reorganize while protecting the left flank of the *11th Panzer Division*'s final

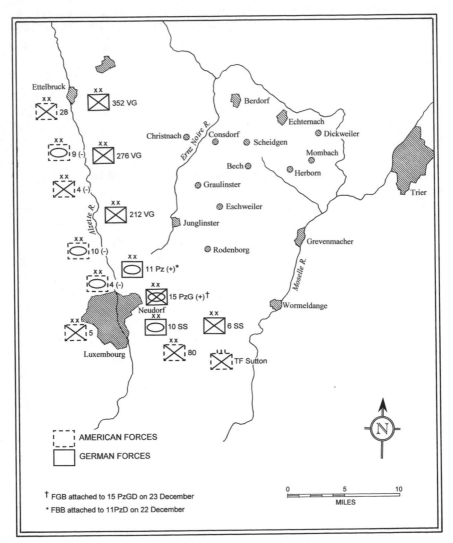

The Battle for Luxembourg

drive to Junglinster. Once reorganized, the *6th SS Nord* would continue the attack to gain the line from Wormeldange on the Moselle to Luxembourg City, the army's main defensive line. With several more bridges over the Sauer River now available, Brandenberger ordered the *15th Panzergrenadier Division* over the river into a reserve position behind the *11th Panzer Division*. *Führer Begleit Brigade* was assigned to the *LXC Corps*. *15th Panzergrenadier Division* now joined the *11th Panzer Division* and *6th SS Nord* in *LXXX Corps* which now added *Panzer* to its title.

The breakout of the troops in the Echternach–Dickweiler pocket began shortly after 11:00 p.m. on 18 December. The pocket collapsed in phases to the west as the troops were pulled back and massed for the breakout attempt. The forces attacked west, meeting only light resistance, and reached the American positions still holding near Berdorf by 1:30 a.m. With the link-up completed, the withdrawal continued southwest through Consdorf *en route* to Christnach. Once at Christnach they would help anchor the new line.

The head of the withdrawing column reached Consdorf by 3:00 and moved off to take up defensive positions on the western side of the Ernz Noirc River. The retreating column was confined to one road which, when passing through Consdorf, was within a half mile of German positions in Scheidgen. Finally realizing something was up, the *212th Volksgrenadier Division* began to launch probing attacks against the withdrawing column, causing it to become strung out.

It was nearly 5:30 a.m. on 19 December when the *Führer Begleit Brigade* began its attack on Consdorf. Attacking over unfamiliar ground, the brigade proceeded cautiously, but it was not long before it was pressing hard against the defenses. The roads leading into Consdorf from the north and south were cut by 9:45. Only the road west to Christnach was still open and the escape route for the last third of the troops from the pocket was cut off. To get around the German blocking positions the retreating troops were forced to abandon most of their heavy equipment and move through the woods to reach the one road out of Consdorf that was still open. The withdrawal maintained good order and most of the troops successfully escaped albeit without much of their equipment.

The *11th Panzer* launched a two-pronged attack to capture Junglinster on the morning of 19 December. Zero hour had to be pushed back from 6:00 to 08:00 because the resupply columns got entangled with the *11th SS Gebirgs Regiment* battalions moving south. The southern prong attacked toward Eschweiler while the northern prong aimed for Graulinster. The southern attack quickly broke through and found itself shooting up surprised U.S. rear elements. But there was no stopping as they pushed on to reach Eschweiler by 10:15. The northern prong had a tougher time and found it difficult to break free of the defending American forces. A morning of hard fighting finally brought the northern prong to the outskirts of Graulinster around 12:15. There CCA finally stopped the forward momentum of the northern prong.

By noon, the *6th SS Nord* had finally sorted itself out and resupplied. Shortly afterward it was back on the attack across a six-mile front, pushing the depleted battalions of the 4th Infantry Division's 22d Infantry before it. By mid-afternoon, Grevenmacher had fallen to the advancing Germans and General Barton's hoped-for new defensive line was already breached.

The southern prong of *11th Panzer's* attack reached the south side of Junglinster just after noon. The Panzergrenadiers advanced into the city while the armored forces swept around both sides. There was some fighting in the city as headquarters and service support troops put up spirited resistance. The armor moving around the northern side of the city spotted the transmitter towers of Radio Luxembourg and raced forward to seize the prize. A U.S. engineer platoon at the Radio Luxembourg compound began to engage the on-rushing Germans to hold them off while members of the radio staff and the engineers placed demolition charges. A couple of bazooka hits halted the initial German rush. The Germans, though, were soon moving into flanking positions and bringing the compound under intense cannon and machine-gun fire. Casualties quickly mounted for the engineers and Radio Luxembourg staff, several of whom took an active role in the defense. The defenders managed to hold the Germans off for nearly 45 minutes, but their position was deteriorating rapidly. Finally, just as they were about to be overwhelmed, there was a huge explosion and the transmitter towers, as if in slow motion, toppled over and crashed to the ground. The surviving defenders made their escape only to be caught in crossfire. Only three engineers made it out.[13]

When Barton learned of the fall of Junglinster, he order CCA to fall back and take up defensive positions behind the Ernz Noire River. With the situation in his sector falling apart, Barton contacted Major General Manton Eddy, commander of XII Corps, who had just taken over control of the forces defending north of Luxembourg City. Barton expressed his fear of being unable to defend the Third Army assembly areas. Eddy decided to ask Patton to have the 4th Armored Division temporarily committed to stabilize the front. As soon as the 80th Infantry Division arrived it would relieve 4th Armored Division. With his depleted 4th Infantry, Barton had gamely battled four enemy divisions (he thought *Führer Begleit Brigade* was another division), and at least one of those was a Panzer division and another was an *SS* division. But he knew he could not keep it up much longer.

For the time being, Barton focused on the task at hand, organizing his new defensive line along the Ernz Noire. With his drastically weakened forces, he held a line from Christnach along the Ernz Noire about half way to Junglinster, where he tied in with the 10th Armored Division. This division with its hard-hit CCA and CCR, extended the line as far as Junglinster. West of there, the division emplaced screening forces. From Junglinster there was a gap of roughly eight miles, screened by a cavalry troop, an anti-tank company, and some air defense, MP, and engineer detachments. East of the gap was the newly designated Task Force Sutton, being built around what remained of the 4th's 22d Infantry. Task Force Sutton was charged with defending from the

Moselle to the eastern approaches of Luxembourg City. Other than a large number of service troops, the only forces in place to defend the city were two military police battalions.[14]

Once he gained a clear picture of the situation, Eddy advised Bradley that it might be prudent to move his headquarters further to the west. Once again Bradley refused, telling Eddy, "I have full confidence in you and the men of the Third Army."

When it was discovered that the *212th Volksgrenadier Division* was holding an empty bag, the division was instructed to attack across the Ernz Noire together with the *Führer Begleit Brigade* and seize Christnach. Once Christnach was secured the two units would attack the flank of the 9th Armored Division's CCA, which had stopped *276th Volksgrenadier Division* dead in its tracks. However, it took so long to get the *212th* into position that the attack had to be postponed until the following morning, 20 December.

To the north of *Seventh Army* things were changing. The *Sixth Panzer Army*'s failure to break through the American lines had resulted in Model, shifting the main effort to *Fifth Panzer Army*. With that shift came greater responsibility for *Seventh Army*. Model rang up Brandenberger on 20 December, informing him about the change and congratulating him on the success of his army, "Everyone is eagerly following progress, you're doing better than *Sixth Panzer*. With change in the main effort, your success takes on even greater importance. The *Führer* has ordered the release of *10th SS Panzer Division* to you. What do you think of that, Erich?" What Brandenberger thought was, "When do I get *21st Panzer Division* and *17th SS Panzergrenadier Division*?" but he bit his tongue. The two divisions had finally arrived in the Trier area and were refitting as rapidly as possible.[15]

There were other significant changes in store for the Germans on 20 December. The newly named *LXXXI Panzer Corps*, attacked at 7:00 a.m. with all three of its divisions on line. The *11th Panzer Division* drove west from Junglinster to sweep around Luxembourg City from the north. The *15th Panzergrenadier Division*, now sandwiched between the *11th Panzer Division* and the *6th SS Nord*, attacked southwest directly on the city itself. The *6th SS* attacked due south with its left flank on the Moselle and its right tied in with the *15th Panzergrenadier Division*.

The *11th Panzer Division* encountered some initial tough resistance from elements of 10th Armored Division's CCR, but around mid-morning was able to break loose. Driving past small detachments trying to slow it down, like so many speed bumps, shortly after noon, *11th Panzer Division* cut the main road from Luxembourg City to the Ardennes.

Smashing through the thinly spread roadblocks and screening forces, *15th Panzergrenadier Division* made a dramatic entrance on the *Seventh Army* stage. The forces arraigned against it were mere odds and sods and the *15th Panzergrenadier Division* was pleased to be in a dominant position for once. Some four miles from the outer villages of the city, lead elements of the *15th*

Panzergrenadier Division, in between bursts of fire from a few American quad-50 anti-aircraft guns, could hear the city's church bells announcing midday.

For the *6th SS Nord* the going was slower. With only 11 of the attached assault guns still operational, *Nord* had neither the punch nor the mobility to match the gains of its corps mates. And then there was also Task Force Sutton to contend with, and Task Force Sutton had more fight in it than any of the forces opposing *11th Panzer Division* or *15th Panzergrenadier Division*. Still, *6th SS Nord* steadily advanced, if at a slower pace. By the end of the day, *Nord* would be within three miles of its campaign objectives.[16]

The Battle of Luxembourg City, 20–24 December 1944

Patton arrived in Luxembourg City that same afternoon. The tension was thick at Bradley's headquarters. There was no panic, but there was a distinct sense of urgency. Seeing Patton enter his office, Bradley came around his desk saying, "Good to see you Georgie, very good to see you." With the sound of fighting off in the distance, Patton half chuckled and replied, "Look, Brad, things aren't so bad we need the Army Group Staff in the line. Take your boys back a few miles, I'll kick these bastards back to Germany and you'll be back at your desk in a couple of days." Bradley finally relented and the headquarters began the move some 30 miles west to Longuyon.[17]

Bradley, Patton, and Eddy stared at the situation map taking in the latest unit dispositions while the staff began packing things up. Patton broke the silence with, "These sons of bitches don't want me to get to the Ardennes. How the hell can my men get to Bastogne with all this on my flank?" he said, waving his hand over the mass of *Seventh Army* units plotted on the map. Bradley looked over and said, "Look George, I'm giving you 28th and 4th Divisions and 10th Armored Division minus and part of 9th Armored Division as well, but truthfully they're pretty banged up and can't hold the line without some help. We need to commit the 4th Armored." Pushing his finger against the map, Patton told Eddy, "Swing CCB around here and have CCA attack on this axis. The 80th Division will be up shortly and we'll finish this business in short order and get on with our real mission. Brad, tell Ike I've taken a detour and may be a day or two late."[18]

After several unsuccessful attempts, *212th Volksgrenadier Division* and *Führer Begleit Brigade* finally took Christnach in the afternoon of 20 December. Many of the units had become intertwined, eliminating any chance for continuing the attack against 9th Armored Division's CCA and CCA then launched a counterattack of its own which took a great deal of effort to beat back. However, *276th Volksgrenadier Division* was now able to make some progress against CCA's front. General Eddy decided it was time to strengthen his line by shortening it. He ordered 28th and 4th Infantry Divisions, 10th Armored Division, and 9th Armored Division's CCA to fall back behind the Alzette and defend from Ettelbruck in the north down to the 4th Armored Division's positions north of Luxembourg City. The movement was accomplished with little interference from the Germans. This new line would remain basically unchanged for the next two weeks, in spite of the best efforts of the *352d*, *276th*, and *212th Volksgrenadier Divisions*.

Brandenberger had little time to savor Hitler's Christmas present—the redesignation of *Seventh Army* as *Seventh Panzer Army*. For the next six days, *Seventh Panzer Army* would be caught up in a ferocious fight with the Third Army. It started on 21 December as the 4th Armored Division launched a counterattack against *11th Panzer Division* and *15th Panzergrenadier Division*. After some initial problems, the two German divisions reacted quickly, halted the Americans and retook most of the lost ground. Over on the east side of the city, 80th Infantry Division committed its regiments, as they arrived, in a series of piecemeal attacks against the *6th SS Nord*, which easily deflected them. *Nord* had reached its objectives and was concentrating on building strong defensive positions.

On 22 December Patton wanted to relieve 4th Armored Division with the 26th Infantry Division, but Brandenberger did not cooperate. The *Führer Begleit Brigade* had been attached to *11th Panzer Division* and together they made serious inroads into 4th Armored Division's CCB positions north of the city, even gaining a small bridgehead over the Alzette. Brandenberger, with the *10th SS Panzer Division "Frundsberg"* starting to arrive, committed the last major unit he had in reserve, the 6,000-man strong *Führer Grenadier Brigade* with over 70 assault guns and tanks. *Führer Grenadier Brigade*'s attack hit the boundary between the 4th Armored Division and the 80th Infantry Division. After some initial progress against the screening cavalry troopers, *Führer Grenadier Brigade* was roughly handled by a task force built around the 80th's tank destroyer battalion equipped with new M36 90mm self-propelled guns. It didn't help that the *Führer Grenadier Brigade* commander, Colonel Hans-Joachim Kahler, was seriously wounded early in the fight. Nevertheless, *Führer Grenadier Brigade*'s attack relieved the pressure on *15th Panzergrenadier Division*'s left, allowing the division to push 4th Armored Division's CCA back into the city proper. The Panzergrenadiers followed quickly to capture the Neudorf section of the city.

Unable to break 4th Armored Division free, Patton beefed up the division's CCR and attached it to 26th Infantry Division for its push on to the now surrounded Bastogne, scheduled to begin on 23 December—a day late and two divisions short.[19] To make up some of the difference for the missing divisions, Patton ordered the 35th Infantry Division to pass west of Luxembourg City through Arlon and join the 26th Infantry Division's attack. Back near Luxembourg City, lead elements of the 5th Infantry Division were closing on the city and were being quickly inserted into the line as need be. Over the next day, 4th Armored Division's CCA would shift its efforts to the north side of the city, while 5th Infantry Division took over responsibility for the rest.

The 23d was another day of intense fighting around and in the city. Clearing weather was allowing Allied fighter-bombers to make it increasingly difficult for the German armored forces to maneuver during daylight hours.

But armored combat dominated the fighting outside the built-up areas regardless. Inside the city, house-to-house, room-to-room, and often hand-to-hand fighting, between armored infantry and Panzergrenadiers, was the order of the day. In spite of the air attacks and the best efforts of CCB, the *11th Panzer Division* managed to expand its bridgehead over the Alzette and also pushed into the northern suburbs of the city, linking up with elements of the *15th Panzergrenadier Division*.[20]

Brandenberger found it increasingly difficult to keep his units supplied with fuel and ammunition. Between a shortage of trucks, air attacks on convoys and bridges, and the massive volume of traffic on the roads at night, it was a wonder anything got to the front at all. Surprisingly, he was able to get the *10th SS Frundsberg* moved up behind the front relatively intact by the morning of the 24th. *Frundsberg* relieved *Führer Grenadier Brigade*, which was now attached to *15th Panzergrenadier Division* and committed to the street fighting. *Frundsberg* and *Nord* formed an SS corps as promised, even if one of the two divisions was not the intended one. *Frundsberg* was pushed around the eastern side of the city to interdict the flow of reinforcements from the south.

On 24 December, German artillery fire noticeably slackened as the resupply effort could no longer keep up with the demands of intense combat. Unable to provide its lead units with adequate artillery support, *11th Panzer Division* was forced to give up its bridgehead, although mysteriously, this development was not reported up to *Army Group B* until several days later. However, the combined attack of *11th Panzer Division*, the reinforced *15th Panzergrenadier Division*, and the *10th SS Panzer Division* captured all of Luxembourg City on the east bank of the Alzette. Fierce fighting continued around the bridges in the city center.

Off to the east the 80th Infantry Division attacked the now well dug-in *6th SS*. The attack made no progress at all. With casualties mounting for no apparent gain, the attack was called off shortly after noon.

On Christmas Day, *15th Panzergrenadier Division* made a successful attack capturing several key bridges. *Führer Grenadier Brigade*'s infantry, with assault gun support, were fed in to expand the bridgehead and were able to take several more blocks, but only at a heavy price in casualties. 5th Infantry Division made several counterattacks the next day but took back only a few buildings.[21]

Clawing to Bastogne, 24 December 1944–3 January 1945

To the north, the drive to Bastogne was not going well for the 26th Infantry Division against the *5th Fallschirmjäger Division* now supported by the newly deployed *79th Volksgrenadier Division*. On Christmas Day the relief force was still 60 miles from Bastogne although, with the arrival of the 35th Infantry Division, the rate of advance was increasing. At the current rate, the relief force would not break through until several days into the New Year. To speed up the progress of the attack, 87th Infantry Division, with its famous all-black tank battalion, was committed to the effort on 27 December. The three divisions, reinforced with CCB from 6th Armored Division and 4th Armored Division's CCR, closed to within 15 miles of Bastogne by 30 December but on that day, a new unit, the *9th Volksgrenadier Division* appeared in the line ahead of them. It took two days to gain an additional three miles.

In Bastogne several days of clear skies around Christmas had allowed substantial resupply of ammunition, but not enough to maintain the fight at the same intensity as in the early days of the siege. On 27 December the *9th Panzer Division* overran most of the besieged garrison's drop zones. The drop zones still available were now under direct fire. With ammunition running seriously low, the resupply drop zones lost or under direct fire, German air defenses thickening around it, and the apparent inability of Third Army to break through, the garrison was ordered to break out on 2 January 1945. During the night of 2 January the artillerymen fired off their last rounds in a blaze of glory and spiked their guns. They formed up into squads and moved to their jump-off positions. The lack of fuel immobilized most of the remaining vehicles defending Bastogne. The crews thermited their tanks and other vehicles and set off to fight their way out on foot.[22]

Attacking southwest towards Neufchâteau they discovered the area was only thinly held by the *26th Volksgrenadier Division*. Encountering light resistance, the lead elements secured Sibret before midnight, but only after a stiff fight from the *26th Volksgrenadier Division*'s reconnaissance battalion. The breakout forces were actually fighting their way along several parallel roads, creating a floating pocket moving across the Belgium countryside. Although ammunition was low and they had to leave the most seriously wounded behind, morale was still high and the troops maintained good order and discipline throughout the movement. By sun-up on 3 January, two regimental columns were converging on Vaux-les-Rosières where an infantry battalion of the *26th Volksgrenadier Division* made a valiant, but hopeless attempt to halt the withdrawal.

Once the Germans realized a breakout was under way, elements of *Panzer Lehr* and the *9th Panzer Division* began probing the receding American rearguards who had been well supplied with bazookas. For the most part, the Germans appeared to be satisfied finally to have taken control of Bastogne and were not all that interested in pursuing their antagonist of the last two and a half weeks.

The 87th Infantry Division battled forward five tough miles against the *5th Fallschirmjäger Division* before tankers of the 77th Tank Battalion finally linked up with the withdrawing troops around 10:00 a.m. The loss of Bastogne was a bitter disappointment for the American command, mitigated only by the fact that 80 percent of those who participated in the breakout on the night of 2 January eventually made it safely back to Allied lines. Nevertheless, Patton's rage was positively Olympian.

In the Ruins of Luxembourg City

Back in Luxembourg City the bloodbath and destruction continued. To the Panzergrenadiers of the *15th Panzergrenadier Division*, *Führer Grenadier Brigade*, and elements of *11th Panzer Division* and *10th SS Panzer Division*, it became known as Stalingrad West. The Germans continued to gain ground, or rather buildings, but at a frightful cost. Outside the city the lines had remained basically unchanged as both sides were drawn into the urban battle like moths to a flame. The 5th Infantry Division was suffering heavy casualties as well, but the numbers paled in comparison to the German losses. There were two reasons for the disparity. First, the Germans were attacking, and attacking a veteran unit at that. The second reason was the massive dominance of U.S. artillery and air power. Not only did the Americans have more than twice the number of guns, but more importantly they had, what seemed to the Germans at least, an endless supply of shells. German gunners found themselves limited to firing only 5 or 10 rounds per gun per day.

Besides the growing loss of human life, the city itself was being battered into submission. The areas converted into rubble grew every day. Fortunately most of the civilian population had started leaving as soon as the fighting appeared to be heading in their direction. The pull-out of Bradley's headquarters had turned the stream of refugees into a flood. Those civilians who remained in the city were now confined to living almost exclusively in their cellars.

Brandenberger knew the urban battle was bleeding his army dry of its precious infantry. Frantically he requested *Army Group B* to release the promised *21st Panzer Division* and *17th SS Panzergrenadier Division*. Those two divisions, coupled with *10th SS Panzer Division*, *11th Panzer Division*, and the still potent *Führer Begleit Brigade*, would be enough to sweep around the city and move the fighting back to the open countryside. He would also be able finally to take Arlon and cut the main road into the Ardennes from the south. However, on 31 December, Model informed Brandenberger that, the imminent fall of Bastogne notwithstanding, the *Führer's* attention was turning elsewhere. There were 63 newly built tanks ready for shipment to the front. The *Führer* had decided not to send them to the Ardennes and was considering sending them to the Eastern Front, a clear sign Hitler was beginning to pay attention to the Russian build-up in the east.

Once Brandenberger heard this he immediately reduced the number, size, and intensity of his offensive operations. He ordered his units to start preparing more permanent defensive positions and to begin planning for additional positions throughout the depth of the ground they had captured over the preceding two weeks. Furthermore, selected items of hard to move or replace equipment were quietly sent to the rear.

His main mission, as he saw it now, was to save as much of *Seventh Panzer Army* as possible. The inevitable order to hold to the last man and not give an inch of ground was bound to come. The troops had fought well and deserved better than that. He was determined to get as many men and as much equipment back for the final defense of the Fatherland as possible, while still appearing to fight for every step of the way. In this effort Brandenberger would be successful, though mainly for other reasons. Throughout January, one mobile division after another would be taken from his command until only his infantry formations remained.

Even though he had not taken all his objectives Brandenberger felt he had done the best he could have done under the circumstances. The blame for the failure of the offensive could not be placed on him. He had kept significant elements of Patton's Third Army tied down. The main offensive had ground to a halt before any Third Army units had reached the main battle area and because of that he credited himself with having a significant impact on the fall of Bastogne.

A Meager Victory

The fall of Bastogne relieved some of the German resupply problems in the salient that became known as the Bulge but, by the time Bastogne fell, the main effort had already been effectively halted. Additionally, the gain of the vital crossroads made the salient more defensible for the Germans. It would take the Allies until 15 February finally to erase the last vestiges of the Bulge. The final assault on the Reich, which Third Army had hoped to start back on 16 December, would not kick off until 16 February, a full two months later. Arriving on the Rhine on 12 March, the Americans found all the bridges had been blown, including the railroad bridge at Remagen, though that was not destroyed until 10 March, only just in time. Fighting their way across Germany, the Americans linked up with the Russians on 7 May along the line of the Weser and Leine Rivers from Bremerhaven south through Hanover and continuing south through Gotha, Nuremberg and on to Munich, which they captured two hours before the arrival of the Soviets. It would be the beginning of 1946 before the Soviets relinquished control over the areas that had been designated for occupation by the Western Allies. The Allies found a wasteland, stripped of everything including most of the population.

The Reality

In the early planning stages of what was to become *Wacht am Rhein*, one of the proposed options had called for an offensive through Luxembourg. The four divisions described here as making up the *Seventh Army*'s right wing, the *5th Fallschirmhager* and the *212th*, *276th* and *352d Volksgrenadier Divisions*, were the actual units in the *Seventh Army* and their advances follow the actual events fairly accurately until the 4th Infantry Division gives way, which of course never happened. Three of the additional divisions used in this scenario, *6th SS Gebirgs Division "Nord"*, *11th Panzer Division* and *10th SS Panzer Division* were in fact in the *OKW* reserve and slated as third echelon divisions for later commitment if the offensive went well. Several of the other units, such as the *15th Panzergrenadier Division* and the *Führer Grenadier* and *Führer Begleit Brigades*, were eventually committed against Patton's Third Army, albeit farther north in the Bastogne area. The use of the divisions from *OKW* reserve would only have been effective in widening the base of the Bulge as was done in this scenario. To have pushed these additional units into the salient would only have added to the already unsolvable logistical problems. Even though Hitler consider the Americans to be the Italians of the Allies, their airpower, the strength of Patton's forces, and the additional units being committed, would have been too much for the Germans to defeat in any case.

Bibliography

Elstob, Peter, *Hitler's Last Offensive*, Secker & Warburg, London, 1971.

Forty, George, *Patton's 3rd Army at War*, Charles Scribner's Sons, New York, 1978.

Hansen, Chet, *Diary*, U.S. Army Military History Research Collection, Fort Leavenworth (unpublished).

MacDonald, Charles B., *A Time for Trumpets: The Untold Story of the Battle of the Bulge*, William Morrow, New York, 1985.

Maertz, J., *Luxemburg in der Rundstedt Offensive*, Grunhalle, Luxembourg, 1948.

Nobecourt, Jacques, *Hitler's Last Gamble: The Battle of the Bulge*, Secker & Warburg, London, 1971.

The Ardennes: Battle of the Bulge, U.S. Army in World War II, Government Printing Office, Washington, 1965.

The Lorraine Campaign, U.S. Army in World War II, Government Printing Office, Washington, 1950.

Notes

*1. Erich Brandenberger, *Too Little Too Late: The Story of the Seventh Panzer Army*, Vowinckel, Heidelberg, 1952, p.13.

*2. *Ibid*, p. 27.

*3. *Ibid*, p. 31.

*4. *Ibid*, p. 38.

 5. MacDonald, *A Time for Trumpets*, p. 190.

 6. *Ibid*, p. 159.

*7. Brandenberger, *Too Little Too Late,* p. 67.

*8. *Ibid*, p. 93.

*9. Cook, *Strong Signal: Radio Luxembourg at War*, Upper Dean Press, Bedford, 1972, p. 42.

*10. Metcalf, Richard, *Unofficial History of the Tenth Armored Division*, Fiddler's Green Books, Elizabethtown, KY, 1961, p. 361.

 11. MacDonald, *A Time for Trumpets*, p. 420.

*12. Metcalf, *Unofficial History of the Tenth Armored Division*, p. 300.

*13. Cook, *Strong Signal*, p.156. All of the Radio Luxembourg staff were either killed or captured. Those captured were transported back to German where they spent the rest of the war until they were liberated by a unit from the 4th Infantry Division.

*14. Shell, Jude, *Studies in Urban Warfare: The Battle of Luxembourg City*, Leatherneck Press, Norfolk, VA, 1992, p. 26.

*15. Brandenberger, *Too Little Too Late,* p. 104.

*16. *Ibid*, p.119.

*17. Shell, *Studies in Urban Warfare*, p. 49.
*18. *Ibid*, p. 63.
*19. Peter G. Tsouras, *Disaster at Bastogne*, Greenhill Books, London, 1995, p. 80.
*20. Shell, *Studies in Urban Warfare*, p. 99.
*21. *Ibid*, p. 124.
*22. Tsouras, *Disaster at Bastogne*, p. 167.

10
ARDENNES DISASTER
The Iron Curtain Falls on the White House

Peter G. Tsouras

The Kremlin, Moscow, 28 December 1944

Stalin hung up the telephone. He paused a moment to light his pipe and take a deep puff. He just sat and let the impact of Churchill's frantic call sink in. Catastrophe had fallen upon the Western Allies. The German offensive had succeeded in capturing Brussels and Antwerp and cutting off almost the entire 21st Army Group.[1]

Bad news, very bad news, he thought. But for whom?

This was the second call in two days from the British Prime Minister. In the first call, Churchill had pleaded for Stalin to begin the planned Soviet Vistula–Oder operation as soon as possible to take pressure off the Western Allies. Stalin had assured him that the Red Army would do everything it could to help. The second call had been to convey the news of Allied disaster. Stalin again assured him that the Red Army would strain every effort to assist its gallant allies.

He lied, of course. Where a lie would serve as well as a truth, he always seemed to prefer the lie. Churchill's desperation was palpable, and desperate men will concede much.

Stalin's mind followed the twists and turns of advantage as the smoke coiled from his pipe. His staff sat stone still through all of it, waiting for the Boss to break his silence. Finally, he grunted and turned his cold eyes on the group. Contempt dripped from his words, "The incompetent Allies have got their dicks slammed in a German door, comrades."

The staff recognized that this was only a preamble and waited.

"For three years we begged them to open a Second Front while we bled rivers to hold off the Fascists single-handedly. Now six months after they actually open the Second Front, and Hitler has turned the tables on them. Now they beg us to rescue them. Get me Zhukov."[2]

Headquarters, First Belorussian Front, on the Vistula River

"Yes, Comrade Stalin, I can delay the offensive," Zhukov stated. He was puzzled. Two days before Stalin had alerted him to advance the offensive from 20 to 12 January. Now he wanted it delayed. Unlike the General Staff in Moscow, Zhukov spoke his mind, within limits, to the Boss. He was the only one, it seemed, allowed that privilege. Stalin recognized an indispensable man who had saved him on many occasions. Still, if Zhukov ever went too far, his past record would be forgotten, but the burly Marshal of the Soviet Union, was adept in many things.

"Comrade Stalin, may I ask why you have made this decision?"

"Of course, comrade marshal." Stalin's normally brusque manner softened for a moment. He was actually enjoying giving Zhukov a peek into the double deception he was planning. "We must let Hitler put his head further into the noose his victory against the Allies has tied for him. I think we shall let his triumph go to his head." Stalin had gained a shrewd and painfully acquired appreciation for Hitler's foibles over the last four years. He paused for a moment to see if his prize commander would pick up the hint.

"Then it is vital for my planning to know exactly when he starts pulling units off our front to send west. My staff will be very busy."

"Good boy," thought Stalin. "Yes, exactly," he replied, "Let him reinforce his victory. We shall be as quiet as mice so as not to disturb his peace of mind." He did not add that his secret police chief, that loathsome child-rapist toad Beria, was already planting disinformation with the Germans to indicate that Soviet logistics were in such a muddle that the offensive could not begin until February at the earliest. Molotov, his foreign minister, was also busy encouraging those vile capitalist toads, the Swedes, to approach Hitler with tentative offers of a peace in the east based upon the situation on the ground. So many loathsome but "useful" toads.[3]

German Headquarters in the West, Ziegenberg, 12 January 1945

Colonel-General Heinz Guderian was the only unhappy German in the *Führer* command group. Everyone else was drunk on the victory in the West. Even the august Field Marshal Gerd von Rundstedt had succumbed to the euphoria. As commander of the German forces in the West, he could claim a sublime victory as all of his references to the hair-brained nature of the operation had been carefully hushed up. After all, his lightning thrust to Antwerp had trapped almost a million Allied troops to the north. Not even the great encirclements in the early days of the war in Russia had netted such a huge bag, though they had not actually marched into captivity. Additionally, he had smashed up the First U.S. Army and brushed its remnants aside.

It had helped that their vaunted Patton was kept very busy on his own front as the critical point in the offensive had developed. Now Allied offensive operations aimed at the German border had ground to a halt. Patton had been pulled north to break through into the Holland Pocket while Patch's 6th Army Group extended its front to cover the new hole in the line. Things were getting desperate for the trapped 21st Army Group (British Second Army and Canadian First Army) which had also assumed control of Ninth U.S. Army and two corps of First U.S. Army also trapped in the Holland Pocket. Supply by air was the only thing that was keeping them going, but it was not by much. Air resupply kept the forces alive, but gave no strength for serious offensive operations. The massive stream of transports flying into the Holland Pocket became a shooting gallery for the *Luftwaffe*'s new jets.

Even sweeter to Hitler's ears had been the wave of despondency that had run through Britain. The word, "Dunkirk" had been the first off the tongue— over five years of struggle and loss, for what? To be right back at the start? Hitler was positively gleeful when the British war coalition almost unraveled. Such was the uproar in the Houses of Parliament that the whips came to Churchill to say he was about to lose a vote of no confidence. The British Lion could see no way out, and went to the King and recommended that Anthony Eden succeed him as Prime Minister.[4] George VI declined the advice and put forward Clement Attlee as the only hope of maintaining the wartime coalition.[5] Hitler's glee had turned to a near orgasm when the news arrived that Roosevelt had died of a stroke.[6] Hitler had gone around the staff exulting that the Empress of Russia had died.[7] His eyes had their old fire back as he waved von Ribbentropp's report that Stalin was making feelers for a separate peace.

As the chief of the Army General Staff, Guderian continued to worry a great deal. He worried that Patton's savage hammer blows at the German coil on the Meuse would succeed in breaking through. He worried more about the *Führer*'s determination not to let that happen. Guderian despaired of inserting any common sense into Hitler's deliberations, especially now that the man's "genius" had once more been affirmed by the victory.

Hitler's answer to Patton was to strip more divisions from the Eastern Front to strengthen the exhausted forces in the West. To Guderian's amazement, even trapped divisions in Courland were being transported by sea across the Baltic to join von Rundstedt's forces. More and more divisions, especially Panzer divisions, were entraining in Poland and East Prussia for movement west. Especially worrying was Hitler's order to transfer Colonel-General Erhard Raus and the staff of his *Third Panzer Army* from East Prussia to the west to organize a new army for further offensive operations. Hitler was talking of another and greater offensive to crush the Holland Pocket followed by attacks to drive the Americans back into France. Raus' departure deprived the Germans forces from Poland to the Baltic of the best Panzer commander left in the east. The man had an extraordinary reputation for clever boldness and ruthlessness in the attack. His *6th Panzer Division* had nearly single-handedly broken into the Stalingrad pocket. He also had a reputation for rescuing his forces from the disasters Hitler's meddling had caused. They said of him, "*Raus zieht heraus!*"—"Raus pulls you through!"[8]

Hitler was full of explanations. Unlike Stalin, he was not guarded in his strategic vision. He was compelled to share it with everyone within earshot.

Guderian thanked his peptic ulcer for the excuse to leave the room and escape those interminable after-dinner monologues.

> "My intention has never been to crush the British, our Aryan brothers. I only wished to compel them to leave me to deal with Bolshevism. But that gangster, Churchill, opposed me and dragged the Americans into the war."

No one commented that it was Hitler who had declared war on the United States on 11 December 1941, even when the Tripartite Pact with Japan had not actually called for it.

> "How much good Aryan blood has been shed on both sides because of that man. Now he has had his come-uppance. And Roosevelt, that Jew... "

He pounded the table in gleeful punctuation.

> "My only goal remains, as it always has been, to crush Bolshevism. We have struck it a great blow, such a blow that Stalin begs me now for a separate peace. That wound and now the crushing defeat of his allies here in the West have taken all the fight out of him. Well, we shall let him think that is what we want as well. When I have done with the British and Americans, then it will be his turn. This time there will be no timid generals to fail in their orders."[9]

And so it went. Hitler's ambitions fed on his victory. Division after division entrained for action in the west, and Stalin bided his time.

Supreme Allied Headquarters, Paris, 20 January 1945

Marshall cleaned house the day he arrived to replace Eisenhower as Supreme Commander, Allied Forces Europe. Bradley, commander of 12th Army Group, and Courtney Hodges of First Army followed Eisenhower back to the States in disgrace. Except for Patch commanding 6th Army Group, there had been almost a clean sweep of senior Allied commanders. Montgomery's capture outside of Namur by a reconnaissance element of the *2d Panzer Division* had contributed to the shock that sent the Churchill government crashing. No British field marshal had ever been captured in the long history of the British Army. Dempsey, commanding British Second Army, had assumed command of the trapped 21st Army Group. The recriminations within the Western Alliance were bitter, with the British and Canadians blaming the Americans for the debacle.

Worse yet, Roosevelt's death had elevated Vice-President Henry Wallace to the office of Commander-in-Chief three months before the inauguration of the Vice-President elect, Harry Truman. Marshall was as worried about Wallace as much as he was about the mess on the Western Front. Harry Truman, Roosevelt's running mate in the 1944 election, would not be inaugurated until early March. Marshall was worried that Wallace's communist supporters were beginning to suggest that Wallace should remain in office until a new election could be called. The Democrats were in complete disarray, splitting into Truman and Wallace camps. It had been interesting to see how Roosevelt's closest aides had jumped. Harold Ickes had been abruptly fired. Lauchlin Currie had moved from administrative assistant to chief of staff. Henry Hopkins assumed the same close relationship with Wallace as he had had with Roosevelt, but a young East Coast aristocrat from the State Department, Alger Hiss, seemed to have become the President's right hand man. Then there was Dexter White suddenly elevated to Secretary of the Treasury. Wallace was stirring up a hornet's nest by firing Democrat stalwarts throughout the government and replacing them with Progressive Party people, many of them outright communists. The last thing Marshall needed was chaos at home.

His final conversation with Wallace had been disturbing to say the least.

Over and over again, Wallace kept emphasizing continuing the offensive as soon as possible not to let the Soviets down.

> "They are our faithful allies, general, and a great force for progress in the world. Why, if the American people only knew the great things that had been done in the Soviet Union before the Germans attacked, they would be shouting the same thing to you."

Hardly a word escaped his lips about the desperate plight of the American troops, much less their allies. At his elbow was Hiss.[10]

Eisenhower's staff car had barely left the headquarters before Marshall ordered his aide, "Get me Patton."

He was lucky. It was one of the rare times Patton had been in his headquarters since he had moved north with two corps to attempt to break open the Holland Pocket. Marshall wasted no words. "General, you will assume command of 12th Army Group. I will meet you at your headquarters tomorrow."

Aboard Marshall's Airplane, 21 January 1945

Marshall knew the details of the disaster even as the operations officer briefed him on the flight to 12th Army Group headquarters. He did not even glance at the swarm of Mustang escorts that flew around his plane in a protective cocoon. Even a man with Marshall's legendary cool head was shaken by the repetition of disaster. The officer went on.

> "Trapped in the Holland is the entire British 21st Army Group—11 British, two Canadian, and one Polish Divisions, plus all of the Ninth Army of 8 divisions and 4 divisions of the First Army. In round numbers of men, over 700,000 British, 100,000 Canadians, 30,000 Poles, Czechs, Dutch, and Belgians... and 300,000 Americans.[11]
>
> Of our seven Allied armies, three and a half are trapped. Patton pulled half his Third Army up to cover the flank of the German encirclement. Patch's 6th Army Group has filled in to the north to cover the front

Patton had to give up. Unfortunately, Patch's U.S. Seventh and French 1st Armies, are small and have had to go over to the defense.

There were five American divisions in Britain or recently landed on the continent.[12] They have been rushed to the open flank left by the encirclement. They are inexperienced and without corps or army level support assets. The strategic reserve of XVIII Airborne Corps is still relatively intact. The German advance was so swift that they were never able to reinforce the vital crossroads towns before they fell to the Germans. The British I Airborne Corps is also in the line, though its 1st Airborne Division has still not fully reconstituted from its mauling in Market-Garden.

Field Marshal Alexander's Fifteenth Army Group has also gone over to the defensive in order to transfer from the Italian front to us the Canadian I Corps, British XIII Corps, and U.S. II Corps, amounting to two armored and five infantry divisions. They are embarking now but lead elements are not expected to begin arriving at the front for another three weeks. It will be two months before they are completely in place.

DeGaulle is rushing three divisions to that sector as well. These divisions were raised from the Resistance to subdue the German fortress garrisons along the Atlantic Wall. They are haphazardly equipped with old French, captured German, and our equipment. He has also reinforced the French First Army with another division raised in Paris."

The briefer paused. Marshall knew what was coming. DeGaulle had defied Patch's order to retreat to the Vosges when the Germans in that sector had attacked. The French stayed and kept Patch nailed to the ground as well.[13] Be that as it may, 6th Army Group had weathered the German attack. Though the French had been pressed back almost to Strasbourg, they had held. Then they had sprung forward to snap the overextended Germans back to the border. Thousands of French troops kept trickling up to the front as fast as DeGaulle could train and equip them. The only bright spot in the disastrous last month had been the French counterattack.

The balance of power among the Western Allies had changed dramatically. Marshall stared out the window and down to the grim winter Belgian landscape as the plane began its descent. But he had more to worry about at the moment than the balance of political power among the Allies or even the perilous situation along the front. The alliance itself was in tatters—its strong poles, Churchill and Roosevelt, were gone. He had stopped in London long enough to call on Prime Minister Attlee and was alarmingly unimpressed.

Worse, though, was the very thought of President Wallace and the apparently disloyal men he was surrounding himself with. It filled him with more disquiet than anything else had in his life. The man himself was too much of a fool to know the extent of the harm he was doing. Those around him had much more a clarity of vision—insidious, single-minded, and ruthless.

Camp Ritchie, Maryland, 14 January 1945

Marshall's mind went back to his clandestine visit only days before to Camp Ritchie in Maryland not far from the presidential retreat. It was one of the Army's most secret installations, shared by Bill Donovan's Office of Strategic Services and the cryptanalysis operation, the Signals Security Agency commanded by Colonel Preston Corderman.[14] The leaves had fallen from the trees on the mountains closely enclosing the post, but the two former ice-harvesting lakes in the center of the little valley sparkled from the reflection of the unusually bright January sky. The front gate was heavily guarded but whisked open as the Chief-of-Staff's car drove up. It was only a few hundred yards to the camp headquarters, a small gem of a building, stone-built in the shape of the insignia of the Army Corps of Engineers, a castle. More guards but no honor guard. Colonel Corderman had stepped outside, saluted, and escorted him inside past more guards. Only these were not soldiers but well-dressed and tough-looking civilians. Corderman led down winding stairs to a small conference room.

Herbert Hoover stood up when Marshall entered the room. Marshall may have been the Chief of Staff of the Army, but Hoover was a power unto himself. He met Marshall halfway across the room before extending his hand. Their relationship had been cordial but correct, once as it had been established that Army Intelligence would not tread on the FBI's turf. But Marshall was aware that Hoover was increasingly irritated by the actions of Donovan and his OSS. Neither trusted the other.

The meeting and its clandestine nature had been requested by Hoover. He had specifically asked that no OSS representative be included. The three men sat at the table. Hoover began in his gruff voice, "General, thank you for meeting me under such unusual circumstances. I thought it best to initiate this meeting outside of Washington through Colonel Corderman. There must be no hint that the three of us have met."

Marshall's face remained impassive as Hoover continued. "I will come to the point, general. For the first time in our history, the American people have a president who is taking orders from a foreign power—a hostile foreign power, the Soviet Union—despite our present alliance. Wallace is Stalin's puppet. He has surrounded himself with communists hiding under the label of the Progressive Party."

Marshall's lips had pursed, and his blue eyes turned into hard agates. "Mr Director, I cannot listen… "

Hoover broke in, "General, with the help of Army Intelligence, we have cracked the Soviet codes being used by the embassy in Washington." He pushed a folder across the table to Marshall. "Read them. They are damning."

Corderman added, "Sir, we were able to break the codes based on a Soviet code book captured by the Finns and turned over to us. The Soviets had tried to burn it, but it was only singed when the Finns overran the headquarters."[15]

Hoover added, "The Bureau has taken these transcripts and put two and two together. There are over 300 Soviet agents, all American citizens, mentioned in these transmissions. We have identified a number so far, and some of them are in the White House, to include this shit Hiss. Another is the Secretary of the Treasury. You remember how White had insisted that the United States transfer 40 tons of uranium ore to the Soviets against the advice of almost the entire government. Well, he had a good reason. The transcripts show that the entire Manhattan Project has been penetrated by Soviet agents as well."

Marshall was stunned. The President was a traitor. Hoover had had the courage to say what he had only feared. Inside that folder was what he dreaded most—that which would question his very concept of duty. Still, the problem seemed to be one that would evaporate with the inauguration of Harry Truman in early March.

Hoover trod hard on that hope. "And we have been picking up an undercurrent of rumor among the Progressives that the inauguration should be postponed until the end of the war."

As he left the building, Marshall gave Corderman a quiet order, "See that General MacArthur is told of this personally by your assistant."[16]

In another part of the post, a man turned off the tape when it appeared that the visitor had left. A lieutenant put it in a briefcase, and chained it to his wrist. A car was waiting for him to take it to Washington.

The next day, the counsel to the head of the OSS, Duncan Lee, was listening to the tape in the privacy of his office. He glanced up to the picture of Robert E. Lee on the wall and smiled.[17]

The Kremlin, 17 January 1945

Beria reminded Stalin of a ghoul when he brought good news. "Our agent *Koch* has informed us of a secret meeting between Marshall and Hoover where they discussed the foothold we have seized in the White House."

Stalin looked up from the report, "*Koch*? Isn't he the one descended from the greatest of their slaveholding generals?"

"Just the one."

Stalin grunted, "Well, history has its jokes."

Beria's laugh was positively lewd. Stalin cut it off, "But Marshall is dangerous, just as dangerous as Hoover. We do not need another Tukhachevskiy to upset our plans in America. Can't you do something about him, Lavarenti Pavlovich?"

"Of course, Comrade Stalin. He is traveling to the war zone, a very dangerous place."[18]

Military Airfield, Spa, Belgium, 21 January 1945

Patton had already inspected the band and the honor guard at the airfield. He had been barely 28 hours in command of 12th Army Group, but he had made sure the Chief of Staff would see a spit and polish display that showed the group was still in the fight. Marshall's plane was overdue, and he paced with long strides, striking his polished boots impatiently with his gloves. Patton was one of many who owed everything to George Marshall. He was also a man eager to please those whom he genuinely respected. Even more he felt vindicated, stepping into Bradley's boots as Bradley had stepped into his. He had barely had time to say goodbye to Bradley—both men were embarrassed and saw no need to dwell on a painful moment. And Patton had much to do to whip 12th Army Group into shape.

He paused in his pacing as he saw an aide sprint towards him from the communications van parked on the edge of the field. The young signals captain ran up, forgetting to salute as he blurted out, "Sir, General Marshall's plane blew up! The commander of the Mustang escort radioed in that he just blew up in midair. The debris knocked down one of his fighters, too."

"There was no German attack?"

"No, sir."

"When?"

The captain looked at his watch, "Sixteen minutes ago, sir. And there were no parachutes, sir."

Red fury rippled across Patton's face, then set into blue steel.[19]

Enter MacArthur

The death of Marshall had been another hard blow to the Western Alliance. The cupboard was nearly bare of the senior leadership of only a month ago. In short order, Montgomery, Eisenhower, Marshall, Bradley, Hodges were all gone. On top of the similar decapitation of the political leadership, it was breeding a crisis of stunning proportions.

Britain was reeling from the disaster of the Holland Pocket and clutched at any straw. The new prime minister demanded that Wallace appoint British Field Marshal Alexander to take Marshall's place. Politically, Wallace could not give in on this demand in the face of public opinion and the advice of both Congress and the Joint Chiefs when it was only the U.S. Army that still held the line in Europe. The name on every tongue was MacArthur, liberator of the Philippines. For Wallace, it was a matter of indifference as long as the Lend-Lease shipments to the Soviet Union continued. Although halfway around the world, MacArthur's contacts had kept him in close touch with events in Washington. He had been especially troubled by the information from Marshall's personal representative. It was all too apparent to him that history was pivoting on multiple events both in Washington and Europe. The Pacific seemed to shrink into a backwater. He immediately flew to Paris to pick up the reins dropped by Eisenhower and Marshall.

Now, at last, Fortune played a good hand for the Alliance. MacArthur's stature and diplomatic skills, not to mention his messianic aura, went over well with the British and French who were staring disaster in the face. Patton and MacArthur were also known quantities to each other, and neither rubbed the other too much the wrong way. Their first meeting had been in France in 1918 when the two young officers chatted while a German barrage crept closer and closer, neither one wanting to flinch first. In 1932 Patton had played an important part as executive officer of the 3d Cavalry Regiment stationed at Fort Myers, Virginia, just across the Potomac River from Washington, while MacArthur was Chief of Staff of the Army. At that time MacArthur had had the unenviable task of driving thousands of destitute World War I veterans, the Bonus Marchers, out of the capital. MacArthur and Patton were both convinced that the Bonus Marchers' demands for payment of a war bonus had been manipulated by communist agitators. Patton led the cavalry in chasing the marchers across the Washington bridges with the flats of their sabers. It was a difficult but tactful job, something MacArthur never forgot.[20]

MacArthur was a great commander of the first order who could take advantage of Patton's aggressiveness and yet guide him with a firm hand. For that reason he had no hesitation in making him overall ground forces commander, the position that Montgomery had so coveted only a few months before. There was no need for MacArthur to tell Patton to succeed or "Don't come back alive," as he had to a corps commander in the struggle for New Guinea. Patton had made quite clear that he would relieve the Holland Pocket or die trying on the point of the assault.

"Sabotage, after all, is a French word," 2 February 1945

To Patton's very colorful distress, the reinforcement of the front slowed to a trickle. By the middle of February, a growing number of inexplicable delays, bottlenecks, and cases of outright sabotage were hindering the movement of reinforcements across France. It was also becoming obvious that the French were behind most it at almost every turn.

If Patton was distressed, Attlee was near panic. A growing despair at rescuing 21st Army Group was becoming palpable in Britain. The prime minister's efforts to counter it seemed increasingly ineffectual. He had confided in MacArthur that the British communists, although relatively few in numbers, were stoking the despair. Attlee himself was no communist dupe. Rather he despised the communists as only a true democratic socialist could. However, the national state of shock made an alarmingly large number of people susceptible to their arguments that the war should be ended on almost any terms.

It was in this growing atmosphere of gloom that MacArthur accepted DeGaulle's urgent request to call upon him.

The French general, and now *de facto* ruler of France, was well-prepared as usual. Although the junior member of the alliance, he was the most strategically gifted and visionary of the national leaders. He was also the most confident in what must be done. He began,

> "*Mon cher marechál* [MacArthur was a field marshal in the Philippine Army], we face a graver threat than the Germans who, at least, are honestly at war with us. I regret to inform you that French communists are behind the campaign to sabotage the transfer of reinforcements to the

front. I assure you of this. The orders are from Moscow. Just as in 1940, Stalin is playing a dirty game to help Hitler by ordering his creatures to sabotage the war effort."

He looked down his long nose at the American who traded him hauteur for hauteur. "And why, *marechál*?" He paused for dramatic effect.

"Because the longer we are stalemated in the West, the more Hitler is tempted to pull forces from the East. Stalin will pour through a denuded Eastern Front and wash up to the Rhine. We cannot afford to be rescued by Bolshevism. And it would be a catastrophe for France for the Rhine to be turned red.

We have the same enemies front and rear. My information is that the same sabotage has begun in your own country."

MacArthur was not surprised by DeGaulle's bluntness. MacAthur was nothing if not politically astute and had had a steady feed of information from the United States on the growing communist influence on Wallace and the rest of the government. Attlee had informed him under the strictest confidence of similar activities in Britain, though they were on a much smaller scale than in France with its powerful communist party.

"You understand that we must clean house if we are not to lose this war twice—both to the Germans and the Russians?" He paused again. Then with a cold, iron glint in his eye, he said, "And I have already begun."[21]

Indeed, as DeGaulle spoke, that very morning the Free French struck swiftly to decapitate the leadership of the French Communist Party. Thousands more in critical positions in the party or the Resistance were also arrested. The communists were taken completely by surprise both in France and in Moscow. In a situation as confused as liberated France, DeGaulle had pulled off the perfect coup. To this day, the maintenance of security of the operation is unparalleled. DeGaulle hardened his heart as French military tribunals and firing squads went to work.

But the communist cell system proved harder to eradicate and, as soon as communications with Moscow were reestablished, lashed back in a spasm of raids and assassinations. Gun battles became all too common on the streets of Paris and other large industrial cities. British, Canadian, and American soldiers all too often were the victims. Never a man to let his conscience stop him from doing what he thought was right, DeGaulle responded with a savagery that stunned the nation but stopped the budding insurgency in its tracks. By the end of February, the movement of Allied reinforcements to the front was going smoothly.

German Headquarters in the West, Ziegenberg, 5 February 1945

Hitler pounded the table, screaming in one of his rages. Von Rundstedt, Model, Guderian, and Raus rode out the storm. All but Raus had seen this performance before. Raus, a former Austrian Army officer, was stunned.

Hitler had become obsessed with destroying the Holland Pocket since the British had refused his peace overtures. He had pinned much hope on Raus' reconstituted *Third Panzer Army* tipping the balance. So now he concentrated much of his wrath on Raus.

"Because of your reputation on the Eastern Front, I brought you to the West. But what have you done with the strong forces I have given you? Nothing! Nothing but losses and failure. The British are trapped, and you cannot crush them."

Guderian stood up. "*Mein Führer*, the British retain a powerful defensive capability. Despite their semi-isolation in the pocket, the British soldier is tenacious in the defense, and enough supplies are getting through by air to keep him going. General Raus has done everything possible."

"More excuses! That's all I get from my generals, excuses!"

Raus' thoughts skipped back to the beginning of his attack, Operation *Sieg*. Hitler thought this would be the *coup de grâce* to the British 21st Army Group. *Third Panzer Army* had been built up to four Panzer and Panzergrenadier divisions and three infantry divisions. He had attacked on a narrow front between *Fifteenth Army* and *Sixth Panzer Army*. But he had never faced the British before and he rubbed his jaw ruefully at the experience. The British had been reduced to about 50 percent of establishment in their infantry battalions before the Ardennes and had had to break up divisions and brigades to maintain even that strength.[22] They had no replacements. Only the wounded had been flown out of the pocket. Yet they had fought stubbornly and intelligently. Two years ago he had crushed two Soviet armies as he led his *6th Panzer Division* in the attempted relief of Stalingrad. Now his Panzers had melted away as they dug deeper and deeper into the British defenses. Then there had been the airpower. "Stunning" had been the only word to describe it. He had never experienced anything so powerful on the Eastern Front. Night and day the British and American bombers had passed in a seemingly continuous flight over the battlefield, turning the soft Dutch polder land into a marsh, reversing a thousand years of reclamation. His *Third Panzer Army* had been trapped in the frozen mud.

His attention was brought back by the scream,

"Excuses! I created the conditions for a German Stalingrad in the West, and you have failed. It was within your grasp! You do not realize the vital political nature of this opportunity. Stalin is watching us. His attention is riveted upon events in Holland. My victory in the Ardennes struck fear into him and stayed his hand in the East. My victory gave us a breathing spell in both East and West. And now both of our enemies teeter, their vaunted Alliance revealed for what it is, a dirty game among gangsters built upon their own ambitions."

He paused to gloat,

"And now that their Churchill and Roosevelt have gone, who are their leaders? Attlee and Wallace! Attlee and Wallace! A filthy socialist and a fool. Did you hear what one American politician said about Wallace? 'Henry's the sort that keeps you guessing as to whether he's going to deliver a sermon or wet the bed.'[23] Wet the bed! I am now opposed to a bed-wetter, and my generals cannot beat his generals!"

The Eastern Front, 28 February 1945

From the Baltic to the Adriatic, the mighty artillery of the Red Army vomited a torrent of firepower on the Germans. The masses of tanks and infantry followed in wave after wave. For Stalin the time had come. It was the moment when all the factors favoring victory converged. The logistics build-up had been enormous; the extra six weeks would give the Red Army much longer legs than if it had attacked on 12 January as Churchill had requested. Stalin had put much importance on getting his agents into the organizations that administered Lend-Lease. Now that emphasis was paying off as the shipments continued and even increased beyond what the Soviets had requested. Hitler had stripped the Eastern Front of as many troops as he could. In the West, Allied reinforcements would soon allow the Anglo-Americans to go over to the offensive. Hitler would be caught between the Red Army's hammer and the Allies' anvil. There was also the troublesome matter of the French. DeGaulle's savaging of the French Communist Party had put an important part of Stalin's postwar strategy at risk. Time here was not on his side.

The German defenses stiffened at first as the few local reserves were committed, then abruptly collapsed to be swallowed in the tidal wave of the Red Army. One by one, Germany's eastern provinces were overrun before the terror-stricken populations had had the chance to flee west—East Prusia, East Pomerania, Silesia, fell into a silent hell of occupation. By 14 March, Zhukov and Koniev had bridgeheads over the Oder River. Zhukov's First Belorussian Front had lunged far enough forward from its bridgeheads to overrun the Seelow Heights, the last high ground between Berlin and the vengeance of the Russians. There they paused two weeks for their logistics to build up for the next great rush forward. This time they would no longer be gobbling up vast spaces of territory. This time they would be in the heart of the beast.

Reshuffling the Deck, March 1945

"Damn! Will you look at that!" PFC Bob Brunsvold exclaimed to his squadmates in their jumping off position. "It's Patton!" And indeed it was Patton, resplendent in polished riding boots and lacquered helmet with its four bright stars. It had been a long time since he had commanded the 3d Infantry Division when it was part of his Seventh Army in Sicily, and he wanted to be there when they jumped off at first light.

The 3d was the best single Allied infantry division, not only in its own opinion, but in the opinion of *OKW* as well which mentioned it by name in its war diary, the only such Allied formation to be so honored. In defiance of convention the men wore their white and blue stripped division patch unsubdued on their shoulders and helmets. They wanted the Germans to know who they were fighting. Reputation gave them an edge, an edge that they took pains to keep sharpened. The 3d had earned the title "Rock of the Marne" in 1918 as it stood like a great rock against which the German 1918 offensive had roared and broken. Patton walked among the Marnemen, as they like to be called, talking to the men. Brunsvold, a tall, lanky young man from Iowa, had landed with Patton in North Africa and was about as much a combat veteran as you could be. Patton was pleased to have him pointed out. "You're lucky to have a veteran like this with you," he said to the rest of the group around him. He did not know specifically, but would not have been surprised to hear that Brunsvold and one other man were the only original members of the company that had landed in North Africa two years before. "Men like this are the reason we are going to rescue our men in the Pocket and then kick the hell out of the Germans."[24]

Another reason they were going to kick the hell out of the Germans was the new British Fifth Army which had taken over the front from First U.S. Army's left to the sea. For the attack, the national components of the First Allied Airborne Army had been transferred to their respective commands. The two British airborne divisions joined the British and Canadian corps that had finally arrived from Italy. Hospitals in the UK and the logistics system had been ruthlessly combed-out to fill the ranks. No men were more determined to win or die than these Britons and Canadians, in order to rescue a million of their compatriots in the Holland Pocket and to rescue victory from defeat. Each corps had a special armored fist in the 5th Canadian Armoured and the 6th British Armoured Divisions.

Patton had carefully reshuffled his forces to concentrate the greatest strength on breaking into the pocket. In the process, almost a million men were shifted along the front in a masterpiece of unit movement. Patton had immediately identified the 3d Infantry Division as his spearhead for Operation Crescendo, the plan to relieve the Holland Pocket, but the 3d was part of the powerful and veteran VI Corps in Seventh Army. And VI Corps was the only American component in Seventh Army; the rest were French. Patton's solution was radical. He transferred the entire VI Corps to First Army. He also transferred the Seventh Army commander, Lieutenant General Lucien Truscott, to take over the rebuilt First. He replaced Seventh Army's American component with the green American divisions that had plugged the breach in the north and the British Fifth Army moved into the line in their place. The three French divisions that he had also rushed into the gap were transferred to the new French Second Army which had been formed in 6th Army Group. DeGaulle had been thoroughly cooperative as French power grew along the southern end of the front. Finally Patton held XVIII Airborne Corps as his reserve.

First Army had been reborn since the Ardennes disaster. Some would say that the Third Army had eaten it alive since only one of its current four maneuver corps, VIII corps, had been part of its order-of-battle before the Ardennes. Two of the others were from Patton's Third Army and the last was VI Corps from Seventh Army. Truscott knew his job and took his new army quickly in hand. They were ready to cross the line of departure that morning of 25 March. Morale was high. It had gone even higher as news of the success of the Red Army came across. A not inconsiderable element of it was the desire to give the Germans a good beating before the Russians finished the job.

Patton was of two minds about the Soviet offensive. On one hand he recognized that every German the Russians killed was one fewer his men would have to deal with. Already that was having a positive effect on the odds his offensive was facing. German units had been pulling out of the line and heading east. On the other hand, it grated upon him that his victory would owe too much to the damned Reds. His glory would be much diminished.

Washington, D.C., March 1945

But overshadowing everything was the upheaval in Washington. The first inkling had made little impression on the troops but had set the general officer corps abuzz. Wallace relieved Marshall's successor as Chief of Staff— he had been replaced, officially "for health reasons," but the general officer back channel said it was an abrupt presidential order. The new Chief of Staff was a non-entity among his peers, a lieutenant general who had been on Marshall's chopping block just prior to his departure. Similar changes had replaced Admiral King, the Chief of Naval Operations, and Hap Arnold, Chief of the Army Air Corps.

Then there had been the President's attempt to fire Hoover. Hoover, like Secretary of War Stanton in 1866, had simply refused to be fired. The country had not noticed the removal of the Chief of Staff who was not familiar to many. They did notice the removal of King and Arnold, both national heroes. The situation had boiled over as the Congress got involved, demanding to know what was behind the purge. Representative Samuel Dickstein (D-NY) led a small but noisy group of Congressmen in support of Wallace. The White House remained obstinate, claiming that the President needed his own team. The attempt to dismiss Hoover, more a national icon hero than a mere national hero, brought the government to a near standstill. The public was both alarmed and outraged, except for the vociferous support given Wallace by the Progressive Party, centered mainly in New York.

In the heated political atmosphere, Wallace stunned the nation by announcing that a plot against the presidency was underfoot and, to secure the nation in this crisis, the inauguration of Harry Truman would have to be postponed indefinitely. Bands of toughs from New York, who had somehow escaped the draft, appeared in Washington. They wore armbands of a group called, "People's Patriots for Wallace." Outspoken public figures and even members of Congress were threatened and some were beaten up. Mr Justice Robert Jackson, appointed to the Supreme Court by Roosevelt, was beaten up outside his home and his arm broken.[25]

The Armed Forces' bedrock loyalty to the Commander-in-Chief was shaken to the core. But with Wallace's replacements now commanding the services, any serious discussion of the obvious conflict in the soldier's oath of allegiance—between loyalty to the Constitution and obedience to the orders of superiors—led to a wave of dismissals across the country.

Patton had literally pissed on the orders from the Chief of Staff to identify and relieve any officer who questioned the authority of the President. He was on the point of fighting the decisive battle of the war, and he could not afford to lose thousands of good men. Furthermore, the enlisted men were just as vociferous in their outrage and confusion. It took superhuman efforts at every level of the chain of command to counter the damage to morale. Basically, the message was that the Republic had a war to win and a million men to rescue. Then the constitutional issues could be addressed as they were being addressed by the Congress at home.

In the meantime, he had a nasty and immediate problem to deal with. Here and there so-called "Soldiers' Committees" had formed in support of Wallace, invariably in line of communications units. Their incessant propaganda efforts were eroding good order and discipline. Officers had been shot in units agitated by the Wallacites. Patton simply ignored the orders from Washington to support the Soldiers' Committees and moved quickly on his own plans. Combat units were withdrawn from the line to surround these Wallacites and arrest them at gunpoint. Not a few were shot in the process. It was at this time that Patton received a personal representative from General MacArthur under the strictest security.

Headquarters, German Seventh Army, Bastogne, 22 March 1945

It did not take a genius to see what was coming. Hitler had held on to the Holland Pocket even after the Red Army had crossed the Oder. The chaos in Washington had given him another false hope to grasp. But then that was always his way—to nail his armies to the ground until a withdrawal was so manifestly necessary that even a blind man could see it. When he could be prevailed upon to authorize a withdrawal, it was then under the most desperate and wasteful circumstances, with huge amounts of equipment abandoned and too many troops lost. The Holland Pocket proved to be no different. Guderian counted it a victory that he had convinced Hitler to transfer Raus' *Third Panzer Army* back for the defense of Berlin. It was quickly followed by *Sixth Panzer Army*, leaving 20 divisions of *Fifth Panzer* and *Seventh Armies* to hold what they could.

Hasso von Manteuffel and Erich Brandenberger, the two army commanders, were left holding the bag. They had met on 22 March at Brandenberger's headquarters in Bastogne. The little Manteuffel was all energy as he stabbed at the air in emphasis.

"This is madness, Brandenberger, sheer madness. Any idiot can tell that the Allied offensive is at best days away. We will be trapped. Most of my best Panzer units have already been sent East... Look, the encirclement is barely 30 kilometers deep at its base in your sector and narrows to less than ten by the time it gets to Antwerp."

Brandenberger was only marginally less alarmed than Manteuffel. His army formed the base of the encircling arm that reached to Antwerp. Manteuffel was literally out on a limb if the Allies cut through anywhere along the coil. "But what can we do. Our orders are to stay put while Raus and Dietrich save Berlin."

"I'll tell you, Brandenberger, the war is lost. Raus and Dietrich will be too late. Our December victory only postponed the end, that's all. Well, I for one am not going to let my boys get cut up for nothing. Beginning tonight, I'm going to start thinning my front and getting my men out. I need your help to pass them through *Seventh Army*."

At All Costs—Operation Crescendo, 25 March 1945

The morning's last hours of darkness were lit with stabbing flames from thousands of guns, sending a crushing barrage into the depths of two German divisions between Antwerp and Namur. Falling through the arcing steel were thousands of bombs dropped by the R.A.F.'s Bomber Command. Thousands of tank and armored vehicle motors revved in the morning cold behind the lines. The infantry battalions of British, Canadian, and American infantry divisions moved forward as the first streaks of dawn were lost in the inferno ahead of them.

Operation Crescendo was an all-out effort to break the German coils that were crushing the trapped Allied forces within the Holland Pocket. From left to right Patton marshaled the British Fifth Army, First U.S. Army, and his old Third Army, totaling 32 divisions from outside Antwerp to Luxembourg City. The plan was simple—pierce the coil and roll it up. Behind the front tens of thousands of trucks waited to rush through and resupply the trapped forces. Within the pocket, 21st Army Group was ready to do its part with carefully husbanded offensive power. Canadian First Army would coordinate its attack with British Fifth Army while Ninth U.S. Army would coordinate with First U.S. Army. The long but narrow German coil would be attacked front and back in two places at once. Already over the preceding few days British Second Army had launched limited holding attacks against the German *Fifteenth Army* on its front.[26]

The Marnemen cut through the hapless wreckage of the *12th Volksgrenadier Division* in front of it within the first 24 hours. They pulled aside as the 4th and 10th Armored Divisions poured through the gap they had created to overrun Dinant and capture its bridges over the Meuse intact and then link up with the 75th Infantry Division attacking from inside the pocket. The breakthrough had taken barely 26 hours.

To the north, the Canadians and British had a more difficult time. They faced the water barrier of the Senne River. An assault river crossing is one of

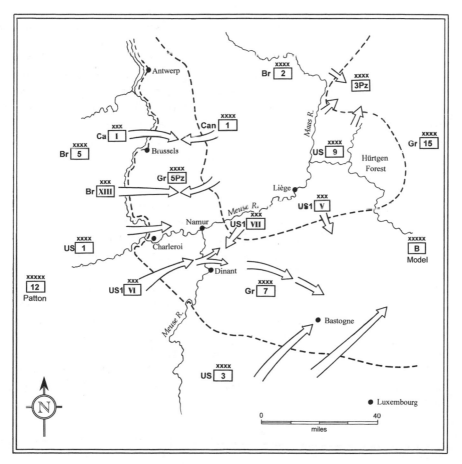

The Relief of the Holland Pocket

the more difficult maneuvers, but they were over in a few hours crossing north and south of Brussels respectively. Their 5th and 6th Armoured Divisions then did a passage of the lines to speed through the chaos of the German rear to take Louvain and Wavre as Manteuffel's *Fifth Panzer Army* collapsed.

First U.S. Army's attack had severed Manteuffel's *Fifth Panzer Army* right at its join with *Seventh Army*. British Fifth Army had then severed it again north and south of Brussels. What made it a disaster for the Germans was that this caught Manteuffel's army in mid-withdrawal. The Allies had cut right through his covering forces and slashed into his columns trying to move out of the coil's arm. Brandenberger had his own hands full as First Army continued its attack deep into the bloody stump of the coil. Then Third Army attacked from the south. The front was disintegrating everywhere as Allied aircraft bombed and strafed everything on the roads. It was like the escape from Normandy all over again, but this time there was not even summer foliage to give a bit of cover. The roads became clogged with burning vehicles, dead soldiers and horses. Units abandoned the roads to strike across the still frozen fields only to scatter in every direction when the artillery or fighters found them.

When news reached Britain of Fifth Army's breakthrough, the church bells rang throughout the kingdom. People rushed into the streets in a spontaneous burst of relief and joy. In tens of thousands of homes, women burst into tears as the crushing weight of despair was lifted from them. The dagger had been removed from the British throat. That evening the King addressed the nation. He was broadcast across the length of a rejoicing Canada as well. The simple eloquence and dignity of his words would be remembered long after his death.

For the trapped men in the pocket who had been on short rations for almost three months, the sight of thousands of trucks stuffed with supplies was met with cheers and a few shouts of "What the hell kept you?"

Patton did not pause to celebrate but kept First and Third Armies hammering at the bloody stump of Brandenberger's *Seventh Army* until it too collapsed.

Berlin and Beyond, April 1945

Manteuffel had been wrong. Raus and Dietrich had been in time, just in time to throw their armies into the defenses of Berlin. Dietrich, though proud and jealous of his SS divisions, was no fool. As early as late June in Normandy, he had hinted to Rommel that he would support him in a coup against Hitler. Dietrich could see even then that the war was lost. In Berlin he could also see that Raus was the better general and actively worked with the Austrian to coordinate the defense of Berlin and the surrounding area. Together they bled Zhukov's First Belorussian Front coming from the east and Koniev's First Ukrainian Front coming from the southeast and fought off every attempt at encirclement. When that fate could no longer be avoided, they evacuated as much of the civilian population as they could, mostly women and children by then. Still, the refugees suffered hideously as the Red Air Force savaged their dense columns.[27]

Now began the great flight to the West by millions of Germans, shielded by the remnants of their armies. Hitler had stayed in the Ziegenberg redoubt rather than rush to Berlin as Zhukov approached. His hopes had pinned him far too long in the West. His absence from Berlin was critical in the wasting away of his authority. The defense of Berlin was fought in disregard of his orders, and a result was the final display of German military prowess in the war. Raus left a wound in the Red Army that would not be forgotten, and he had got the Berliners and his army out, confirming the epithet that his troops had given him long ago.

The situation crumbled quickly after that. Hitler had made the great mistake of staying in his Ziegenberg cave complex. His absence from the capital of the Reich in its death throes had given his subordinates far more latitude to think and act. Berlin's fiery death and the loss of so many of its people in the flight to the West had convinced Dietrich that the situation called for action. It was out of character for the old street fighter to be a conspirator. That function was provided by Admiral Dönitz, Hitler's chosen successor. With Raus' support as well, Dietrich lured Hitler out of his cave and shot him at point blank range. For the Germans, the war was now over.

MacAthur's gracious acceptance of Dönitz's surrender in the American sector had followed Patton's announcement that he would take the surrender of any Germans that presented themselves. No one was to be turned back to surrender to the Red Army. The State Department's advisors in theater threw a fit and cabled Washington of every so-called slight Patton made against the Soviets. They were half right. Patton stepped on a lot of Red toes by aggressively representing his country's interest better than the orders coming out of Washington. He was, however, acting with MacArthur's silent approval.

The situation in Washington had frozen into two stalemated camps. The Congress, the Republicans and most of the Democrats were against the Wallacites, the Progressive Party, stalking horse for the Communist Party, U.S.A., and now the senior levels of the armed forces. The Wallacite thugs had been reinforced by gangs of the so-called "Soldier and Sailor Councils" culled by the new leadership from various Stateside posts and camps. These thugs, made up of stockade leavings and the impressionable, took over the barracks of the 3d Infantry Regiment at Fort Meyer near Arlington Cemetery. From there they joined the Wallacites in strong-arming the population. The forces in the field continued to concentrate on fighting the war, though Admiral Nimitz, to whom command of the entire Pacific Theater had devolved after MacArthur's transfer to Europe, had as little truck with the "SSCs" as Patton.[28]

Patton, unlike MacArthur, stuck in Wallace's craw, or rather in that of the group of agents controlling Wallace. Patton was poking a sharp stick in Stalin's eye in the middle of Germany at every opportunity, while MacArthur was uncharacteristically avoiding the limelight. Two weeks after the German surrender, Patton received the telegram that relieved him. He gathered his army and corps commanders together to show them the paper. The silence was stony. Hard men with hard faces.

The Inauguration, Washington, D.C., 24 April 1945

Patton flew home in a cramped Dakota, shorn of all but one aide. He landed at Bolling Airfield across the Anacostia River from Washington and was met by a representative of the Chief of Staff who strutted up to him and waved a contemptuous salute that Patton would never have tolerated from a recruit. "General, as per Presidential order you have been placed on the retirement list. The President wants you to retire quietly. That means go home, stay home, and shut up if you know what is good for you," then he sneered, "and for your family." As the creature lectured the old soldier, out of the corner of his eye Patton saw the beginning of a huge flight of transports making their landing approach. As the first flight landed, armed men in combat gear exited quickly and ran across the field. Patton had been enjoying the man's performance, actually smirked through some of it. A jeep with a machine gun drove up. Out jumped Iron Mike O'Daniel with that blue and white patch on his shoulder and helmet.

O'Daniel saluted. "General, the 15th Infantry Regiment will be landed within an hour. The trucks are ready to load up the men as they arrive."

"Excellent, general." A flight of Mustangs hung in the air over the field as the transports landed. Patton looked up and said, "I see Hap is back, too." Then he turned to look at the Chief's representative. "And arrest this," he paused as if the next word had suddenly been dirtied, "officer."

Patton walked over to the nearby base headquarters to stretch his legs after his long flight. A man in rumpled khakis stepped out. His greasy cap had scrambled eggs on its brim. There was a corncob pipe in his mouth. He stepped forward to offer his hand as Patton saluted, "Glad you could make it, George."

"Wouldn't miss it for the world, general."[29]

The coup was a complete success. The 15th Infantry Regiment roared over the bridge into Washington to secure key points as FBI agents fanned out to make hundreds of arrests. Patton strode down the halls of the Pentagon as staff officers scurried out of his way. He took the Wallace-appointed Army Chief of Staff under protective custody. A body of Marines removed the Chief of Naval Operations at the same time. Iron Mike O'Daniel seized Fort Meyer where the military thugs of the "Soldiers and Sailors for Wallace" had been garrisoned. They surrendered without a shot.

Hoover himself led the team that seized the White House, supported by a rifle company of the 15th Infantry, commanded by 1st Lieutenant Audie Murphy, the most decorated soldier of the war. The Wallacites had fled, and so all the Tommy guns and Garands proved unnecessary. Hoover found Wallace alone in the Oval Office. There would be no courtesy of "Mr

President'" only a terse, "Henry Wallace, you are under arrest for treason." A special FBI team had rescued Truman from house arrest, and he was flown immediately to Washington by military aircraft with a suitable fighter escort.

He landed at National Airport to be met by MacArthur whose only change of uniform had been to a pressed set of khakis. The pipe, though, was not in evidence. As Truman stepped off the plane, MacArthur saluted and said, "Mr. President-Elect, your inauguration awaits."[30]

A half hour later, Truman was standing on the steps of the Capitol surrounded by most of the Congress and thousands of citizens as Mr Justice Robert Jackson, arm in a sling, swore him in to office as the 34th President of the United States to wild cheers. His speech was not long or polished, but it ended with the heartfelt words, delivered as he looked at MacArthur and Patton,

> "I stand here today as your President because the Constitution, as the will of the people, has been fulfilled. And the Constitution and the concept it enshrines of civilian control of the military has no greater servants than these two men who stand next to me—men who have restored the lawful government of the United States."

With that he enthusiastically shook Patton's and MacArthur's hands. The cameras flashed at the historic moment. Unfortunately, a tall guard stood awkwardly in front of Patton and spoiled his pictures. The waters parted more naturally for MacArthur whose photograph with Truman would become a classic. It was the picture splashed across every paper in the country the next day. "Constitution Saved: Truman Thanks MacArthur!"

Epilogue

With the crushing of the Wallacite Conspiracy, Truman firmly took up the reins of the Presidency, and MacArthur returned to the Pacific to crush Japan. Patton was, in effect, appointed a proconsul of the American sector in Germany. He made it a priority, amid all the other pressing duties of occupation, to plan on the reconstitution of the German Army.

In June, the Big Four—Truman, Attlee, DeGaulle and Stalin—met in Potsdam outside Berlin to settle the fate of postwar Europe. Truman and Attlee had insisted on the presence of DeGaulle whose two armies had done so much to secure the Allied victory in the West. All three were fully aware of Stalin's duplicity during the war. When the roundup of the Wallacites netted most of the Soviet agents in the United States and a similar roundup occurred in Britain, the Soviet codes were changed abruptly. Stalin knew that they knew, and they knew that he knew that they knew. Still, diplomacy is a whore's game of false smiles and affability. So Truman, despite his Missouri bluntness, attempted to make small talk with Stalin, who could be very affable when he wanted to charm. Today he was gruff. Truman persisted and stated that Stalin must be amazed at the turn about of his fortune. Why, only a few short years before, Hitler had been at the gates of Moscow while now

Stalin was ensconced right outside of Hitler's capital. Stalin only gritted his teeth as he replied, "[Czar] Alexander the First got to Paris."[31] DeGaulle was not amused.

The Reality

This story pivots on the dog that did not bark—complete German success in the Ardennes Offensive. The British and Americans were not a growing steamroller by the middle of December 1944. The British had scraped the bottom of the manpower barrel and had actually to break up major army formations to provide replacements. The U.S. Army's well of replacements was equally dry because of the determination years before that the war in Europe would be over by this point. A German victory would have caught them at their weakest. The scope of the catastrophe here advances the stroke that actually killed Roosevelt barely three months later. The level of exhaustion and war weariness in Britain was such that a catastrophe on the scale of the trapping of almost all of Britain's field army in a second and far greater Dunkirk could conceivably have brought down Churchill and put Attlee in his place only six months before the British people in the full flush of victory actually turned Churchill out in their first postwar election.

The Soviet codes were not significantly broken until 1947, under what eventually was to be called the Venona Program, when they began to reveal the extent of Soviet penetration of the U.S. Government. An indispensable tool was the badly burned code book the Finns turned over to the U.S. in late 1944. In this story, the code book is intact. Soviet agents such as Alger Hiss, Lauchlin Currie, Dexter White, Samuel Dickstein, and Duncan Lee (a descendant of Robert E. Lee) were, indeed, identified as agents in the Soviet cables.

Henry Wallace had been a disastrous choice as vice-president, and those around Roosevelt, such as Mrs Roosevelt and Harold Ickes, were desperate to get him off the ticket in the 1944 election because of his generally bizarre ideas and pro-Soviet attitudes. As a sop, Roosevelt appointed him to a cabinet position from which he brazenly attacked Truman's policies towards the Soviets. Truman fired him. In the 1948 election he ran on the Progressive Party ticket. The Progressives were essentially a front organization for the Communist Party, U.S.A., taking orders directly from Stalin. This story explores the opportunities that lay before the communists had there suddenly come to power a man who fit Lenin's classic description of a "useful idiot."

Bibliography

Blumenson, Martin, ed., *The Patton Papers, 1885–1940*, Vol. I, Houghton Mifflin, Boston, 1972.

Cole, Hugh M., *The Ardennes: Battle of the Bulge*, Office of the Chief of Military History, Washington, D.C., 1965.

DeGaulle, Charles, *The Complete War Memoirs of Charles DeGaulle*, Da Capo, New York, n.d.

Harriman, W. Averell, *America and Russia in a Changing World*, Allen & Unwin, London, 1971.

Haynes, John Earl, & Klehr, Harvey, *VENONA: Decoding Soviet Espionage in America*, Yale University Press, New Haven, CT, 1999.

Pogue, Forrest, *The Supreme Command*, Office of the Chief of Military History, Washington, D.C., 1954.

Ready, J. Lee, *World War Two: Nation by Nation*, Arms and Armour Press, London, 1995.

Tsouras, Peter G., ed., *Panzers on the Eastern Front: Erhart Raus and His Panzer Divisions in Russia*, Greenhill Books, London, 2001.

Notes

*1. Harry R. Porterfield, *Ardennes Disaster: The Defeat That Nearly Doomed the Allies*, Collins, New York, 1960, p. 287.

*2. Presidential Archives of the Russian Federation, *The Stalin Conversations During the Great Patriotic War*, Kremlin Press, Moscow, 1997, pp. 512–15.

*3. *Ibid.*, p. 576.

4. Under emergency wartime laws there was to be no British general election until after the defeat of Germany. A vote of no confidence in the government would not have triggered a new election. Normally, the outgoing prime minister would recommend a successor for formal appointment by the king, as Chamberlain did in 1940 when he resigned and was replaced by Churchill.

*5. However, on 14 January 1945, the King exercised his prerogative to throw his support to someone other than Anthony Eden, whom Churchill had recommended. Clement Attlee was the leader of the Labour Party and an important member of the War Cabinet, a British wartime institution which included members of all parties. Attlee may well have been the only man who would have held the wartime coalition government together

*6. Within days of the news of the Ardennes disaster, Roosevelt's health visibly deteriorated. He was speaking with Mrs Roosevelt when he put his hand to his head and said, "I have such a terrible headache." Within seconds he slumped in his chair and was dead.

7. Hitler had convinced himself that he would be vindicated by Providence just as his hero, Frederick the Great had been at the end of the Seven Years War, when the Empress of Russia had died—to be succeeded by her son who promptly took Russia out of the anti-Prussian coalition. The coalition then promptly fell apart, saving Frederick who was on the verge of utter defeat.

8. Tsouras, *Panzers on the Eastern Front*, p. 19.

*9. Helmut von Harzburg, ed., *The Hitler Transcripts: Transcripts from OKW*, Leopard Press, London, 1962, pp. 722–5.

*10. Howard Elliot, *I Remember Marshall: A Memoir of George C. Marshall's Military Aide*, Rutledge University Press, Washington, 1952, p. 179. Marshall dictated an account of his last interview with Wallace immediately after the event.

11. Pogue, *The Supreme Command*, p. 543.
12. Cole, *The Ardennes*, p. 334.
13. DeGaulle, *Complete War Memoirs*, pp. 831–9.
14. John P. Finnegan, "Corderman Led Intelligence Effort in World War II," *INSCOM Journal*, April–June 1998, Vol. 21, No. 2, pp. 1–2.
15. Finland was in a delicate position in World War II; it had only joined the Germans in their attack on the Soviet Union to retrieve territory seized by the Soviets in the Winter War of 1940–41. That alliance, in turn, earned the Finns war with the Western Allies. By turning over the Soviet code book, they wanted to ensure that they had some good will to draw upon should Germany lose the war.
*16. Elliot, *I Remember Marshall*, pp. 199–202.
*17. William H. Longstreet, *A Legacy Betrayed: The Life of Duncan Lee*, University of Lexington Press, Lexington, VA, 1999, p. 242.
*18. *The Stalin Conversations*, pp. 734–5.

*19. Harrison Williams, *Victory Redeemed: Patton and the Holland Pocket*, Parker House, New York, 1955, p. 42.
20. Blumenson, *The Patton Papers*, pp. 585–6, 888–9, 893–896,
*21. Rene Foucault, *Fratricide: DeGaulle and the French Civil War*, London, Leventhal Books, 1992, p. 76.
22. Ready, *World War Two: Nation by Nation*, p. 302. From D-Day to the end of the war, the British infantry battalions in the Northwest European Campaign lost 63 percent of their fighting strength.
23. Arthur Schlesinger, Jr., "Who Was Henry Wallace: The Story of a Perplexing and Indomitably Naïve Public Servant," *Los Angeles Times*, 12 March 2000.
*24. Robert Brunsvold, *I Served With Patton*, Infantry Press, Washington, D.C., 1959, p. 199.
*25. Martin J. Coletti, *The Wallacite Conspiracy*, Parker House, New York, 1949, p. 190.
*26. Edward Harris, *The Rescue of a Million: Operation Crescendo*, Whitney & Sons, New York, 1952, p. 292.
*27. Karl Kitzinger, *Erhard Raus und der Berlinschlact*, Stahlhelm Verlag, Munich, 1963, p. 233.
*28. Coletti, *The Wallacite Conspiracy*, pp. 341–5. The 3d Infantry Regiment was and is Washington's garrison and under the personal command of the President. However, the Wallacites saw it as a possible counter-revolutionary threat. Wallace ordered it sent to the Pacific to get it out of the way. In the 3d's absence the SSCs ignored the duty to guard the Tomb of the Unknown Soldier. When this was discovered, walking wounded from Walter Reed and Bethesda Naval Hospitals took over. They only relinquished their post when relieved by the 15th Infantry Regiment.
*29. George Patton, *One Day in April*, Oliver & Stone, Los Angeles, 1949, p. 324.
*30. Robert C. Lowery, *How Douglas MacArthur Saved the Constitution*, Windham House, Boston, 1964, p. 435.
31. Harriman, *America and Russia in a Changing World*, p. 44. Stalin was referring to the occupation of Paris by the Imperial Russian Army, accompanied by Czar Alexander I, in 1814 following the defeat of Napoleon.